D1480132

TECHNOLOGY
IN SCHOOLS

DEBATING ISSUES
in American Education

EDITORIAL BOARD

TECHNOLOGY
IN SCHOOLS

VOLUME EDITOR

KEVIN P. BRADY
NORTH CAROLINA STATE UNIVERSITY

10
VOLUME

DEBATING ISSUES
in American Education

SERIES
EDITORS

CHARLES J. RUSSO
ALLAN G. OSBORNE, JR.

⑤SAGE reference

Los Angeles | London | New Delhi
Singapore | Washington DC

Los Angeles | London | New Delhi
Singapore | Washington DC

FOR INFORMATION:

SAGE Publications, Inc.

2455 Teller Road

Thousand Oaks, California 91320

E-mail: order@sagepub.com

SAGE Publications Ltd.

1 Oliver's Yard

55 City Road

London EC1Y 1SP

United Kingdom

SAGE Publications India Pvt. Ltd.

B 1/I 1 Mohan Cooperative Industrial Area

Mathura Road, New Delhi 110 044

India

SAGE Publications Asia-Pacific Pte. Ltd.

3 Church Street

#10-04 Samsung Hub

Singapore 049483

Printed in the United States of America.

Library of Congress Cataloging-in-Publication Data

Technology in schools/volume editor, Kevin P. Brady.

p. cm.–(Debating issues in American education; v. 10)

"A SAGE reference publication."
Includes bibliographical references and index.

ISBN 978-1-4129-8759-2 (cloth : alk. paper)

1. Educational technology—United States—Planning. I. Brady, Kevin P.

LB1028.3.T3972 2012
371.330973—dc23   2011031313

Publisher: Rolf A. Janke

Acquisitions Editor: Jim Brace-Thompson

Assistant to the Publisher: Michele Thompson

Developmental Editors: Diana E. Axelsen, Carole Maurer

Production Editor: Tracy Buyan

Reference Systems Manager: Leticia Gutierrez

Reference Systems Coordinators: Laura Notton

Copy Editor: Amy Freitag

Typesetter: C&M Digitals (P) Ltd.

Proofreader: Allyson Rudolph

Indexer: Mary Mortensen

Cover Designer: Janet Kiesel

Marketing Manager: Carmel Schrire

SUSTAINABLE FORESTRY INITIATIVE
Label applies to the text stock

Certified Sourcing
www.sfiprogram.org
SFI-00341

12 13 14 15 16 10 9 8 7 6 5 4 3 2 1

CONTENTS

ABOUT THE
EDITORS-IN-CHIEF

Charles J. Russo, JD, EdD, is the Joseph Panzer Chair in Education in the School of Education and Allied Professions and adjunct professor in the School of Law at the University of Dayton. He was the 1998–1999 president of the Education Law Association and 2002 recipient of its McGhehey (Achievement) Award. He has authored or coauthored more than 200 articles in peer-reviewed journals; has authored, coauthored, edited, or coedited 40 books; and has in excess of 800 publications. Russo also speaks extensively on issues in education law in the United States and abroad.

Along with having spoken in 33 states and 25 nations on 6 continents, Russo has taught summer courses in England, Spain, and Thailand; he also has served as a visiting professor at Queensland University of Technology in Brisbane and the University of Newcastle, Australia; the University of Sarajevo, Bosnia and Herzegovina; South East European University, Macedonia; the Potchefstroom Campus of North-West University in Potchefstroom, South Africa; the University of Malaya in Kuala Lumpur, Malaysia; and the University of São Paulo, Brazil. He regularly serves as a visiting professor at the Potchefstroom Campus of North-West University.

Before joining the faculty at the University of Dayton as professor and chair of the Department of Educational Administration in July 1996, Russo taught at the University of Kentucky in Lexington from August 1992 to July 1996 and at Fordham University in his native New York City from September 1989 to July 1992. He taught high school for 8½ years before and after graduation from law school. He received a BA (classical civilization) in 1972, a JD in 1983, and an EdD (educational administration and supervision) in 1989 from St. John's University in New York City. He also received a master of divinity degree from the Seminary of the Immaculate Conception in Huntington, New York, in 1978, as well as a PhD Honoris Causa from the Potchefstroom Campus of North-West University, South Africa, in May 2004 for his contributions to the field of education law.

Russo and his wife, a preschool teacher who provides invaluable assistance proofreading and editing, travel regularly both nationally and internationally to Russo's many speaking and teaching engagements.

Allan G. Osborne, Jr. is the retired principal of the Snug Harbor Community School in Quincy, Massachusetts, a nationally recognized Blue Ribbon School of Excellence. During his 34 years in public education, he served as a special education teacher, a director of special education, an assistant principal, and a principal. He has also served as an adjunct professor of special education and education law at several colleges, including Bridgewater State University and American International University.

Osborne earned an EdD in educational leadership from Boston College and an MEd in special education from Fitchburg State College (now Fitchburg State University) in Massachusetts. He received a BA in psychology from the University of Massachusetts.

Osborne has authored or coauthored numerous peer-reviewed journal articles, book chapters, monographs, and textbooks on legal issues in education, along with textbooks on other aspects of education. Although he writes and presents in several areas of educational law, he specializes in legal and policy issues in special education. He is the coauthor, with Charles J. Russo, of five texts published by Corwin, a SAGE company.

A past president of the Education Law Association (ELA), Osborne has been an attendee and presenter at most ELA conferences since 1991. He has also written a chapter now titled "Students With Disabilities" for the *Yearbook of Education Law*, published by ELA, since 1990. He is on the editorial advisory committee of *West's Education Law Reporter* and is coeditor of the "Education Law Into Practice" section of that journal, which is sponsored by ELA. He is also on the editorial boards of several other education journals.

In recognition of his contributions to the field of education law, Osborne was presented with the McGhehey Award by ELA in 2008, the highest award given by the organization. He is also the recipient of the City of Quincy Human Rights Award, the Financial Executives Institute of Massachusetts Principals Award, the Junior Achievement of Massachusetts Principals Award, and several community service awards.

Osborne spends his time in retirement writing, editing, and working on his hobbies, genealogy and photography. He and his wife Debbie, a retired elementary school teacher, enjoy gardening, traveling, attending theater and musical performances, and volunteering at the Dana Farber Cancer Institute in Boston.

ABOUT THE
VOLUME EDITOR

Kevin P. Brady is currently an associate professor in the Department of Leadership, Policy and Adult and Higher Education at North Carolina State University in Raleigh, North Carolina. Previously, he was an assistant professor in the Department of Educational and Community Programs at the City University of New York–Queens College.

His current research interests include student and teacher free speech and expression, legal issues involving student discipline, special education law, school finance, blended learning distance education course development, and educational technology issues involving today's school leaders.

Brady's peer-reviewed scholarship appears in a wide array of leading educational law, policy, and technology journals, including the *Brigham Young University Education and Law Journal, Children's Legal Rights Journal, Distance Education, Education and the Law, Education and Urban Society, Journal of Education Finance, Journal of Interactive Online Learning, Journal of Online Learning and Teaching, Journal of School Leadership, International Journal of Educational Reform, NASSP Bulletin, Review of Research in Education,* and *West's Education Law Reporter.*

ABOUT THE CONTRIBUTORS

Leanna Matchett Archambault is an assistant professor of Instructional Technology at Arizona State University. Her research interests include K–12 online teacher preparation, the nature of technological pedagogical content knowledge in online environments, and the use of innovative technologies to improve teaching and learning.

Michael Barbour is an assistant professor in instructional technology and educational evaluation and research at Wayne State University. He has been a K–12 online learning researcher, teacher, course designer, and administrator in several countries for more than a decade. Barbour researches the effective design, delivery, and support of K–12 online learning.

Justin M. Bathon is an assistant professor of educational leadership studies at the University of Kentucky, where he is a director of the University Council for Educational Administration Center for the Advanced Study of Technology Leadership in Education.

Christine M. Battista received her PhD in English, general literature, and rhetoric at Binghamton University in 2011. She is currently a lecturer and a writing associate at Binghamton University. Her interests and fields of research include American studies, feminism, ecocriticism, and studies in composition. Her essay is based on her own experiences in the classroom, and she currently is researching the intersections between areas of globalization, environmentalism, technology, and literary studies.

Steven M. Baule is superintendent of North Boone Community Unit School District 200 in Poplar Grove, Illinois. He has written and presented on a variety of educational technology and historical topics. He was named one of the Ten Tech Savvy Superintendents in 2009 by eSchoolNews.

Jill Castek is a postdoctoral scholar at the University of California, Berkeley. She has taught striving readers in grades K–12 for more than a decade. Her research examines the skills and strategies needed for online reading comprehension and explores instructional techniques for inquiry learning and online collaboration among academically diverse learners.

Margie W. Crowe spent 30 years teaching general and special education in public and private schools before joining the special education faculty at the

University of Southern Mississippi. Her interests include assistive technology, differentiating instruction, and curriculum design.

Philip T. K. Daniel is the Flesher Professor of Educational Administration and an adjunct professor of law at the Ohio State University. He is the author of numerous refereed publications and is coauthor of the books *Law and Public Education, Education Law and the Public Schools: A Compendium*, and the upcoming *Law, Policy, and Higher Education*.

A. Jonathan Eakle is an associate professor of The Johns Hopkins University School of Education. His research involves communications and cultures; in particular, the relations among images and words used in formal and informal learning environments and how these relations create various subjects, including education policy, philosophy, curriculum, and instruction.

Margaret Hagood is an associate professor of literacy at the College of Charleston. She teaches undergraduate and graduate courses in early childhood, elementary, and middle grade literacies, focusing on new literacies, pop culture, and digital technologies relevant to life in the 21st century.

Abigail Hawkins is a senior instructional designer at Adobe Systems Incorporated, where she designs learning solutions for Adobe managers and employees. Her research interests include K–12 online learning, learning analytics, and management development. In 2011, she completed her PhD in instructional psychology and technology from Brigham Young University. Prior to that, she earned her MS in the same field from Indiana University. Hawkins has authored several articles on the subject of K–12 online learning and interaction.

Geraldine R. Johnson graduated with a PhD from Texas A&M–Commerce. She presently serves as chair of the Educational Instruction and Leadership Department at Southeastern Oklahoma State University, Durant, Oklahoma, and teaches educational technology. She is a former secondary science teacher, librarian, and principal.

Kathryn Kennedy is an assistant professor at Georgia Southern University. She holds a PhD from the University of Florida in curriculum and instruction, with a concentration in educational technology. Her research interests include teacher preparation for technology integration and instructional design in traditional, blended, and online learning environments.

Jerrid W. Kruse, assistant professor in the School of Education at Drake University, teaches courses in educational technology, science education, learning and assessment, and chemistry. His research interests include the natures of learning, science, and technology, and how students of all ages might come to understand these natures.

Robert Stewart Mayers, former teacher and high school department chair, is an associate professor in the Department of Educational Instruction and Leadership at Southeastern Oklahoma State University in Durant, Oklahoma. His research interests include legal issues in education and teacher evaluation. He earned his PhD at the University of Georgia.

Timothy E. Morse is an associate professor at the University of Southern Mississippi Gulf Coast, where he directs the Mississippi Department of Education's Autism Project. In addition to having taught undergraduate and graduate special education courses at the university, he has worked as a public school special education administrator and teacher.

Curtis R. Nash has an MA in communication from Illinois State University and is a doctoral student in the Educational Leadership program at the University of Dayton (UD). He is currently a graduate assistant at UD. His current research interests focus on legal aspects of university student codes of conduct.

Kevin M. Oliver is associate professor of curriculum and instruction at North Carolina State University.

Patrick D. Pauken is vice provost for Governance and Faculty Relations at Bowling Green State University, where he teaches school law, higher education law, special education law, and ethical leadership. He has presented and published in various areas of ethics and law, including school violence and technology.

Allison Powell is the vice president for State and District Services of the International Association for K-12 Online Learning (iNACOL). Before joining iNACOL, she helped build the Clark County School District's Virtual High School and an online professional development program. She completed her PhD from Pepperdine University in educational technology.

Jayson W. Richardson is an assistant professor in the Department of Educational Leadership Studies at the University of Kentucky. He researches educational leadership, emerging technologies, technology leadership, and technology in less developed countries. He is the associate director of the Center for the Advanced Study of Technology in Education.

Raymond Rose is cofounder of Rose & Smith Associates of Austin, Texas. He is an online learning evangelist and a fierce advocate for the radical reform of

U.S. education. He has been a classroom teacher and school administrator, and he now focuses his career to working for school improvement nationwide.

Nick Sauers is currently a graduate student at Iowa State University and the leadership training coordinator for the Center for the Advanced Study of Technology Leadership in Education. Prior to his current position, he had served as a classroom teacher and a principal.

Meredith Stewart teaches middle and high school history at Cary Academy in Cary, North Carolina, where she developed the school's first blended learning class. In addition to her teaching responsibilities, she serves as an instructional technology facilitator. She holds both a graduate theology and a law degree from Duke University.

Anne F. Thorp is the regional educational media center director and an instructional technologist for the Ottawa Area Intermediate School District in Holland, Michigan. Blended and online instruction are areas of specialization commonly taught through related professional development opportunities at the Ottawa Area Intermediate School District.

Bruce Umpstead serves as the state director of educational technology and data coordination at the Michigan Department of Education. He is responsible for implementing Michigan's online learning graduation requirement and the State Educational Technology Plan. His formal education includes a BA in public administration, an MBA in finance and general management, and professional certifications in management accounting, project management, and online instruction.

Korrin M. Ziswiler has an MBA from Wright State University and is currently a doctoral student in the Education Leadership program at the University of Dayton in Dayton, Ohio. She is currently a graduate assistant for the University of Dayton and has taught numerous online classes for Sinclair Community College in Dayton, Ohio.

INTRODUCTION

TECHNOLOGY ACCESS IN TODAY'S K–12 SCHOOLS

In the past decade, considerable progress has been made in terms of increasing student access to technology in public K–12 schools across the country. In 1993, for example, approximately two-thirds of public K–12 schools in the United States could claim that they had Internet access for both their students and staff (Wells & Lewis, 2006). A decade later in 2003, K–12 public schools across the United States could boast nearly universal Internet access in their schools (Wells & Lewis, 2006). According to the National Center for Education Statistics (NCES), a national count of computers in public schools across the country revealed a ratio of 3.8-to-1, compared to a ratio of 5.7-to-1 in 1999, for the number of students sharing a computer for instructional purposes with Internet access (Wells & Lewis, 2006). While it is evident that overall student access to technology in public K–12 schools in the form of a computer with Internet access has improved, there still exist significant disparities in student access to technology across states. For instance, in states with high student technology access, such as Maine and South Dakota, there is only a 2-to-1 ratio of students sharing a computer with Internet access compared to an estimated 5-to-1 ratio in states with low student technology access, such as California, New Hampshire, and Utah.

EQUITY: THE CONTINUING "DIGITAL DIVIDE" OF TECHNOLOGY IN SCHOOLS

The well-documented "digital divide" in technological access between wealthier and poorer school districts, based on the unequal access to computers in schools, has substantially diminished. While the existing research demonstrates an improvement in the availability of computers with Internet access in schools, the research also indicates great inequities in the availability of certain technologies and the quality of technology-related instruction. For example, access to high quality professional development in the use of technology for instruction for both teachers and school administrators varies widely among school districts. In order to reduce this existing "digital divide," improved efforts need to be made, especially in poorer urban and rural school districts, to offer improved and quality technology training opportunities for educators who are attempting to use technology in the classroom, especially if previous technology training initiatives were inadequate and ineffective.

In terms of equity, there is still much work to be done involving the proper and educationally beneficial adoption of technology in schools to see that all students have both fair and extended opportunities to utilize school technology in rich and educationally productive ways. Currently, leading private technology companies, including Apple, Google, and Microsoft as well as the U.S. Department of Education, continue to invest hundreds of millions of dollars into providing schools across the country with the newest technology gadgets ranging from e-books to iPads. In 2011, for example, the Bill and Melinda Gates Foundation donated $20 million to develop a "tech revolution in education" and the U.S. Department of Education contributed more than $7 million to fund technology-based learning programs in schools across the country.

Despite a nationwide economic downturn, the financial rate of investment in technology for today's K–12 schools continues to increase. Unfortunately, however, much less research-based evidence is currently available, detailing the actual return on investment in terms of time and financial resources into technology adoption in our schools, especially in terms of outcome performance predictors of either student or school-based success, including improving student academic performance, best professional development practices for teachers and school administrators using technology as part of the instructional process, the viability of national and state-level technology standards for today's teachers and school administrators, best practices for using assistive technology effectively for students with special needs and disabilities, the cost-effectiveness associated with virtual schools, proper school policies and procedures for teaching students the responsible and ethical use of technology, and ensuring that technologies in schools are used in ways that ensure student safety and school security.

The 13 chapters that comprise this volume titled *Technology in Schools* vigorously debate many of the present and controversial issues surrounding the proper role of technology in today's schools. All of the chapters in this volume address whether certain aspects of technology adoption or practices in schools provide an appropriate return on investment based on whether technology has a favorable impact on factors such as student performance, budgeting, professional development, and safety and compared to a traditional brick-and-mortar student learning environment.

GROWTH IN ONLINE LEARNING, BUT CONCERNS OVER EDUCATIONAL QUALITY REMAIN

In 2011, 48 of the 50 states and the District of Columbia provide full-time or part-time online learning opportunities to approximately 3 million K–12 students with access to either supplemental or full-time online learning opportunities (iNACOL, 2011). In a national report by the Sloan Consortium titled *K–12 Online Learning: A Survey of U.S. School District Administrators,* online and blended courses, or those courses that combine online and face-to-face course delivery, grew 47% between 2005–2006 and 2007–2008 (Picciano & Seaman, 2009). In fact, blended courses, or those courses that combine both online and traditional, face-to-face instruction has emerged as the model believed to be the most effective in merging the best instructional practices from both online and traditional, face-to-face instruction (Staker, 2011). Although more technology is needed for this, the principal need is for development of the right goals, curricula, pedagogy, assessment, and overall educational vision.

In their provocative 2008 book *Disrupting Class: How Disruptive Innovation Will Change the Way the World Learns,* authors Clayton Christensen, Michael Horn, and Curtis Johnson highlight the significance of online student learning as a technology that can allow educators to customize instructional experiences for individual learners. The authors claim that by 2019, 50% of all high school courses will be delivered fully online. This pattern of growth is characteristic of a disruptive innovation—an innovation that transforms a sector characterized by products or services that are complicated, expensive, inaccessible, and centralized into one with products or services that are simple, affordable, accessible, convenient, and often customizable. More specifically, the authors argue that disruptive innovation, such as emerging technologies being used in today's schools, will force schools to abandon traditional curricula and pedagogical approaches to using technology. According to the Sloan Foundation's report, *K–12 Online Learning: A 2008 Follow-Up of the Survey of U.S. School District Administrators,* it is estimated that 1.03 million K–12 students took at least one online course during the 2007–2008 school year, a statistic that grew 47% from only 2 years earlier (Picciano & Seaman, 2009).

While it is clear that there is growth in the provision of online education to K–12 students, a cautionary review of the existing research reflects that only a few rigorous studies have been done thus far at the K–12 level detailing the educational effectiveness and overall quality of online education in terms of improving achievement and educational outcomes for K–12 students. One of the most controversial research reports was a meta-analysis of more than 1,000 controlled studies comparing online and traditional, face-to-face instruction in K–12 school environments, released by the U.S. Department of Education. The Speak Up National Research Project, which annually polls K–12 students, parents, and educators about the role of technology for learning in schools, identified factors that school administrators believed were barriers to offering quality online courses to students. These five barriers to effective online student courses include the following:

1. Limited state funding

2. Difficulties associated with evaluating the quality of online courses and the curriculum

3. Lack of experience to create student online courses

4. Teacher compensation

5. Teacher discomfort with, or lack of teacher training in, teaching online student courses

Despite an increased demand for and interest in online courses for K–12 students, there are still barriers that schools must address before online learning will effectively engage, enable, and empower a new paradigm for student learning (Project Tomorrow, 2011).

CUSTOMIZING STUDENT INSTRUCTION USING ASSISTIVE TECHNOLOGY AND UNIVERSAL DESIGN

In the first chapter of this volume, the authors debate whether assistive technology or universal design is a more effective method of technology implementation for students with special needs and disabilities. As more students with special needs and disabilities are spending a larger part of their day in general education classrooms, it is imperative that teachers learn how certain technologies can assist students in the learning process. In fact, the U.S. Department of Education currently funds two agencies, the National Center for Technology Innovation and the Center for Implementing Technology, which research and promote the use of technology specifically to improve the education of students with special needs and disabilities. Recent research suggests that as technologies evolve to help customize instruction, some assistive technologies that were traditionally used by students with special needs and disabilities are now being seriously considered useful learning tools for the general student population (Ash, 2011).

For example, Apple's iPad has applications, such as text-to-speech and speech-recognition software, which can be used by both students with disabilities and the general student population. Clearly, the advancement of newer technology in schools minimizes the distinction between assistive technology devices and general education technology tools. The universal design approach xx Technology in Schools

to technology relies on using elements of support for some student populations, including students with disabilities, that can benefit everyone. As the number of special education students in regular education classes increases across the country, it is even more imperative that teachers and school administrators learn how technology can help customize or individualize instruction for potentially all students.

THE EDUCATIONAL PROMISE OF E-BOOK TECHNOLOGIES

The second chapter in this volume, titled "Should E-Books Replace Traditional Textbooks and Paper-Based Books in Schools?" details the benefits and concerns associated with some schools' decisions to replace traditional, hardcopy textbooks with e-books. Since the 2007 release in the United States of Amazon's e-reader device, called the Kindle, the increased availability and low-cost of using e-book technology has become a reality. This increased availability and low-cost of e-book devices has made them particularly attractive to K–12 schools across the country. However, the potential of e-readers as effective technology tools for student learning has not yet been determined. As with many issues involving the implementation of technology in K–12 schools, there is much discussion of the potential of these technologies but sparse information on the documented educational effectiveness of these technology devices as effective student learning tools. As school districts across the country experience budgetary deficits like no other time in recent memory, it will be interesting to see whether cost considerations affect a shift toward e-readers over traditional textbooks. A central concern must continue to be the educational benefits associated with today's e-readers, especially in terms of student learning.

STATE AND LOCAL POLICIES AND THE IMPACT ON TECHNOLOGY IN SCHOOLS

Chapter 4 of this volume debates the issue of whether today's policies and procedures governing online student course offerings are appropriate to realize the unique technology advantages of these online classes. Some argue that K–12 education in the United States is at a policy crossroads when it comes to educational technology policy (Quillen, 2011). As momentum for online instruction grows at the K–12 level, many K–12 school- and district-level policies reflect the traditional brick-and-mortar, physical classroom that never envisioned terms such as distance learning, blended learning approaches, or virtual schools. Many of these existing state and local policies, such as school funding models, textbook adoption procedures, and teacher certification requirements, actually hinder the growth of the emerging online-based learning models. For example, while many publishing companies are adapting to digital textbook formats, most school districts do not have policies in place that address how to combine traditional print and digital textbooks in an effective way. Even fewer districts have policies in place that would facilitate the technological integration of all digital textbooks.

THE EDUCATIONAL VIABILITY OF VIRTUAL SCHOOLS

Several chapters in this volume debate the current viability of today's virtual schools, either as effective student learning environments or as cost-effective compared to traditional brick-and-mortar schools. Chapter 5 debates the controversial issue of whether virtual schools, either full-time or supplemental, are effective student learning environments. As the number of states with virtual K–12 schools continues to grow, some researchers maintain that virtual schools provide unique and increased educational benefits to students compared to traditional brick-and-mortar schools, including the ability of K–12 virtual schools to meet the specific academic needs of students who previously struggled academically in traditional, face-to-face classroom settings, as well as students with special needs and disabilities. Additionally, public K–12 virtual schools have the ability to increase student access to specific classes, such as Advanced Placement (AP) or credit recovery classes, that students would not otherwise have the opportunity to take at their traditional brick-and-mortar schools, especially in rural school communities. The primary counterargument to the existing educational benefits of today's virtual schools as effective student learning environments is that there is not enough rigorous, empirical research being done on virtual schools. A major critique against the existing limited research studies that examine whether virtual schools are effective student learning environments is that they are not representative of today's diverse K–12 student virtual school population.

Chapter 6 addresses whether today's virtual schools are more cost-effective compared to traditional brick-and-mortar public schools. Unquestionably, there is very little research detailing how today's virtual schools are funded. It is important to recognize that virtual schools have unique costs and do not share some of the daily operating cost considerations of traditional brick-and-mortar schools, such as capital and construction-related costs or transportation-related expenses. However, both virtual and traditional brick-and-mortar schools face some similar costs necessary to become successful student learning environments, including teacher professional development expenses, quality assurance, instruction, and continuous research, development, and planning associated with curriculum development (Anderson, Augenblick, DeCescre, & Conrad, 2006). As this debate concerning the funding of virtual schools compared to traditional brick-and-mortar schools reveals, many of the costs associated with providing a high-quality education are identical in both online as well as face-to-face classroom environments.

NATIONAL AND STATE TECHNOLOGY STANDARDS FOR EDUCATORS

Chapter 8 addresses the controversial issue of whether national or state-level technology standards should be required for today's teachers. The International Society for Technology in Education (ISTE) has been and continues to be the primary organization that has advocated the movement toward national technology standards for both educators and students. Since 2007, ISTE has developed a set of National Educational Technology Standards (NETS) for students, teachers, and school administrators.

Clearly, a central question in the debate about whether to have national and/or state-level technology standards for educators is whether the standards will actually help teachers across the country properly use technology to improve instruction. Another issue involving the adoption of national and/or state-level technology standards for educators is what impact, if any, such standards might have on quality or credibility. For example, the growth of virtual schools across the country and the need to ensure that these online-based schools are credible and of high quality has prompted the need to consider technology-based standards. Some argue that the use of national or state-level technology standards for teachers from a legitimate accreditation agency would verify that students who are receiving online instruction or instruction using emerging technologies are meeting the same educational standards expected in traditional brick-and-mortar school environments (Ash, 2011). A potential downside to national or state-level technology standards is that they would be set too low and not allow for innovation by teachers. Nevertheless, the debate over whether national or state-level technology standards should be mandatory for today's teachers addresses the issue that technological investments in schools raises questions of quality and credibility of technology as a student learning tool. Whenever the educational community loses sight of the importance of quality and credibility when using emerging technologies, it minimizes the high priority of student learning.

DIGITAL CITIZENSHIP: RESPONSIBLE STUDENT TECHNOLOGY USE IN A WEB 2.0 WORLD

While many of the contributors to this volume actively debate issues involving the effectiveness of certain technologies on student learning and educational quality, several of the chapters debate the issue of whether certain technologies, such as social networking sites and smart phones should be banned in schools or whether educators should develop policies and procedures that focus on the responsible use of technology in schools by students. Currently, many K–12 school administrators across the country view the use of mobile technologies and social networking sites, such as Facebook and Myspace, as inappropriate in schools and these sites are banned. While concerns about student safety on the Internet is certainly a valid concern for today's educators, some of the authors in this volume question whether there is a more balanced approach to consider the educational benefits of technologies such as social networking sites.

Some of the contributors to this volume argue that both the media and critics of the use of mobile technologies and social networking sites in schools give far more attention to what is wrong with these emerging technologies compared to the potential educational benefits these technologies can provide students in an increasingly global 21st-century world. For example, a growing number of media reports highlight the misuse of social networking sites for the purposes of cyberbullying and cyberharassment, or the use of mobile devices for sexting—the act of electronically sending sexually explicit messages or photographs. Rarely do the mainstream media concentrate on the ways social networking sites or mobile technologies are being used by students and teachers to enrich learning in schools.

For instance, a 2007 report by the National School Boards Association (NSBA), titled *Creating and Connecting: Research and Guidelines on Online Social and Educational Networking,* details the difference in opinion between school administrators compared to students and parents regarding the use of social networking sites in schools. In the report, more than half of the school administrators surveyed wanted to prohibit the use of social networking sites in schools. Nearly 60% of students surveyed indicated that they used social networking sites for online discussions to assist with their schoolwork. Additionally, a majority of both the students and parents surveyed expressed high expectations regarding the positive role social networking technologies can play in a student's education.

Since social networking is increasingly playing an important role in education at both the K–12 and higher education levels, there are alternatives for students and educators who want to experience the potential educational benefits of social networking without the student safety and school security concerns often associated with using mainstream social networking sites, such as Facebook or Myspace. For instance, worries about security, information-sharing, and safety have led some educators to turn to the use of social networking sites such as Edmodo, which was specifically designed to be used in schools. The increasing development of education-based social networking sites, such as Elgg, Edmodo, Gaggle, and Ning might serve both students and educators as a viable alternative to the commercial social networking sites, such as Facebook and Myspace, that many people are familiar with. It seems that education-based social networking sites provide a safer and more secure environment that can be monitored by the school district while simultaneously allowing students and educators the opportunity to participate in the use of 21st-century social networking technologies (Brady, 2010).

SAFETY AND SECURITY ISSUES INVOLVING TECHNOLOGY IN SCHOOLS

In addition to debating whether current investment levels in certain technologies, such as virtual schools or pocket assistive technologies in schools, are yielding high returns in terms of educational productivity for students, several chapters in this volume concentrate on whether the use of certain technologies, such as video camera surveillance or commercial social networking sites, pose school safety or security concerns that outweigh any educational benefits they might provide. Several chapters in this volume debate the appropriate legal rights of teachers and school administrators and the use of social networking sites. For instance, Chapter 9 addresses the issue of whether today's teachers have the legal right to create and post online content about their school on commercial social networking sites.

Chapter 7 of this volume examines whether the use of video surveillance cameras in today's schools is an invasion of student privacy. One contentious issue involving the use of video surveillance cameras in schools is whether these surveillance cameras violate a student's right to privacy or provide today's school officials greater control to manage school safety and security on school premises. For example, in Chicago, video surveillance cameras in 14 public high schools with a history of school violence have been linked directly to local police stations in an effort to create a safer environment in those schools. As surveillance technologies become more sophisticated and less costly, the question becomes, will school officials be more likely to use video camera surveillance in lieu of actual security officials located physically in the schools?

As a continuing economic downturn forces school districts to make drastic budgetary cuts, including in personnel, some reformers are turning to online-based technologies, such as social networking sites, as potentially valuable educational resources. Simultaneously, however, increased reports of sexual predators and cyberbullying on the Internet have raised concerns for some parents and state legislators about whether the safety concerns of using social networking technologies outweigh the educational benefits these technologies might provide. As a result, many states across the country have passed legislation to address incidents of cyberbullying and cyberharassment in schools, as well as to limit the use of social networking sites in schools. Chapter 9 of this volume debates the legal issues concerning whether or not teachers should have the right to create and post online content about their school on social networking sites, even when the teachers post the online content on their own time and without the use of any school resources.

Similarly, what levels of legal authority do school administrators have in terms of regulating the online-related activities of their students as a means to protect student safety and the overall security of the school. Chapter 10 examines whether school administrators should have greater legal authority to discipline students for online behavior resulting in cyberbullying or cyberharassment. Similarly, Chapter 11 examines whether school administrators should have greater legal authority to discipline students for false online statements regarding school personnel on social networking sites. A problem in the current legal landscape is that the U.S. Supreme Court has not yet ruled on or developed legal guidelines associated with either teacher or student free speech and expression in an online environment. As a result, today's school administrators are in a state of legal limbo regarding the handling of teacher and student conduct involving the use of certain technologies. Arguably, one effective means of handling such misuse of technology is not through the adoption of tougher laws or policies. Instead, educators need to take the responsibility of teaching proper "digital citizenship" to both students ands school staff. Possibly, responsible technology usage and online behaviors are more effectively taught than legislated.

SUMMARY

Based on the current investment, in both time and monetary resources, the next decade promises to be a defining period for the use of technology and online learning in today's schools. In their provocative book *Disrupting Class: How Disruptive Innovation Will Change the Way the World Learns,* authors Clayton Christensen, Michael Horn, and Curtis Johnson proclaim that the educational system of the United States is at the point of an online learning revolution. The authors make this controversial prediction regarding the technology landscape for U.S. K–12 schools in 2018:

> The result of these four factors—(1.) technological improvements that make learning more engaging; (2.) research advances that enable the design of student-centric software appropriate to each type of learner; (3.) the looming teacher shortage; and (4.) inexorable cost pressures—is that 10 years from the publication of this book [2008], computer-based, student-centric learning will account for 50 percent of the "seat miles" in U.S. secondary schools.... Given how long some have been in the trenches of school reform, this will be quite a breathtaking trip. (p. 103)

The increased infusion of technology in today's schools is pushing the boundaries of customized student learning. The educational community needs to consider technology's return on its investment in terms of factors such as student achievement, student safety, school security, and emerging technology's contributions to creating an effective student learning environment that meets the expectations of educators. This diverse and interesting series of 13 debates involving many facets of technology in schools hopefully will provide readers an opportunity to reevaluate, retool, and rethink how we use emerging technologies in the classroom.

Kevin P. Brady
North Carolina State University

FURTHER READINGS AND RESOURCES

Anderson, A., Augenblick, J., DeCescre, D., & Conrad, J. (2006). *20/20 costs and funding of virtual schools.* Atlanta, GA: BellSouth Foundation. Retrieved from http://www.apaconsulting.net/uploads/reports/9.pdf

Ash, K. (2010, April 23). Accreditation is seen as high priority. *Education Week.* Retrieved August 15, 2011, from http://www.edweek.org/ew/articles/2010/04/28/30edtech_accountability.h29.html

Brady, K. P. (2010). Lifting the limits on social networking sites. *The School Administrator, 67*(2), 8.

Christensen, C. M., Horn, M. B., & Johnson, C. W. (2008). *Disrupting class: How disruptive innovation will change the way the world learns.* New York: McGraw-Hill.

International Association for K-12 Online Learning (iNACOL). (2011). *Research, trends, and statistics: K-12 online learning and virtual schools.* Washington, DC: Author. Retrieved from http://www.inacol.org/press/nacol_fast_facts.pdf

National School Boards Association (NSBA). (2007, July). *Creating and connecting: Research and guidelines on online social and educational networking.* Washington, DC: Author.

Picciano, A. G., & Seaman, J. (2009, September). *K–12 online learning: A 2008 follow-up of the survey of U.S. school district administrators.* Newburyport, MA: The Sloan Consortium.

Quillen, I. (2010, April 23). E-learning delivery debated. *Education Week.* Retrieved August 15, 2011, from http://www.edweek.org/ew/articles/2010/04/28/30edtech_daily.h29.html

Speak Up Project. (2011). *Learning in the 21st century: 2011 trends update.* Washington, DC: Project Tomorrow.

Staker, H. (2011, May). *The rise of K-12 blended learning: Profiles of emerging models.* Mountain View, CA: Innosight Institute.

Wells, J., & Lewis, L. (2006). *Internet access in U.S. public schools and classrooms: 1994-2005* (NCES 2007-020). Washington, DC: National Center for Education Statistics.

Is assistive technology or universal design a more effective method of technology integration for students with disabilities?

POINT: Timothy E. Morse, *University of Southern Mississippi Gulf Coast*

COUNTERPOINT: Margie W. Crowe, *University of Southern Mississippi*

OVERVIEW

In this chapter, authors Timothy E. Morse (University of Southern Mississippi Gulf Coast) and Margie W. Crowe (University of Southern Mississippi) debate whether assistive technology or universal design is a more effective method of technology integration for students with disabilities and special needs. The authors Morse and Crowe debate the relative strengths as well as weaknesses of each approach to technology integration, particularly as it impacts students with disabilities. During the past decade, evolving technologies and their integration into the classroom have unquestionably changed former approaches in which students with disabilities and special needs were educated. Although not a novel concept or practice in the educational community, assistive technology, commonly referred to as AT, has made a notably dramatic impact in increasing the functional as well as educational capabilities of students with disabilities. The type of assistive technologies available to students with disabilities is extensive, including not only computer hardware and software, but technology applications and tools exclusively available on the Internet. Most recently, for example, relatively low-cost applications, commonly called *apps* on Apple's iTunes or a host of other open-source application-based websites have become available for use on mobile technology devices, including smartphones or tablet-based computers, such as Apple's iPad.

In his position that AT is a more effective approach to technology integration for students with disabilities, Morse argues that AT is a considerably more effective method of technology integration compared to universal design mainly because AT is a process that is "highly individualized, comprehensive, and self-validating" than universal design's concentration exclusively on design and access issues associated with technology integration. While acknowledging the valid concerns of design and accessibility linked to technology integration, an AT-oriented approach to technology integration, Morse argues, incorporates the individualization necessary for the rigid data collection and analysis required for an effective means of technology integration for the highly individualized educational needs of students with disabilities.

Since AT is so focused on the individual student with a special need or disability, Morse asserts, technology integration can be uniquely and individually fitted and adapted to the specific educational strengths and weaknesses of each student with a disability. In this respect, Morse contends, an AT approach to technology integration for students with disabilities is more effective than a universal design–based approach to technology integration for students with disabilities. Another argument Morse advances for the use of AT as a more effective method for the integration of technology for students with disabilities is the fact that the current and primary federal law governing students attending elementary through secondary schools, the Individuals with Disabilities Education Act (IDEA), specifically authorizes the use of AT for qualified students with disabilities who receive special education services, including those services involving the integration of technology.

In her counterpoint essay, Crowe asserts that universal design, often referred to as Universal Design for Learning, or UDL, is a better and more appropriate approach to technology integration than the highly individualized approach of AT. Unlike the individualized approach of AT, the universal design approach focuses on the creation of products, including technology, that are designed from the outset to accommodate individuals from a wide range of abilities as well as disabilities. The primary objective of a universal design approach to technology integration for students with disabilities would be to develop technology products that are more accessible to all groups of students as well as flexible for all students. Additionally, unlike AT, the universal design approach to technology integration in education is relatively new and was previously applied in the area of architecture. Given today's diversity of student learners, Crowe asserts that universal design is a more effective method of technology integration than AT because this particular approach is designed to be available from the very beginning to students with disabilities. Instead of providing AT's individualized approach to technology integration, a universal design approach is developed to be flexible and inclusive, as well as to actively accommodate the wide diversity of student learning needs.

In the complex educational setting, both authors seem to find some middle ground in their discussion of the potential benefits associated with the technology integration of both AT and universal design for students with disabilities. For example, both authors admit the inherent disadvantages of focusing exclusively on either a too individualistic AT approach or a purely universal design approach where inefficiencies occur when trying to develop technology integration and accommodations for all students, especially students with so-called low-incidence disabilities. Both Morse and Crowe acknowledge the strong link between AT and universal design and discuss how both approaches can be used to develop technology integration solutions for students with disabilities and special needs. In a complex educational environment where technology is constantly changing, the authors believe an optimal approach to technology integration for students with disabilities and special needs will be one that uses both AT and universal design. Both authors suggest that both approaches suffer from a lack of clarity as the approach relates to technology integration, especially among students with disabilities and special needs. This debate provides some of this necessary clarity by pointing out that the AT approach highlights an individualized approach to technology integration while the universal design approach concentrates on the importance of technological design and the increased access to technology for a larger diversity of student learners, including students with disabilities and special needs.

Kevin P. Brady
North Carolina State University

POINT: Timothy E. Morse
University of Southern Mississippi Gulf Coast

E ffectively and efficiently providing every student access to an education without barriers is clearly a goal that everyone with a vested interest in our nation's public schools can support. The realization of this goal is currently captured by a concept that is being referred to as Universal Design for Learning, or UDL. Given the diversity that exists among our nation's school-age public school population that allows for universal access, many elements will need to come together for this concept to be fully realized. At the very least, accessible technological environments will need to be properly constructed and configured to work in concert with one another. For example, both the design of a computer workstation and the computer within it—the machine and its software—will have to be accessible.

Yet, while the inherent design of learning environments and technologies will make them more universally accessible and afford an opportunity for students with disabilities to be integrated into mainstream environments that are based on the principles of UDL, design alone and the access it affords will not necessarily result in effective methods of technology integration. Rather, as will be argued in this point essay, AT is the more effective method of technology integration for students with disabilities. AT defined by the Individuals with Disabilities Education Act (IDEA, 2006) refers to any piece of equipment that can be used to support or enhance individuals as they achieve, improve, or continue the skills necessary for learning, daily living, and recreation. AT results from a process that is highly individualized, comprehensive, and self-validating. AT, as it is addressed by the federal mandate that authorizes its use for qualified students with disabilities who receive special education services (i.e., IDEA), allows for the individualization, comprehensive design and implementation, and data collection and analysis necessary for ensuring an effective method of technology integration.

Before debating the reasons why this is so, two overarching topics must be addressed: (1) the strong link between AT and UDL and (2) the proper contextual definition for the term *effectiveness* as it applies to this discussion.

Regarding the link that presently exists between AT and UDL, it must be noted that it is not possible, or even necessary, to put forth arguments in favor of the use of AT at the expense of UDL. Rather, given that the use of AT by students with disabilities leads to the realization of the ultimate goal of UDL, what must be understood are the reasons why AT solutions are a necessary and more effective method of technology integration for students with disabilities compared to the more global and less specialized technology integration construct of universal design, or UDL. An explanation of these reasons is the focus of this debate.

The definition of the term *effectiveness* as it applies to this debate focuses on the use of technology that directly results in desired outcomes for students with disabilities. The desired outcome for students with disabilities using AT would be the improved functional capabilities that allow them to be both more independent and access additional mainstream environments.

There are many reasons why an AT approach is considered a more effective method of technology integration for students with disabilities compared to a universal design approach. First, the incredible range of unique situations that AT solutions can address is highlighted and discussed. Second, the wide-ranging provisions that are put forth in the IDEA legislation that pertain to the comprehensive design and implementation of a unique AT solution for a student with a disability, and an ongoing validation of the solution's effectiveness, are delineated. Third, these provisions and their relationship to additional, complementary supports that are allowed for in the IDEA are examined with respect to how they permit for an individualized and comprehensive solution. Collectively, these issues combine to explain why AT is a more effective method of technology integration compared to a universal design approach for students with disabilities.

ASSISTIVE TECHNOLOGY EFFECTIVELY ADDRESSES UNIQUE STUDENT DISABILITY-RELATED NEEDS

By definition, a disability refers to some sort of limitation. Hence, interventions that are provided to students with disabilities seek to mediate the impact of their disability. For instance, multisensory instructional strategies are used to teach students with specific learning disabilities how to acquire basic reading and more advanced literacy skills, and devices such as hearing aids enable students with hearing impairments to enhance their ability to process auditory input.

The latter instance is an example of the application of AT. The use of AT by students with disabilities enables them to increase their functional capabilities that have been limited by their disability. *Functional capabilities* refer to the performance of skills that would have to be performed wholly, or in part, by someone else if the individual with a disability could not perform them.

The inherent nature of a number of disabilities for which students can qualify to receive special education services uniquely limits the functional capabilities of those who experience them and, in turn, historically has presented barriers to their access to an appropriate education. For instance, consider each of the following scenarios:

1. A student with a specific learning disability and resulting fine motor difficulties that prevent him from producing legible text using a pen or a pencil cannot satisfactorily complete writing assignments, such as an essay for English class or a short-answer science quiz.

2. A student with an orthopedic impairment who is a quadriplegic cannot complete required reading assignments because he cannot access the textbook that contains them.

3. A student who has multiple disabilities can neither speak nor write and, therefore, has no way of expressing her knowledge via traditional means.

4. A fourth grade student, who is mildly mentally retarded, can only decode and comprehend text that is written at a kindergarten level, yet his listening comprehension skills are between a second- and third-grade level.

Without the provision of an AT solution tailored to each of these students' situations, they would be denied the opportunity of access to an appropriate education. However, when each student is provided an appropriate AT solution—the student with a specific learning disability is given access to a keyboard for the purpose of creating legible text, the student with an orthopedic impairment is enabled to use a switch-operated page turner so that he can read the course's textbook, the student with multiple disabilities is provided with an augmentative communication device that enables her to produce both speech and text, and the student with mental retardation uses a text-to-speech conversion program to have grade-level texts read to him—he or she is able to access the same education as his or her non-disabled peers using a uniquely tailored technological solution.

Thus, as is the case with respect to every issue that is addressed in special education, the first step toward designing an effective intervention is identifying the unique circumstances that pertain to each student's case. In accordance with the language of the IDEA, this is referred to as *individualizing instruction*. A global, one-size-fits-all solution, such as the one implied by the concept of universal design, is, by definition, the antithesis of special education. Consequently, it must be acknowledged that the individualization that is afforded by AT to students with disabilities is an essential first step to a method of effective technology integration.

THE IDEA'S WIDE-RANGING ASSISTIVE TECHNOLOGY PROVISIONS

Individualizing instruction on behalf of students with disabilities entails the comprehensive design and implementation of an intervention, followed by data-based validation of its effectiveness. With respect to the use of AT by students with disabilities, the IDEA contains a number of relevant provisions that address these very issues.

First, the law identifies AT as a special factor, which means that its use by every student with a disability must be considered. More specifically, the law requires that when there is reason to believe that a student with a disability will benefit from using an AT, he should undergo an appropriate evaluation that is to be conducted across all customary environments. Investigating the possible use of AT across all customary environments, which in a school setting would include general education classrooms, restrooms, gymnasiums, playgrounds, and the cafeteria, highlights the fact that AT fundamentally is considered to be an effective method of technology integration for students with disabilities, a means by which technology truly is a tool that enhances one's functioning.

Moreover, an AT evaluation serves two primary purposes related to the integration of the technology. The first is the selection of an appropriate AT. The second purpose is to collect data that are to be used as a baseline measure against which data pertaining to the future use of the AT can be compared. Data that verifies the effectiveness of the AT validates its use, while nonsupporting data result in a reexamination of the appropriateness of the AT solution that was selected.

Third, to ensure that the AT solution is effective, the IDEA contains provisions that address the comprehensive design and implementation of the chosen AT solution. In accordance with the IDEA, not only the student with a disability but also significant others in his life, such as teachers, peers, and family members, are to be taught their role with respect to the use of the AT. Moreover, schools also are responsible for ensuring that the AT remains in good working order by performing repair and maintenance activities as necessary. And, as noted previously, formative data must document the effectiveness of the AT solution.

RELATED AND SUPPORTING STIPULATIONS IN THE IDEA

Though not specifically identified as provisions that pertain to AT, other related stipulations in the IDEA combine to support AT as an effective method of technology integration. In fact, one could reasonably argue that some of these stipulations are, by definition, additional low-tech assistive technologies.

As states have developed assessment systems for the purpose of addressing relevant parts of the No Child Left Behind (NCLB) Act of 2001, they have created lists of allowable accommodations that can be used by students with disabilities when they participate in statewide assessments of student achievement of the content area standards that have been established in accordance with the NCLB Act, as well as protocols for the use of these accommodations on a daily basis in the classroom. Accommodations do not enable a student to alter the content standards he is required to master but do allow him to use different ways to demonstrate mastery of the content (e.g., orally state rather than write responses), or to demonstrate mastery of the content during different, yet acceptable, testing conditions (e.g., complete the exam in a small group arrangement rather than a large group arrangement). In some instances these accommodations serve as low-tech AT solutions, such as when a student dictates his responses to short-answer questions into a digital recorder rather than writes these responses. In other instances, these accommodations are not assistive technologies in the sense that they enable a student to independently improve his functional capabilities; rather, these accommodations work as an additional tool school personnel can use to allow a student with a disability to be integrated into the general education curriculum. As such, they can be considered to be supplementary aides and services that are applied uniquely to the case of each student with a disability so that he realizes an effective method of technology integration in the general education classroom. While the concept of UDL aims for this integration by designing universally accessible environments "on the front end," this concept does not address the case study analysis that is necessary to establish its effectiveness.

CONCLUSION

As has been documented throughout this point essay, the AT provisions in the IDEA are another example of how this law calls specifically for individualized instruction and the collection of supporting data that documents the effectiveness of this instruction to ensure that a student with a disability realizes meaningful benefit from the special education services he receives. With respect to AT, these provisions include proper evaluations, comprehensive program design and implementation, and validating data collection and analysis.

Furthermore, as the concept of universal design has emerged and continues to develop, it appears as if there is a recognition that it will coexist alongside AT as well as subsume its intended outcomes. The justification for this assertion rests with the fact that the IDEA addresses both universal design and AT, but has not sought to completely eliminate one in favor of the other.

Rather, it appears that the effective use of one (AT) leads to the other (universal design).

Additionally, the IDEA's AT provisions call for the use of accommodations and supplementary aides, services, and supports to enable students with disabilities to be educated in a general education classroom is balanced by calls in the professional literature for the use of differentiated instruction. Thus, there seems to be an understanding that many tools will be brought to bear in an attempt to realize the goal of universal design, and this means that this general concept, by itself, cannot be deemed to be the most effective method of technology integration for students with disabilities.

While it is appropriate at the outset to design educational environments so that they allow the maximum amount of student access possible, it is extremely difficult to imagine that any environment could be designed once to account for the nuances of various disabilities as well as the changing nature of education (e.g., emerging instructional materials and strategies). Rather, these progressive environments will have to be updated and supplemented (such as with the provision of AT) to enable the goal of universal design to be realized. Consequently, the use of AT is best for each student with a disability because this technology is especially crafted to meet each individual student's needs. As was emphasized throughout this point essay, the IDEA's specific AT provisions call for detailed case studies in each instance of its use, with the end result being clear documentation of its effectiveness in each instance. A major shortcoming of the universal design technology integration approach is that it assumes incorporation of every individual rather than requiring a detailed study of each individual student case. Based on this presentation of the debate, AT emerges as the more effective method of technology integration for students with disabilities.

COUNTERPOINT: Margie W. Crowe
University of Southern Mississippi

Providing access to education is not only a fundamental principle woven into the tapestry of our society, it is also the law. This is evidenced by the federally mandated programs aimed at today's diversity of student learners. Today's schools are mandated to provide educational services to students who are academically gifted, poor, and migrant and speak languages other than English, as well as to students with disabilities. As a result, one of the major daunting challenges to 21st-century schools is that they provide educational programming that meets the needs of a wide range of student learners and simultaneously determine, according to the No Child Left Behind Act (NCLB, 2006), challenging standards for all students with success measured against these standards.

Students receiving special education services under the Individuals with Disabilities Education Act (IDEA, 2006) are perhaps the largest single group of these diverse student learners. Students with disabilities represent a group within themselves that are as individually diverse as each of the current 13 eligibility categories under the IDEA. Under the best of circumstances, providing for these students is a daunting task. However, as a result of these needs, options for learning designs, pedagogies, and learning environments emerge. Within the field of special education, two growing technology integration methodologies are the use of AT and the use of universal design, often referred to as Universal Design for Learning (UDL). While there is considerable overlap in AT and UDL, there is also a fundamental difference. AT is individualized and, thus, limited in scope, whereas UDL is universal in application. For that reason, UDL can afford methodologies to meet a range of student needs on a daily basis that might include AT for individual students but also meet the various needs of other students in the classroom. Universal design strategies for technology integration provide flexible means of engagement supporting various student interests, as well as learning modality diversity that challenge and assess each student. Every student benefits from a universal design approach to technology integration, including those students with disabilities. Universal design often includes technology but it also includes a myriad of other techniques, materials, and pedagogies. Using universal design means meeting these high individual leaning expectations and the individualized needs of students with disabilities from the onset while simultaneously considering the very realistic restraints of cost, availability of equipment, support, and training.

ASSISTIVE TECHNOLOGY

Although effective, AT in some cases may involve little or no technology, such as adapted pencils. It can also involve higher-level technology. It is individualized, which incurs maintenance, possible training, and ongoing individualized student assessment. While AT has been a part of special education services for years, it has, for the most part, been underutilized. The 2004 reauthorization of the IDEA requires that all students receiving special education services be considered for AT. In many schools, this has been a simple "yes/no" question. Now, however, schools are required to not only consider whether or not to use AT but provide a justification as to why AT is appropriate or not for each student receiving special education services. AT, in some cases, makes the difference in access to learning, such as in the case of speech to Braille accommodations for a student who is blind. Students can be included by using switch-activated devices in activities that would, without AT, leave them as observers instead of active participants in the learning process. This has brought AT more to the forefront of individual planning. It is, like much in special education and education in general, underfunded. It is, because of its limited scope, only one tool in the major concept of universal design. There is no doubt that AT is one essential tool.

Special education requires the individual assessment and observation of the student in various settings. It requires the focused attention of a team of professionals and family members to ascertain the most effective goals, settings, and methodologies. To determine the best use and proper assignment of AT requires the same ongoing assessment and evaluation to make sure adequate progress is being accomplished. Evaluation and assessment linked to progress are the elements that make special education "special." This same process must be repeated for effective AT to be available to a student. Once again, a specialized team must be assembled, evaluations and observations must be conducted, and goals for the technology, at this time, must be determined. Using the technology integration approach of AT often begins a lengthy and complicated process for the needs of one individual student.

UNIVERSAL DESIGN

Originally, universal design was limited to the disciplines of architecture and construction. This meant, in the case of established buildings, reconstructing elements of the building to provide access. It meant ripping out such things as a wall to build a larger door to the restroom to make it wheelchair accessible. It is now a broader concept in other fields, including technology integration in education. Technology, for example, struggles with accommodations that are expanded in each new operating system or word processing program. The field of education soon saw the implications of the universal design approach for technology integration. One of the major efforts was in the form of federal grant monies to investigate universal design. More specifically, UDL is the intentional and systematic process by which curriculum in its entirety (goals, materials, methods, activities, assessments) is designed from beginning to end to address individual learning differences (Center for Applied Special Technology, 2008). UDL basic assumptions focus on the concept that students with disabilities are not a separate category of learners but a part of a larger learning difference continuum that allows the teacher to focus on the needs of the entire classroom as well as the individual needs of students with special needs. UDL is not focused on remediation or "retrofitting" but in creating a learning environment from the very beginning that accommodates learner needs or is "smart from the start."

The term *universal* can be misleading. It is not intended to presume that there is one methodology or way for every person but rather to support the understanding that all (universal) learners have unique needs and implies a range of methodologies and materials. There is no limitation on the type of equipment or technology necessary. While technology may and should be an integral part of a universal design classroom, it is only one option. It would be senseless not to consider the concept of universal design in construction. New construction from the blueprint stage is now required to include these elements of universal design. It is a matter of planning the building originally rather than reconstructing after the fact. It is also a matter of financial consideration. Any businessperson would conclude that the costs of originally constructing a building that meets these needs is more economical in time, labor, and materials than the costs of these same resources to make the changes once the building is constructed. While this seems very sensible and logical in construction and business, often these same sensible and logical conclusions are not applied to educational settings. Students are required access to a curriculum that is not designed to meet their needs. A considerable number of resources are expended to make a classroom work for a student when the original "construction" of the class elements, namely instructional strategies and planning, could eliminate this retrofitting.

UNIVERSAL DESIGN PRINCIPLES

The Center for Applied Special Technology (2008), a charter organization centered on universal design, describes universal design as a blueprint for student lesson design. The basic premise of universal design is to proactively consider the barriers to learning rather than using a medical model of curing or fixing the student learning problems once they occur. Foundational to universal design is the construct that curriculum should include a range of alternatives to make it available to all learners with different backgrounds, learning preferences, abilities, and disabilities. Universal design is a concept or a philosophy for designing lesson delivery and all its elements in such a flexible manner that it meets the needs of all learners rather than a select few (Spooner, Baker, Harris, Ahlgrim-Delzell, & Browder, 2007). Efficient use of resources in UDL, like that of universal design in construction, is a logical conclusion.

While universal design is described as a concept, it has framing principles that offer parameters for consistent implementation. Frank Bowe (2000) suggested equitable use for all learners, flexibility (or variety) of materials, simple and consistent expectations avoiding unnecessary complexity, perceptible information using all of the senses, tolerance for errors, low physical effort, and size and space for appropriate use. While these principles overlap in function, they can be applied in both pedagogical and technological ways.

UNIVERSAL DESIGN AND STUDENTS WITH DISABILITIES

In IDEA (2006), general education was established as the source or foundation for all children. It became the guideline whereby students should be measured. Therefore, it became common for students in special education to be placed in a general education classroom with "nondisabled peers" as required by IDEA (2006). It was obvious that for students requiring special education services there would need to be accommodations or modifications to make this a productive setting. So it most often became a task of making the student fit the classroom rather than the classroom fit the student. Planning for this "goodness of fit" requires resources, including time, personnel, and material, that can be more efficiently streamlined if the initial planning is universally designed.

The understanding that students with disabilities have limited functional capabilities in the specific area of their disability is foundational to AT and special education in general. It also falls within the parameters of universal design. UDL, at its foundation, is considering the needs of all learners. With more students in inclusive educational settings with more involved disabilities, universal design allows the student to be a part of age-appropriate activities with as little spotlight as possible. Basic to UDL are multiple means of representation, multiple means of expression, and multiple means of engagement that allow for a viable plethora of services provided in a natural and least restrictive environment from the beginning.

UNIVERSAL DESIGN VERSUS ASSISTIVE TECHNOLOGY

UDL requires training and a change of assumptions and paradigms. As with any new method, these changes require support. Many skills, tools, and scaffolds are readily available from publishers. Lesson plans and instructional guides are available online for teachers. It would be a mistake, illegal, and perhaps naive to abandon AT or to consider it unusable or archaic. AT can be an essential part of the education plan for that a student, affecting the quality and usefulness of life. However, because of the cost and specialized skills required for training, and limited information, comprehensive AT may not efficiently be available to students or it may not be maintainable. Both universal design and AT are about making learning and functional skills accessible. A universally designed curriculum is one that has been designed from the very beginning to be available for students. Finding barriers and designing a curriculum that aligns with NCLB and IDEA can be a better use of resources.

Further, a universally designed curriculum is designed to meet the needs of a wide range of students with sensory, motor, cognitive, linguistic, and affective abilities and disabilities (Rose, 2001). These disabilities are very different in the scope of accessibility. AT is focused on a skill or set of skills. UDL is focused on the designing pedagogies and environment, learning or physical. Each has their place. It is not a matter of the "chicken and the egg." It is, rather, a matter of best practice. UDL may enable students to access content designed from the beginning to accommodate their instructional needs, such as listening to chapters in electronic text while their peers are reading chapters from print texts. How well the students with and without disabilities comprehend from those texts formats is attributed to effective pedagogy that can either stand alone as universal design or stand with the technology (King-Sears, 2009). Thus, AT alone without the support of a UDL environment is only a part of the blueprint for effective support and education of students with disabilities.

Further Readings and Resources

Bausch, M. E., & Ault, M. J. (2008). Assistive technology implementation plan: A tool for improving outcomes. *TEACHING Exceptional Children, 41*(1), 6–14.

Bowe, F. (2000). *Universal design in education: Teaching nontraditional students.* Westport, CT: Bergin and Garvey.

Center for Applied Special Technology. (2008). *Universal Design for Learning guidelines* (Ver. 1.0). Wakefield, MA: Author.

Cook, A. M., & Polgar, J. M. (2007). *Cook and Hussey's assistive technologies: Principles and practice.* Maryland Heights, MO: Elsevier.

Council for Exceptional Children. (2005). *Universal Design for Learning: A guide for teachers and education professionals.* Boston: Pearson.

Johnston, L., Beard, L. A., & Carpenter, L. B. (2007). *Assistive technology: Access for all students.* Upper Saddle River, NJ: Pearson.

Julnes, R., & Brown, S. (1993). The legal mandate to provide assistive technology in special education programming. *Education Law Reporter, 82,* 737–748.

King-Sears, M. (2009). Universal Design for Learning: Technology and pedagogy. *Learning Disability Quarterly, 32*(4), 199–201.

Lahm, E. A. (2003). Assistive technology specialists: Bringing knowledge of assistive technology to school districts. *Remedial and Special Education, 24*(3), 141–152.

Rose, D. (2001). *Testimony: Hearing on education technology: Committee on appropriations subcommittee on labor, health and human services, and education hearing on educational technology.* Wakefield, MA: Center for Applied Special Technology.

Spooner, F., Baker, J., Harris, A., Ahlgrim-Delzell, L., & Browder, D. (2007). Effects of training in Universal Design for Learning on lesson plan development. *Remedial and Special Education, 28*(2), 108–116.

Zabala, J. S. (1995). *The SETT framework: Critical areas to consider when making informed assistive technology decisions.* Houston, TX: Region IV Education Service Center. (ERIC Document Reproduction Service No. ED381962)

COURT CASES AND STATUTES

Individuals with Disabilities Education Act, §§ 1400–1485 (2006).

No Child Left Behind Act, 20 U.S.C. §§ 6301–7941 (2006).

Should e-books replace traditional textbooks and paper-based books in schools?

POINT: Meredith Stewart, *Cary Academy*

COUNTERPOINT: Christine M. Battista, *Binghamton University*

OVERVIEW

An electronic book, or e-book, is defined as a book-length manuscript published in a digital format, consisting of text, images, or both, and produced, published, and readable on a computer or other electronic device, commonly referred to as an e-reader. In today's high-tech marketplace, an e-reader device called the Kindle was released in the United States in 2007 and marketed by the online bookseller Amazon.com, which started a competitive movement to deliver e-books and other written materials in fast, inexpensive ways that fit more easily into today's modern digital age. Shortly after the release of Amazon's Kindle, other e-reader devices from Sony and Barnes & Noble were developed. More recently, the Internet giant Google has developed Google ebooks, a service offering millions of e-books available for free Internet download to users.

In a 2009 *Education Week* article titled "Reimagining the Textbook: The Risks and Rewards of Electronic Reading Devices," educators Michael L. Miles and Bruce S. Cooper maintain that the availability of portable e-readers, such as the Kindle, provide us with a glimpse into the classroom of the future, where e-books could possibly replace the traditional, print copies of textbooks used in schools across the country. However, while these authors highlight some of the potential benefits of e-books over traditional textbooks in schools, including lower costs, increased access to more books, eco-friendliness, and increased instructional options using e-books, the authors warn that the educational community must weigh these benefits with the limitations and unknowns of e-books before we envision an e-book in every class of the nation's 56 million schoolchildren.

Similarly, the point and counterpoint authors of this chapter, Meredith Stewart, a Language Arts and World Cultures teacher at Cary Academy in Cary, North Carolina, and Christine M. Battista, a lecturer and writing associate at Binghamton University in Binghamton, New York, argue different positions regarding the benefits as well as limitations and drawbacks of e-books for today's students. In her point essay, Stewart notes one of the biggest policy advantages associated with e-books is that students have increased access to books electronically compared to the traditional print book format. Stewart cites research that indicates that since e-readers have become significantly more affordable, a younger audience for e-readers has developed, namely teenagers. Additionally, some libraries are providing e-book loans to their patrons, and this service has become extremely popular.

Along with increased access to books, e-books are, on average, less expensive compared to the cost of a comparable textbook. Stewart argues that lower book costs would certainly be an incentive for not only students but school officials as well. Another advantage of the e-book in an educational environment is that it is fairly easy to create customizable reading selections for students. For example, teachers or librarians can select e-books they believe would appeal to certain students and load them on e-readers or computers. According to Stewart, there is much greater potential to customize instruction to students using e-book technologies compared to traditional textbooks.

From the perspective of a current teacher, Stewart argues that a compelling advantage of e-books is their technological flexibility. For instance, Stewart maintains that e-books are much less likely to become outdated compared to traditional paper-based textbooks. According to Stewart, the significance of this benefit of e-books being contemporary and not outdated is that it directly counters the commonly held assumption by students that what they learn in schools is irrelevant to what is happening in the "real world." The ability of the authors of e-books to quickly update information and content electronically provides a significant advantage to teachers, especially in subjects such as history or American government, where the student curriculum content is continually changing.

Stewart contends that the greatest motivation for educators who are against the e-book movement in education is fear. She maintains that this belief by some educators is both ironic and misguided because it is easier to label these educators as "out of touch." Both teachers and librarians, for example, need to reexamine the modern experience of student learning. While school librarians will and should not be eliminated, the modern digital age has significantly altered how we retrieve and store information, and many school districts have recognized this shift by changing the job title of "school librarian" to "school media specialist."

Disagreeing with Stewart, the counterpoint author, Battista, a writing associate and lecturer of English literature, states that advocates of e-books incorrectly believe that reading texts online will "humanize the learning experience of students." According to Battista, the implication is that today's students will connect with e-books similar to how they can connect with the printed version of a book. Given the current economic climate, schools across the country are more than willing to introduce the less costly option of e-books. According to Battista, certain subject disciplines, including the humanities, are at a distinct disadvantage.

Contrary to Stewart's position that an author's intent is not lost in a digitally based presentation of their work, Battista firmly believes that the digital format compromises not only the author's intentions but also the intellectual process. One of Battista's central arguments against e-books in the educational environment is the negative impact they have on the student-teacher intellectual relationship. As Battista states, "if students simply read the text at face value, they are not challenging the constructed ideologies of the text itself—nor are they actively questioning their own subjectivity within this process."

Both authors clearly disagree on the future status of today's school libraries if e-books become a preferred method in which students choose to read. While Stewart believes that traditional brick-and-mortar school libraries can coexist in an age of digitized textbooks and e-readers, Battista disagrees. Clearly, there is not clear consensus as to the viability of universal e-books for all students. Even among educators who tout the advantages of e-book technologies, it is recognized that it is premature, based on limited research studies, to say that e-books should replace traditional textbooks and paper-based books in school environments. Rather, most experts agree that more time and studies need to be conducted to ascertain whether e-books provide the major educational benefits that some claim they do.

Kevin P. Brady
North Carolina State University

POINT: Meredith Stewart
Cary Academy

S ome students experience the traditional brick-and-mortar library as a place of joy, a cocoon in which to spend long, warm afternoons getting lost in the stacks of books. But the traditional library can just as easily prove a place of frustration—needed pages ripped out of a journal, the futility of spending hours looking for information only to come up empty-handed, the one needed book only available through a painfully slow interlibrary loan process. The recent and increasing availability of electronic books, or e-books, has begun to shift what the experience of reading a book looks and feels like in libraries and classrooms across the country. E-books are often beneficial to students because of the access and flexibility they provide. This new access and flexibility requires shifting roles for both teachers and librarians. Although different, these roles are no less important than those needed to help students navigate paper-based resources. Despite the promise of e-books, there are also con-straining forces that need to be considered and, in some cases, guarded against. While these forces are more grounded in economic and legal spheres, educa-tors can still be advocates to help ensure e-books evolve in a way that will benefit all students. This point essay will advocate the major policy and tech-nology issues involving the adoption of e-books in today's schools.

E-BOOKS AND GREATER ACCESS FOR STUDENTS

One of the greatest assets of e-books and digital texts is the ease with which they may be accessed. Students and the public are no longer bound by the limits of their local public or school library. Instead, anyone with a computer or phone can access any book he or she owns whenever they want. Digital texts also have the ability to revive texts that have been long out of print and often difficult to access. Authors whose work has been abandoned by publishers have the opportunity to make their writing available again through e-book versions. Since the cost to the publisher of creating digital versions of books is relatively low, many publishers may embrace e-books as an additional revenue stream.

The question of the ability to legally share e-books is important to consider. Initially, manufacturers of e-book readers made the sharing process difficult or impossible. Recently, however, this has begun to change, as major manufactur-ers have announced deals with publishers to allow the sharing of e-readers they have purchased. For example, some libraries have begun acquiring and lending e-readers for patrons' use both inside and outside of the library. These libraries have used the e-readers to expand their collections without requiring additional space and often at a lower cost compared to acquiring print versions of books.

E-books also offer the potential to create easily customizable reading selections for students. Teachers or librarians can select books that they believe will appeal to particular students and load them on e-readers or computers. While a student need not limit his or her choices to preselected suggestions, a list like this can give some direction to students for whom a traditional brick-and-mortar library is a bewildering, overwhelming place. Individualized digital libraries can also be used to track students' reading choices and to facilitate reading circles.

Recently, *The New York Times* has noted that the popularity of e-books with teens for recreational use is rapidly increasing. Initially, e-readers were purchased primarily by adults, but with dropping prices they are becoming more accessible to a younger audience. Teens are reading e-books as a replacement of paper books and some teenagers are even using e-books as a replacement for television or other forms of digital media. Because books now in the public domain are available for free on e-readers, teens reported exploring these older books, even though they might not have been previously interested in them.

Some might counter by saying that e-books actually limit access because to read digital texts one needs both a digital device and access to a particular text. The need to have access to digital devices to access e-books does create an opportunity gap between the haves and the have-nots. While e-books may highlight this gap, the e-book does not create it. One need only browse websites where teachers in schools with lower levels of funding post requests for a class set of books to see that the gap exists not because of the use of electronic texts, but because of the funding inequalities that exist in education as well as because of disparities in income generally.

THE INCREASED FLEXIBILITY OF E-BOOKS

Many students have had the experience of opening a history or science text only to find the information therein woefully out of date. A periodic table missing newly discovered elements or a history text that doesn't mention the attacks of September 11 and the death of Osama bin Laden are almost laughable to media-savvy students. Outdated texts are frustrating not only insofar as they present content that students know is incorrect but also in that this omission or error creates the concern, whether rightly or wrongly, that the content in the rest of the text may be untrustworthy. Outdated traditional paper texts also reinforce the assumption of many students that what they learn in schools is irrelevant to the "real world."

Electronic, or digital, texts significantly shorten the time between the occurrence of an event or discovery and the point at which a student has the ability to read about it. They allow the ability to update texts without the time or expense required to produce a completely revised edition of a text. They also ease authors' fears that the content that they write risks being out of date soon after it is printed.

When educators take the lead in creating digital texts, they have flexibility in determining how material will be presented to students. This process of acting as a curator for students is not a new development. College professors have long assembled course packets, and secondary school teachers have spent thousands of hours in front of a copy machine to provide students with articles or selections of writing that they wish had been included in the textbook but were not. E-books make this process considerably quicker and simpler, allowing teachers to customize materials for each course. These electronic or digital texts can be easily modified to respond to students' specific needs.

While e-books can simply replicate print editions, they also create the possibility of embedding additional forms of media within text to enrich the educational content. A foreign language e-book, for example, could use embedded video to highlight recent cultural events from countries where the language is spoken. A math text might include screencasts of a teacher working out practice problems alongside problems for students to tackle on their own. Video elements within texts allow students to "replay" instruction and can be especially useful for students who need multiple iterations to absorb instruction. Several education textbook companies have begun to realize the potential that e-books hold and have begun offering them to supplement or replace current textbooks.

Some have worried that the flexibility of e-books eradicates the author's intent in writing a text. While a discussion of the notion of authorial intent is outside the scope of this point essay, it is worth noting that students often read texts in forms other than those in which they were originally created. While reading Jack Kerouac's *On the Road* on a continuous scroll of paper no doubt gives a different feel than reading it in paperback; that does not suggest that it should only be read in scroll form. For instance, William Shakespeare's plays were written specifically to be performed on stage, but they are read by thousands of students every year. To suggest that a text is somehow stripped of authorial intent if it is read in a form other than print assumes the notion of a book as a fixed, self-contained entity totally controlled by an author. In reality, however, this has never been the case.

FORCES OF CONSTRAINT WITH TODAY'S E-BOOKS

There are reasons to be cautious and thoughtful about the implementation of e-books, but they do not fall under the category of bemoaning the technological appetites of the young, the diminishing role of the traditional library, or the fading influence of the author. Instead, we ought to consider the cultural, technological, and economic forces constraining digital texts. In a way, these forces are nothing new. In earlier times, the gatekeepers of knowledge were publishers and the admissions committees of universities. In the era of e-books, educational technology companies and publishers have the potential to create similar barriers to access.

The digital era of publishing also has to come to grips with the fact that copyright law was written during a time when the possibilities currently available had, in some cases, not been imagined. Consumer use has far outpaced the ability of the law to devise workable solutions. While many would never think of stealing a book from the library, they are less hesitant about illegally downloading a copy posted on the Internet. Licensing schemes, such as Creative Commons, hold great promise for some authors and works. Creative Commons licensing allows authors to grant permission to use their works in particular ways outside of the scope of traditional copyright arrangements. For example, an author might grant permission for his or her book to be used and freely distributed, so long as it is used for noncommercial purposes.

For those book titles that are not in the public domain or available under Creative Commons licenses, digital equivalents of public libraries need to be created. There are exciting proposals for projects, such as the National Digital Library, which would offer access to many more volumes than are available in local libraries. Proponents of the National Digital Library have argued that energy needs to be focused in this area to ensure that books are available to the public and not limited to those who can purchase them.

CHANGING ROLES FOR TEACHERS AND LIBRARIANS

Much of the current literature arguing against the use of e-books is undergirded by a sense of fear. The fear posits that if students begin using e-book libraries and librarians, teachers and classrooms will no longer be necessary. Those sounding the death knell for traditional brick-and-mortar libraries worry that with the advent of electronic texts, libraries will become relics. However, this position evidences a very narrow view of the function of libraries. If libraries are simply those places to which people go for solitary interaction with dead trees, then yes, e-books may signify their demise. However, libraries and schools serve many more purposes. Libraries are places where people gather to share ideas and access information. The library can be the only place where some have easy access to the Internet and devices on which to access it. To deny patrons access to these things risks impoverishing them in the way that those without access to books might have been disadvantaged 100 years ago.

Paradoxically, those resisting e-books with all their might are creating the very condition that they fear. It becomes easier to stereotype them as woefully out of touch, and their arguments as protectionist fear-mongering. This is lamentable because important roles do remain for teachers and librarians. Students still need guidance in learning how to read carefully and critically.

Access to literary materials will remain an important issue and the resources of depositories of learning will be crucial in ensuring access to them. While some might lament the transformation of libraries into what they perceive as essentially coffee shops, there will always be the need for spaces to both read carefully and collaborate. Spaces may need to change to meet changing demands, but to suggest that libraries remain in a pre-21st-century time warp is contrary both to the modern experience of learning and the vision of many librarians and curators. While libraries may continue to hold paper volumes, they can also become spaces where students congregate to work collaboratively or to research with the assistance of their peers and librarians.

With publishers no longer acting as the gatekeepers of knowledge, teachers and librarians will have the important task of helping students sort through this information. Many school librarians are on the forefront of this shift. Some institutions have changed librarians' titles to "Media Specialist" to reflect the more diverse role they play in an Internet age where the vast majority of resources are accessed digitally. These roles require assisting students in locating resources in digital spaces and helping them think critically about information they encounter and its trustworthiness. These skills will be important for students in both work and college, so having training in them early will help make them better prepared for what lies ahead.

Books such as *Distracted* by Maggie Jackson and *The Shallows* by Nicholas Carr have suggested that digital devices result in greater distraction for students and hinder close reading. But reading distractions have always existed. Students stared out windows, surreptitiously scribbled notes to be passed to classmates, and calculated the number of days until graduation. Students need to be given guidance about how to manage these distractions. By talking honestly with students about strategies for managing these distractions and for adopting work habits, teachers have an opportunity to help students create lifelong habits. Part of being successful in college and in the world of work is taking advantage of the knowledge available by the swipe of a screen or stroke of a key without becoming overwhelmed by the volume of resources.

Even if technology is typically thought of as favoring a faster pace, this doesn't mean that teachers and librarians who adopt digital texts will have to speed up or lose the race. There is still a place in our society for close reading and careful annotation. Indeed, e-books can actually facilitate enhanced annotation. Readers can discover the meaning of unfamiliar words quickly and easily without having to shift focus from the text. Through social bookmarking and annotation sites, such as the Kindle app, annotations can be stored and, if readers wish, shared with others in their class or across the world. Such collaborative note-taking offers the possibility of enriched classroom discussions because, prior to the class, everyone has had the opportunity to get a sense of the feeling of the class. Also, those students who are reticent to speak up in class have opportunities to make their thoughts on the text known before the discussion begins. Teachers can use the annotations to check for student understanding and to clear up misperceptions about the text. This sort of conversation within or near the text doesn't serve to cheapen authorial intent or result in superficial readings. Instead, it highlights the dialogue with the text that might otherwise only happen internally or in notes scribbled in the margins and forgotten.

THE END IS NEAR (AND IT ISN'T)

While worries about the demise of the traditional paper-based book may seem very current, the end of the print book has been predicted for many years. As early as the 1960s, futurists were envisioning the possibility of digital texts, and by the late 1990s, some within the publishing industry predicted that publishing was going to undergo a significant shift in the coming years. A recent announcement by Amazon.com that sales of e-books have outpaced sales of print texts seems to suggest that this is indeed the direction of the trend (Miller, 2010).

The forces of economics and culture are powerfully arrayed behind digital devices. For teachers and librarians to sit on their haunches and bemoan the demise of the glory days of the paper book does a disservice to students. To support the adoption of digital texts for some aspects of students' learning does not have to imply unconditional endorsement of the changes a digital medium ushers in.

We should look to nurture the next generation of avid readers, students in our schools. Staunchly dictating what the book they read looks like is a guaranteed way to turn them off of reading and drive them farther from the texts we want to encourage them to explore. It is clear, given the many policy and technological advantages of e-books, that they should be welcomed into the educational community.

COUNTERPOINT: Christine M. Battista
Binghamton University

This counterpoint essay addresses some of the major concerns associated with the educational community embracing the use of e-books over traditional print books by today's students. A recent collaborative article addressing the relationship between electronic texts and education, "Online Learning and Intellectual Liberty: A Mixed-Mode Experiment in the Humanities," argues that the recent surge in the proliferation of e-books will increase the possibilities for learning, creative inquiry, and intellectual openness, leading to a more emancipatory form of educational liberation: "[web-based learning] can be used in post-secondary teaching in ways that humanize the learning experience of students" (Breton et al., 2005, p. 102). What's most concerning to many educators is the belief that reading texts online will "*humanize* the learning experience of students," implying that young scholars will connect with electronic texts in a more intimate way than with printed books. This position is not only erroneous but also dangerous, as it could lead to the elimination of printed books altogether—an evident sign of a swiftly decreasing concern and appreciation for the humanities. Already we are seeing the result of national budget cuts leading to the loss of funding to English, language, art, and philosophy departments across the spectrum. If we no longer have value for our textbooks—the true bread and butter of the humanities—then where will this leave us? Have we gone too far?

As we have already begun to see, electronically mediated forms of communication have taken our school systems by storm. In fact, most scholars depend on the use of technology to administer assignments, instruct classrooms, and conduct discussions. However, what is lost is the live, vivid, discursive exchange that occurs between student and teacher—an exchange that is fundamental to the type of open intellectual inquiry the humanities fosters. If textbooks, discussions, and instruction will soon all be available online, why would a student care to visit the library—arguably one of the last great tangible cultural archives of Western civilization? Are we willing to risk abandoning what artists, writers, and intellectuals fought for years to have printed, produced, and circulated?

Although many argue that electronic texts provide students with a myriad of educational opportunities, there is a concern that as technology pervades our educational institutions, we will be increasingly constricted in terms of what we are able to read, research, and access. Those who determine, for instance, what *may* be available via the computer can also decide what gets eliminated—and can also decide *if* we will continue to have libraries that house printed texts. If we allow for this kind of control to be administered in the hands of a few, we could be facing a very bleak academic future, a future determined by an authoritatively mediated infrastructure. It is precisely the generative interplay between student and text that provides for critical inquiry—and keeping textbooks in the classroom, and in the library, is essential for maintaining this level of discursive inquiry.

SHIFT TO DIGITAL MEDIA

Having been a student and educator for more than 10 years, I have experienced firsthand the university's increased reliance on all forms of technological and digital media. Online instruction is just one example of this shift—a shift that has altered the very way students and educators communicate and interact. This transformation is a detriment to the entire learning process. It seems we are experiencing a far more apathetic, disinterested sense of critical awareness—and the increased dependence on technology seems to be fostering this level of apathy. What is needed to keep learning and critical awareness alive and generative is a rigorous engagement with texts, theory, and live dialogue. William V. Spanos (1989) claims in "Theory in the Undergraduate English Curriculum: Towards an Interested Pedagogy" that "it is the activation of 'critical consciousness,' which liberates student and teacher from the invisible oppression of the discursive practice of hegemony: of received ideas taken to be natural but which, in fact, have been historically constituted by the dominant social order" (p. 46).

The humanities and English departments, in general, have historically been the creative, critical space for social issues to be examined, contested, and challenged—and these courses should have, at their end, "the activation of a consciousness aware of its historical occasion" (p. 46). This is the purpose of reading, of analyzing texts: to open up and examine one's own subject-constitution in a world that has become increasingly hegemonic and oppressive. Indeed, authors have been writing for centuries about their own unique sociohistorical concerns—but how can the richness, complexity, and vitality of the text truly be analyzed and explored if we neglect to interact with the text in a tangible way? Isn't there something to be said about holding a book, flipping through its pages, making notes in the margins, reflecting on our ideas and thoughts through an intricate dialogue *with* the book itself? If all books become digital, the humanities will merely become a watered down version of our increasingly corporatized historical present.

Not only are we experiencing a shift in our current historical consciousness, but the way in which students are molded and produced by the educational system has witnessed a tremendous shift as well. As Bill Readings (1996) remarks in his groundbreaking text, *The University in Ruins*, the educational apparatus has become more interested in producing students of "excellence," a symptom of an increased emphasis on standardization and capitalist consumption:

> Excellence is clearly a purely internal unit of value that effectively brackets all questions of reference or function, thus creating an internal market. Henceforth, the question of the University is only the question of relative value-for-money, the question posed to a student who is situated entirely as a *consumer*, rather than as someone who wants to think . . . excellence draws only one boundary: the boundary that protects the unrestricted power of the bureaucracy. And if a particular kind of department's excellence fails to conform, then that department can be eliminated without apparent risk to the system. (pp. 29–33)

With an increased focus on excellence, students are groomed to focus on marketability; critical consciousness, the student who "wants to think," who wants to actively engage and interact with the philosophical issues of our contemporary sociopolitical ethos, is no longer considered of value. As the university begins to further represent and mimic a corporate infrastructure, the possibilities for active critical agency will surely be eradicated. The electronic appropriation of textbooks is a red flag; it reveals the ways in which educational standards are becoming more malleable, managerial, and, therefore, ideologically concentrated in the hands of a select few. If departments such as English and philosophy, for instance, do not resist acclimating to these technological standards, they are in danger of being eliminated altogether.

IMPACT OF ELECTRONIC TEXTS

Many educators and proponents of English—especially literature and literary theory—cannot imagine leading a discussion without holding a text in their hands, without engaging in a discussion with students about the texts. A literature course simply cannot be taught or managed efficiently without *books*. Likewise, many cannot imagine pouring over a Yeats poem on a laptop or Virginia Woolf's *A Room of One's Own* on a Kindle. Relegating literature to the realm of technology completely eradicates the original intentionality of the author. Think of authors such as Woolf, James Joyce, T. S. Eliot, Charles Dickens, John Keats, Nathaniel Hawthorne, and Herman Melville: these writers produced their work in handwritten form. They pored over endless notes and pages for months, years, to complete their work so that it would have the chance to make it to the presses.

Digitally relegating novels to the world of cyberspace seems not only antithetical to the author's original intentions—intentions educators should hold sacred—but it also greatly disrupts the intellectual process. Studying novels to their fullest requires careful, meticulous attentiveness; it requires cognizance, ambition, patient reflection, and concentrated attention. The layers of details, richness, and complexity in the text are completely eradicated through the digital process. Furthermore, students lose their active agency in the interpretation of the text, translating into a form of "disinterested inquiry," which is "inscribed by a hidden Ideology, more specifically, by a regulated and totalized system" that is based on the normative values of the dominant cultural consciousness (Spanos, 1989, p. 50). If students simply read the text at face value, they are not challenging the constructed ideologies of the text itself—nor are they actively questioning their own subjectivity within this process. If all texts become electronic, students will more widely read texts at face value, which will surely result in an increased level of critical apathy.

So far this counterpoint essay has addressed the unfortunate impact of electronic texts on the humanities, in the classroom, and on the student-teacher intellectual relationship. But what bears emphasizing even more than these issues, it seems, is the future of our library system. What will the future of research look like? Will everything be available online? Will libraries no longer be necessary? What would it mean to no longer have a library filled with books, a library filled, instead, with digital databases, computer labs, stretches of tables, simulated books, perhaps a coffee kiosk, a juice bar, and a virtual reading room? In other words, a library transformed into a glorified Starbucks, a sea of students lost in their iPods and Blackberries while sipping on their mocha triple lattes, virtually chatting with other students and digitally browsing Shakespeare's *The Tempest*. What would distinguish this virtual library from a Starbucks or a wireless café? There would be no more books, no more endless pages of information to leaf through casually. Instead, one's research would always be mediated by a technological device that would supply the answers to the researcher's questions.

This would be, in this writer's mind, the irrevocable, devastating fall of the humanities, the arts, the literary sciences—it would be the end of any kind of intellectual communalism, openness, or connectivity. Being that our age is increasingly virtual—we can virtually farm, cook, design houses, create human avatars, all from the comfort of our own isolated cubicle—it seems as if it is easier for us to settle into our computers, tune out the person next to us, and control our virtual worlds while ignoring the problems that pervade our actual world. If we give up on live, human communication, if we no longer have books to look through and study, if everything becomes technologically mediated, how would we separate ourselves from our microcosmic *Sims* worlds? Would we really be any different than the robotic virtual humans on our computer screens?

As a researcher, I admittedly appreciate the ease of searching and downloading an article within minutes. However, some of my most lively, generative moments of clarity have occurred while spending time in the library, among the tangible printed texts. In fact, my most organic, original ideas have been inspired by the times where I have been able to pause and scan through rows of books, leafing through pages of subjects I never would have given much thought to, books that were secretly hiding beneath the canopy of an obscure subject. These moments have truly inspired some of my best work, my best writing. So if there are no more books to leaf through, no more categorized subjects to peruse, what happens to the creative process? Isn't research intended to *open* up the creative process? If we no longer have actual aisles of books to search through, if the entire research process becomes mediated by computers, we lose out on these lively and inspiring possibilities. All disciplines, regardless of the field, are predicated on research. Cutting-edge innovations and advancements in *any* discipline wouldn't be possible without hours of research—knowing our fields inside and out, acquainting ourselves with the predominant scholars in our discipline and building bridges to new forms of knowledge and advancement—these are central tenets to the advancement of scholarship. If we cannot immerse ourselves in the active, scholarly process, the meticulous process of pouring over a myriad of texts, we greatly lose out.

Another important aspect to consider is the rapidity of technological evolution and its impact on the student. Now more than ever, technology is moving at an increasingly fast pace. So if the books utilized in educational institutions become electronic, we are forcing our youth to follow this stringent pace—a pace that puts an unprecedented amount of pressure on students to conform to fairly unrealistic technological standards. And while convenience and time are certainly a positive aspect for students who struggle with a hefty course schedule, it nevertheless keeps students moving at a quick and uneasy pace, without much time for reflection or thought. Indeed, it's the *process* of research that teaches students not only critical thinking skills but also patience and concentration—all of which are essential for students as they enter the workforce. It is an educator's responsibility to teach students the importance of critical thinking. But if students spend most of their time on their computers, they will eventually have a more difficult time distinguishing between actual research and their online social networks. In other words, if we relegate books to the realm of the Internet, they lose their intellectual efficacy; they lose their unique and powerful singularity—both of which are crucial for producing thoughtful, critically engaged young minds.

CONCLUSION

Many would disagree with this counterpoint essay's position. In fact, scholars have argued that the recent surge in electronic texts and online distance learning has increased the means through which students have been able to foster open critical inquiry. As authors of "Online Learning and Intellectual Liberty" argue,

> In our version of the mixed-mode course and in our use of discussion boards, we stress the need to constantly undermine the final and fixed conclusions, or assumptions of objective truth. Because answers to queries are collectively assembled through the compilation of postings, we can emphasize process as opposed to product, and give form to our rejection of mechanistic, pre-given, spatialized, linear, vertical modes of knowledge. The vastness of cyberspace and the sheer number of possible windows on a site also convey the idea that the truth does not stop anywhere. (Breton et al., p. 104)

Soon, this kind of instruction will become the norm. And while cyberspace enables "process" over product, the relegation of books to digital media will inevitably result in the deterioration of educational standards. In the generative interplay between reader and book, thoughtful, imaginative inquiry is opened when we are given the opportunity to step away from our technologically mediated world. It is from within these moments where we can open a text and feel the paper between our fingertips while taking in the tradition and histories of Plato, Jean-Paul Sartre, and Henry David Thoreau that true creative imaginings can unfold—imaginings that can only be achieved from beyond our cubicles, our desks, our chat rooms, and within our slow, thoughtful, and curious walk through one of our civilization's last cultural archives: the library. If we are to keep critical inquiry alive and generative, we must do everything in our power to maintain a strong degree of academic authenticity, to keep printed books sacred and widely accessible to everyone, not just students. The future and integrity of our schooling system, our nation's youth, depends on it.

FURTHER READINGS AND RESOURCES

Breton, R., Doak, S., Foster, W., Lundström, D., McMaster, L., Miller, J., et al. (2005, Summer). Online learning and intellectual liberty: A mixed-mode experiment in the humanities. *College Teaching, 53*(3), 102–109.

Creative Commons: http://creativecommons.org

Darton, R. (2009). *The case for books.* New York: Public Affairs.

Ehrenreich, B. (2011, April 18). The death of the book. *Los Angeles Review of Books.* Available from http://lareviewofbooks.org

Miles, M. L., & Cooper, B. S. (2009). Reimagining the textbook: The risks and rewards of electronic reading devices. *Education Week, 29,* 24–25.

Miller, C. C. (2010). E-books top hardcovers at Amazon. *The New York Times.* Retrieved from http://www.nytimes.com/2010/07/20/technology/20kindle.html

Powers, B. (2010). *Hamlet's BlackBerry.* New York: Harper.

Readings, B. (1996). *The university in ruins.* Cambridge, MA: Harvard University Press.

Rose, F. (2011). *The art of immersion.* New York: W. W. Norton.

Spanos, W. V. (1989, Winter–Spring). Theory in the undergraduate English curriculum: Towards an interested pedagogy. *boundary 2, 16*(2/3), 41–70.

Do pocket assistive technologies, such as the iPod, iPhone, and iPad, provide mainly educational benefits or distractions to students in today's schools?

POINT: Nick Sauers, *Iowa State University*

COUNTERPOINT: Jerrid W. Kruse, *Drake University*

OVERVIEW

The history of assistive mobile technologies can be traced back to World War II, when the military used radio telephony on airplanes for air traffic security and in tanks to communicate on the battlefield. In 1973, Motorola developed the first modern mobile phone. The modern era of mobile technologies is historically divided into three generations. In 1979, the first generation of mobile technologies introduced cellular networks, which allowed for the transfer of telephone calls from one site to another while the user traveled during the transmission of these calls. Beginning in 1991, the second generation of mobile technologies introduced digital networks, which allowed digital instead of traditional analog transmission of telephone calls and a new method of communication, text messaging using a cellular phone. The current third generation of mobile devices introduced high-speed Internet–enabled data networks and mobile broadband.

Released in June 2007, the Apple iPhone is one of the most popular examples of the current third generation of mobile technologies. In the context of education, some argue that the use of mobile learning technology makes sense for school-age children, especially those students living in rural areas or who have certain learning disabilities. A mobile learning device that can be mass-produced at an affordable price, along with a solar cell charger, can be of great use even without current ability to connect to the Internet. Yet others argue that pocket assistive mobile devices pose significant distractions to students and negatively impact the student learning process.

In this chapter, authors Nick Sauers (Iowa State University) and Jerrid W. Kruse (Drake University) debate the issue of whether today's popular pocket assistive technology devices, such as the Apple iPhone and iPad, provide mainly educational benefits or distractions to today's students. Sauers's point essay begins with the premise that, historically, society and educators have reacted with both fear and apprehension to new, emerging technologies but the majority of these fears have been unfounded. However, these same fears and distrust of technology have significantly influenced the mindset of many educators as it relates to the use of new technologies in schools, such as assistive mobile devices.

According to Sauers, the majority of educator fears and distrust of technology revolve around unwarranted perceptions involving the negative role technology plays in increasing student distractions and misbehavior, as well as facilitating inequities between groups of students who have access to emerging technologies compared to those students who do not. The existing mindset of educator fear and mistrust of emerging technologies, including assistive mobile devices, Sauers argues only helps conceal and hinder the educational benefits of these devices, including increased student access to information, collaboration, and engagement. Sauers argues that today's adults already acknowledge the benefits of these pocket assistive devices and the impact they have in creating a more efficient and effective workplace.

In his counterpoint essay, Kruse argues that today's educators need to be much more mindful of how emerging, new technologies, such as assistive mobile devices, affect the nature of student learning. New, emerging technologies are often adopted in haste by today's educators. While Kruse concedes that assistive mobile devices may be "transformative innovations for learning futures" (Pea & Maldonado, 2006, p. 437), educators should not automatically assume that transformation and student improvement are synonymous with one another. Kruse argues that educators need to increasingly make more informed decisions regarding the adoption of technology in their schools. While Kruse agrees that one potential benefit associated with the use of assistive mobile devices by students is that they increase the speed of access to information, he asks what is lost in the student learning process. In the specific case of assistive mobile devices, Kruse believes that with the increased speed of access to information, the proverbial trade-off is that students do not engage nearly enough in reflective thought.

While Sauers argues that the educational benefits associated with assistive mobile devices far outweigh the distractions they may provide to some students, he readily concedes that the majority of educators do not rate pocket assistive devices highly in terms of the educational benefits they provide. In teacher surveys, portable technologies, such as laptops, are more often perceived by educators as technologies with the greatest potential for educational benefits in the classroom. In his counterpoint essay, Kruse argues that pocket assistive technologies, including the popular Apple iPhone and iPad, do little to nothing to improve face-to-face interaction among students. Additionally, Kruse maintains that while developing and enhancing student communication skills using digital technologies, such as pocket assistive devises, is useful, it is important in the educational process to maintain an emphasis on facilitating students' face-to-face communication skills.

One of the more interesting arguments advanced in this chapter on pocket assistive technologies was the relative failure of today's educators to address the issue of teaching students *digital citizenship*, or the proper use and role of technology in an increasingly global society. Sauers argues that educators have essentially failed at preparing today's students in the responsible and ethical use of technology. This failure by educators to prepare students to become good digital citizens has resulted in students attempting to navigate the new digital landscape with little assistance from teachers or school leaders. This lack of digital citizenship inevitably results in some negative behaviors by students who use emerging technologies, such as pocket assistive devices. While Kruse does not take as extreme a viewpoint as Sauers regarding digital citizenship, he does mention that teachers should actively assist students in the process of becoming better and more critical consumers of emerging technologies. Kruse maintains that educators and students should not automatically assume that new technologies improve student learning. Technological innovation should not immediately equate with student learning improvement.

Overall, Sauers's point essay details what he believes to be to the current, untapped educational benefits associated with pocke assistive mobile devices compared to the noticeably more skeptical viewpoint of Kruse's counterpoint essay. Sauers strongly believes that educators need to encourage the responsible and ethical use of emerging technologies by students through digital citizenship. By adopting all-or-nothing zero tolerance school- and district-level policies banning the student use of assistive mobile devices, educators are only focusing on the negative aspects of these technologies, such as increasing student distractions. Banning the use of assistive mobile devices, Sauer contends, will never allow educators to explore the existing, potential educational benefits of these devices. In his counterpoint essay, Kruse maintains that pocket assistive devices are more of a distraction to today's students because not enough consideration is given by today's educators to how technology actively improves the student learning environment. Kruse's primary argument is that educators must always consider the trade-offs associated with using technology in the classroom. While both authors would agree that you cannot blame student distractions exclusively on the use of emerging technologies, such as assistive mobile devices, the authors disagree on how educators should think about the integration of emerging new technologies, such as pocket assistive devices, in schools.

Kevin P. Brady
North Carolina State University

POINT: Nick Sauers
Iowa State University

There is much debate concerning the use of pocket assistive technologies in schools. Most of today's schools have taken a "just say no" approach to the use of personal mobile devices in schools, ranging from cell phones to mobile tablet devices, such as the popular Apple iPad. Some schools have begun to purchase various mobile devices for their students for educational purposes, but allowing pocket assistive technology devices in schools for student personal use is still quite rare. For example, if you stand outside most schools, you can see evidence of these school- and district-level policies that ban the use of pocket assistive technologies through an amazing phenomenon. Across the country as students exit schools, you will see students reach into their pockets to power up their pocket assistive devices, such as an Apple iPhone, after being required to disconnect these devices during the day while they are at school.

This point essay will argue that pocket assistive technological devices provide educational benefits to students from two perspectives. First, many of the commonly held beliefs and concerns of integrating mobile devices into a classroom will be addressed. The second part of this point essay will highlight some of the potential educational benefits commonly associated with using mobile devices. The challenge facing today's schools is to truly weigh both the concerns and the benefits of using pocket assistive technologies in today's classrooms. Too often, policy decisions, especially in areas involving technology in schools, are made based simply on the concerns associated with an issue. For instance, today's school leaders instead need to decide if a slight risk may be worth taking if that risk can lead to monumental educational gains and improvements in their schools.

COMMONLY HELD BELIEFS AND CONCERNS

In his 2010 article, Vaughan Bell, a clinical and research psychologist, highlighted the fearful and often unwarranted ways society has responded to new technologies. Bell begins with Swiss scientist, Conrad Gessner, who might have been the first to raise the alarm about the effects of information overload. Gessner died in 1565, and his warnings referred to the seemingly unmanageable flood of information unleashed by the printing press. Bell documents the historical concerns of schools and the changing uses of technology by students, ranging from radio and television to the more recent impact of the Internet, including e-mail and the use of social networking websites, such as Facebook. Bell's book argued that the majority of the technology-related fears expressed by schools over the years proved to be largely unfounded. The fears expressed by school leaders were not based on fact, but rather speculation that often came from people who knew very little about the emerging technologies, not the educational potential of these technologies in the classroom.

A similar mindset of premature fear and distrust involving the use of new technologies in today's schools currently seems to be embraced by many educational leaders and stakeholders when thinking about the use of assistive mobile devices in the student learning process. Although many fears and concerns exist among educators, most fall into the following three groups: (1) student distractions, (2) student misbehavior, and (3) equity.

Student Distractions

The primary concern many people have with using assistive mobile devices in education is that students will be distracted. This concern doesn't seem to be based on empirical research, and it also fails to realize the actual status of student engagement in our schools today. A recent study conducted by Learning 24/7, with over 1,500 classroom observations, found that in 85% of the classrooms observed, fewer than half of the students were paying attention (Schmoker, 2006). These alarming results would align with comments that you would most likely hear if you talked to a group of students. Our schools are doing a terrible job engaging students today! A pocket assistive device is not the cause of further student distraction, nor will it be an automatic solution to the various problems associated with student distraction. Instead, today's teaching practices will need to change to get our students more engaged in the classroom. In section two of this point essay, some of the ways using technology to change instruction, which can actually help improve student engagement, are highlighted.

Student Misbehavior

The mass media have not shed a positive light on the impact of technology in schools, especially as it relates to improving student behavior. For example, there have been numerous media reports detailing the negative impact cyberbullying is having in today's schools. While these concerns should not be ignored, the question that we must ask is are these inappropriate student behaviors due to technology, or are they just a new form of an old problem? Is there more student bullying and harassment because of technology? If so, is that due to technology or other societal changes? Is it more hurtful because of technology? There isn't a simple answer to any of these questions. This author's experience as a former teacher and principal indicates that this isn't a new experience, and it cannot be blamed exclusively on students' use of technology.

Unfortunately, many schools have completely failed to address appropriate "digital citizenship" in teaching students the proper use and role of technology in an increasingly global society. Digital citizenship can be defined as a concept that assists teachers, technology leaders, and parents to understand what students, children, and technology users generally should know to use technology appropriately. Digital citizenship is more than just a teaching tool, it is a way to prepare students to interact with others in a technological society. We have expected students, who have had very limited access to technology while in school, to leave school and act like responsible users, or digital citizens, of technology. Students are trying to learn this new digital landscape with little help from school personnel or any other adult. Some schools implement a very basic digital citizenship curriculum, but rarely does that go deep into the topic.

There is also a fear about the anonymity that students can have online. Although this can be a problem, it isn't unique to technology. A student writing a nasty message on the restroom wall is surely just as anonymous as a student who has a hidden identity on his or her computing device. Many tech-savvy educators will actually tell you that in most cases it is much more difficult for students to hide their identities online, although there are certainly exceptions. There have been cases where students and even parents have gone to tremendous lengths to create false online identities and then used those identities to hurt students. Again, it is important to note that these cases are unique and not common occurrences. This entire issue is an extremely important one for schools, but it certainly is not just a technology issue. Quite simply, digital citizenship is an issue that today's schools need to address.

Equity

Many educational stakeholders worry about equity, or fairness, when we allow students to bring in their own assistive mobile devices. This concern seems somewhat odd. Because some students don't have access to a pocket assistive device, some school officials argue that we should ban all students from using their pocket assistive mobile devices. What other devices that help students learn do we put the same limitations on: books, eyeglasses, art supplies? Obviously, schools don't force all students to have as little as the student who has the least access to supplies. Instead, some educators provide all students with at least basic access to the student learning device. If we would do this with assistive mobile devices, the cost may actually be less than many would imagine. A massive survey of various educational stakeholders, including parents, revealed that 62% of parents said they would provide a pocket assistive device to their son or daughter if the school allowed it for educational purposes (Project Tomorrow, 2010). If leveraged appropriately, schools could potentially see a cost savings even if they provide assistive mobile devices to students who don't have their own device. There could be drastic savings by reducing or eliminating the number of computer carts, labs, and servers. Printer and copy machine costs could also be reduced when students and teachers begin to exchange products and resources digitally rather than relying on expensive printing and copying machines. If schools value mobile devices, the equity issue should focus on raising the bar for all students rather than lowering the bar for many students.

EDUCATIONAL BENEFITS

The first part of this point essay addressed many of the leading concerns and misconceptions that educators have about using assistive mobile devices in education. However, reducing or eliminating those concerns is not reason enough to actually use the devices. There must be a genuine educational benefit in using assistive mobile devices if today's schools are going to invest time and limited resources into putting these devices into the hands of students and teachers. Currently, many educators simply don't believe educational benefits exist with pocket assistive devices. In a recent study, educators were asked to use a 10-point scale to rate various portable devices on their education potential, with 10 being the highest rating (PBS & Grunwald Associates LLC, 2011). Eighty-one percent of those educators surveyed rated laptops as an 8, 9, or 10, while only 28% rated an iPod touch, a popular pocket assistive device that high, and only 11% gave mobile cell phones a similar high rating. The perceived lack of educational benefit and value associated with pocket assistive technologies may be due to a failure to realize the educational potential of those devices in a classroom setting. The remainder of this section will separate these educational benefits into the following three categories: (1) access to information, (2) collaboration, and (3) engagement.

Access to Information

Many students currently have a technological tool in their pocket that gives them nearly unlimited access to information. Unfortunately, many schools choose not to allow students to use that tool while at school. Students are instead limited to textbooks, which may potentially be outdated or inaccurate, or sporadic computer use only when a computer lab is available. Students are often forced to use information that may be irrelevant to them, and they are limited by the educational resources available to them by the school. By allowing students to use assistive mobile devices, a floodgate of educational opportunities is opened. Teachers can easily have students research a topic from a multitude of perspectives. Additionally, it becomes much easier to differentiate instruction. Teachers can recommend online sites or students, with coaching, can find online sites that are the most appropriate for them. Inquiry-based and project-based learning also becomes much easier. Often, this type of learning is limited because few resources are readily available to the students as well as the teachers. Students can truly become digitally literate when we do not restrict them to the existing educational resources within a school building. The ability to evaluate, synthesize, and reflect on the information students find will prove to be an invaluable skill as they progress to the technology-infused workplace.

Collaboration

Embracing a pocket assistive learning device in school naturally leads to more collaboration outside of school. Students and educators begin to see learning as something that is not limited to a traditional 6-hour day in a physical brick-and-mortar building when they use a pocket assistive device. Although many business leaders and education reformers see collaboration as a true 21st-century skill, many school leaders do not always reflect this belief (Wagner, 2008). Instead, students are told that homework is meant to be done independently. We miss a big learning opportunity when we fail to let students collaborate and learn from one another outside of school. Often, a fellow student is the best teacher available after school hours. Many students, as well as adults, learn best by working with others. This does not mean that all work needs to be done in groups; educators can certainly develop guidelines depending on the specific task. However, it does imply that students often benefit from working together, especially when they are experiencing academic difficulties in the classroom. Educators can also use e-mail, wikis, a class social networking page, blogs, and myriad other technology tools to better connect with students not only within their own schools but across the world. Each of those technology tools allows students to connect better with one another as well as their teacher. Learning can truly become something that is not limited to the school building during school hours when educators embrace the use of today's assistive mobile learning devices.

Engagement

Having access to better information and meaningful collaboration both help increase student engagement. When students have access to more relevant personalized information, they usually become more engaged. One major benefit of a pocket assistive device is that students can learn in ways that are the most beneficial for them. Digital devices allow students to learn through reading, viewing pictures, watching video, connecting with others, and listening to audio files. Most of today's classes deliver information in one or two mediums, and students who do not learn well with those mediums are often not successful in the classroom. Educators need to ensure that our students become familiar with learning in more than simply one instructional delivery method, and also that they can identify their own most effective learning style. If you see a student in public with a pocket assistive device, it becomes quickly apparent that they are very engaged. The challenge to today's educators is to design student instruction that harnesses that engagement around learning.

CONCLUSION AND DISCUSSION

Across the country, many schools have made major investments in technology for their schools. Some schools have gone so far as to provide a laptop computer for each of their students. School and community leaders have decided that it is important to develop students who are fluent users of technologies. Unfortunately, very few schools have permitted the use of an effective and efficient assistive mobile device that many students already use outside of the school setting. The number of students with pocket assistive technologies is growing quickly, yet many schools still insist on strictly banning their use while students are in school. Many school officials still focus on the fears that exist about using assistive mobile devices at school, and they fail to see the educational benefits these devices offer student learning. Educators often say they want their students to learn to become digital citizens but block students from using their own technology.

Not only do more students own assistive mobile devices today, but the technological capabilities of those devices are becoming increasingly more powerful. It is truly difficult to imagine some of the learning possibilities that already exist, and even more difficult to imagine the technological possibilities of the future. The current position that many school officials have taken on assistive mobile devices is contrary to what is happening in the real world. For instance, adults have embraced pocket assistive technologies in their personal and professional lives because they realize both the effectiveness and efficiency of these devices. Currently, schools have a significant opportunity to transform our system by embracing assistive mobile devices, a technology that the majority of today's students already possess.

COUNTERPOINT: Jerrid W. Kruse
Drake University

Many people do not spontaneously consider the disadvantages of technology. Articulating the disadvantages of technology is not a popular endeavor, but too often educators at all levels claim that technology is "just a tool" and that any positive or negative use is simply a matter of decision making. While educators might desire technology to be neutral, or value-free, this simply is not the case. While philosophical arguments between technological instrumentalism and determinism are beyond the scope of this counterpoint essay, it must be acknowledged that the value in understanding that our decisions regarding technology use are important and, in some ways, technology makes many decisions for us—shaping teachers, students, and learning environments in profound ways. The dismissal of these deep impacts by educators is troubling.

While the nature of this counterpoint essay is to raise concerns regarding the use of assistive mobile devices, I am not against using such technological devices. In fact, I have encouraged students to use assistive mobile devices in my 8th-grade classroom and now teach an educational technology course to pre-service teachers that discusses assistive mobile platforms extensively. Yet, important issues must be considered to make more informed decisions regarding technology adoption and use in education. The aspects raised here are an important part of technological literacy referred to as *the nature of technology*. Unfortunately, few educational technology frameworks include the nature of technology ideas. A more robust educational technology framework must include understanding the relative trade-offs, values, and limits of technology.

RATIONALE FOR CONSIDERING TECHNOLOGICAL DOWNSIDES

While this counterpoint essay is chiefly concerned with mobile technologies, the concerns raised apply to all technologies, including "low tech" devices, such as pencil, paper, books, and so on. In many ways, the integrated nature of today's digital technologies requires thinking about them as holistic. That is, mobile devices are essentially minicomputers, both of which are essentially portals to the web and web applications. Because technology is ubiquitous in society and schools, being able to critically examine technology's effects is of the utmost importance.

Often, educators assume that the introduction of new technologies will revolutionize student learning environments. Unfortunately, this deterministic view ignores the impact of people's beliefs on how technology is used. Traditional teachers often use technology to support traditional methods, and more reform-based teachers likely use technology to support reform-based instruction. Yet, the "it is how we use it" rhetoric is problematic and overly instrumentalist.

Today's educators must carefully consider how new technologies, including pocket assistive technologies, might deeply affect the nature of our students' learning for both good and bad, in both explicit and implicit ways. It is in this deep reflection on how technology might transform student learning in unexpected ways that technology might be truly disruptive and may initiate education reform. Too often, new technologies are adopted in haste to "start somewhere."

GO DEEPER

Most critiques of technology use in schools are fairly superficial—aimed at the lack of technology in schools or restrictions being placed on teachers' use of technology. Some critiques go slightly deeper, noting the limitations of technology. For example, Yeonjeong Park cites Agnes Kukulska-Hulme (2007) to summarize limitations of mobile technology as

> (1) physical attributes of mobile devices, such as small screen size, heavy weight, inadequate memory, and short battery life; (2) content and software application limitations, including a lack of built-in functions, the difficulty of adding applications, challenges in learning how to work with a mobile device, and differences between applications and circumstances of use; (3) network speed and readability; and (4) physical environment issues such as problems with using the device outdoors, excessive screen brightness, concerns about personal security, possible radiation exposure from devices using radio frequencies, the need for rain covers in rainy or humid conditions, and so on. (Park, 2011, pp. 82–83)

While these kinds of critiques are important, they are not at the heart of teaching and learning. These superficial problems have technological fixes.

Educators must consider more fundamental problems. Problems that require deep reflection on how technology affects teachers and students will not likely have technological fixes. Like the obese individual at risk for heart attack, taking Lipitor does not solve the root cause of the risk, obesity. Neither shall a technological fix address the problems that need to be carefully considered when adopting technology in educational settings.

Park (2011) even demonstrates the superficial nature of the issues typically raised when noting, "looking at how rapidly new mobile products are improving . . . the technical limitations of mobile devices may be a temporary concern" (p. 83). While the technical limitations might be easily addressed with technological improvements, the metaphysical and epistemic limitations require teachers and learners to wrestle with deeper issues, such as how using assistive mobile devices, such as an Apple iPhone or iPad, might change students' conceptions of learning; how assistive mobile devices might undermine reflective thought; or how decisions regarding the use of assistive mobile devices might serve to maintain the status quo in education.

To more carefully assess the possible role of assistive mobile technology in education, educators must move beyond superficial discourse. While not all issues raised will come to fruition, not all possible concerns can be raised. Instead, awareness must be raised concerning the possible downsides of technology in education. To make more informed decisions regarding our implementation of assistive mobile technology, educators must carefully consider the trade-offs of mobile technology, the values inherent in mobile technologies, and the limitations of mobile technologies. While many of the negative aspects of technology cannot be avoided, we do not have to go blindly into the night.

TRADE-OFFS OF ASSISTIVE MOBILE DEVICES

While assistive mobile devices may be "transformative innovations for learning futures" (Pea & Maldonado, 2006, p. 437), educators should not naively assume that transformation and improvement are synonymous. Going further, even when advantages are clear, corresponding disadvantages exist. For example, television made instant and far-reaching information dissemination possible, but compressed the information into short, decontextualized bits. In America, the public could be more easily informed of presidential candidates, but premium is placed on appearance rather than substance of message.

Educators must ask of each technology, "What is lost?" If they do not ask, they risk not making well-reasoned decisions about technology adoption and implementation. So, what are some gains and possible trade-offs of assistive mobile technologies in schools?

First, students will gain instant access to information. This information may be useful in satisfying curiosity, looking up unknowns, and making decisions. Yet, what of reflective thought? What happens to students' ability to deduce from context clues? While access to information is important and liberating, access to information must never replace wisdom.

With mobile technologies, students and teachers gain new communication avenues outside of class. The walls of the classroom can "come down," and learning can be extended beyond the school day. New technologies, particularly mobile technologies, have reduced "the dependence on fixed locations for work and study, and consequently change the way we work and learn" (Peters, 2007). While benefits exist for connecting school learning to everyday life, students do not need to be constantly tethered to school as many adults are constantly tethered to work. Students should have a childhood!

As a science teacher, I see great possibility in having students use assistive mobile devices to take pictures of nature to use as data to discuss. For example, students might go off school grounds to take pictures of various types of plants or leaves. Before assistive mobile devices, students would have to draw pictures of plants they observe. Pocket assistive devices clearly improve the speed and accuracy of student data, but what is lost? When students snap a picture of a plant, the task is rather mindless; they do not need to pay any attention to detail. If students had to draw the same plant, they would be encouraged to attend to detail. The mobile technology might actually change the kind of thinking encouraged during the collection of samples. While the drawings would not be as accurate, the thinking that goes into drawing is so much more valuable than the thinking that goes into snapping pictures.

With the many possible advantages of mobile technologies in education, educators easily dismiss or ignore the trade-offs. Trade-offs are always present with technology use. For every advantage there is a corresponding disadvantage. The question is not how to avoid the disadvantages. The question is whether the advantages are worth the disadvantages.

EFFECT OF TECHNOLOGY ON VALUES AND BELIEFS

Marshall McLuhan famously noted that the medium is the message. While this phrase succinctly summarizes important ideas concerning technology, its full implications are not often considered. Technology carries inherent values and biases. Educators must realize that the technology medium we use for learning carries powerful messages about the nature of learning. These implicit messages are powerful agents that can change conceptions of teaching and learning.

Overly simplistic instrumental views of technology must be avoided. How technology is used is important; however, careful consideration must be given to how technology might use us by shaping learning environments. Too often, focus is placed on technology's affordances without recognizing technology's cues—the subtle ways in which technologies tell us how to use them. For example, Park (2011), when thinking about mobile devices in education, sets out to "describe its technological attributes and pedagogical affordances" (p. 79), but makes no mention of the subtle cues these devices have that steer learning environments in powerful ways. The dialogue in educational technology circles has focused on what is possible with technology while ignoring what might be *encouraged* by technology.

Eric Klopfer and Kurt Squire (2008) note the affordances of mobile technology including, "portability, social interactivity, context, connectivity, and individuality" (p. 204). While these affordances have their pros and cons, considering the cues of these devices might highlight how they may negatively shape learning environments and conceptions of learning. For example, small screens do not support creation of lengthy arguments. Instead, short exchanges are encouraged by both screen size and typing interface, not to mention the limits placed by applications such as Twitter. One must wonder how the length of our communication might reflect or impact the depth of our thinking.

The individuality afforded by mobile technologies creates new opportunities for students. Yet, educators must not lose sight of the importance of social interaction for learning. While mobile learning tools might increase the flexibility of digital tools, the notion that these technologies make learning "just in time, just enough and just for me" (Peters, 2007, p. 15) should not necessarily be equated with improvement. Indeed, our definition of improvement, or any definition, ought to be carefully scrutinized. The increased emphasis on individuals and the "just for me" attitude may easily lead to increased ego. Of course, this outcome is not fixed, but people must recognize both the technology's bias and in what ways these biases might impact our thinking.

The instantaneous nature of mobile computing may also undesirably alter beliefs about learning. Access to instant information can satisfy students' curiosity, but might inadvertently send the message that all answers are easily "Googled," reducing the value placed on deep reflection. For example, a recent application sends students study questions via text message. The advertisement noted that students could study anytime—even while doing other things. This is a nice sentiment, but it ignores the value of setting aside dedicated study time and feeds the myth of multitasking. Furthermore, questions that can be answered via text and evaluated by a computer are not likely the kind of questions worth answering—feeding the all-too-common problem of reducing education to memorization. As the lines between professional and amateur continue to blur, such pseudo-educational apps are likely to proliferate.

Often, the use of mobile technologies is rationalized using student interest in such devices. However, using students' interest in technology to generate student engagement is a dangerous approach. Relying on technology for student engagement quickly becomes entertainment. While students should see learning as worthwhile and engaging, deep learning is often difficult and frustrating. Edutainment might cause students to think that worthwhile activities must be fun. Of course students seem engaged when using mobile technology—most students like using mobile devices. However, engaged by a device and engaged in learning are not necessarily the same things.

LIMITATIONS OF TECHNOLOGY

Beyond asking "What is lost?" and "What are technology's biases?" educators must consider what technology cannot do, or what things technology ignores. Education is a deeply nuanced endeavor. One would not expect any technology to be able to address all aspects of an educational setting. However, identifying what things a technology does not explicitly address can help maintain balance.

Mobile technologies do little to enhance face-to-face interaction. In some ways, mobile devices encourage reduced emphasis on face-to-face education. While developing communication skills using digital technologies is important, maintaining emphasis on developing students' face-to-face communication skills is prudent. Excitement about technology should not distract from providing students with a well-rounded education.

Mobile technologies ignore all forms of input that cannot be made digital. Students must continue to interact with real objects. While digital technologies might provide high-quality visualizations, real objects are more concrete and provide important experiences for the development of children.

In the previous section, concerns were raised about mobile technology placing too much emphasis on individuals. However, the implementation of mobile platforms might also ignore individuals. That is, if a single device is purchased for every student, students are forced to fit yet another mold to be successful. This seeming contradiction between too much focus on individuality and ignoring individuals serves to illustrate the nuanced and contextualized nature of technology issues in education and as well as why philosophical thinking must inform practical decisions regarding technology.

Finally, educators must know what educational technology dialogue often ignores: the importance of teacher decision making. This problem is illustrated when Park (2011) concluded "that instructional designers and individual learners will continue to incorporate mobile technologies into their teaching and learning effectively . . ." (Park, 2011, p. 79). This conclusion is better classified as a dangerous assumption. This assumption encourages educators to not critically evaluate technology and to assume that technology will always be used effectively. Instead, educators must recognize that they need to make decisions about instructional tools based on their goals for students and an understanding of how people learn.

SUGGESTIONS FOR THE USE OF ASSISTIVE MOBILE TECHNOLOGY

Based on the issues raised, some suggestions can be made. First, students should be allowed to choose their device. Second, the device should not become the center of instruction. Teachers must resolve to use strategies and tools that best fit the content to be learned and the goals for particular lessons. Too often teachers ask, "How can I use X technology?" rather than, "How can I best teach Y?" Third, schools should consider having the devices stay at school. This step may help maintain boundaries between school and home and might restore childhood. Last, teachers should help students become critical consumers of technology. The International Society for Technology in Education (ISTE) standards note students should "understand human, cultural, and societal issues related to technology." Engaging students in explicit activities and discussion regarding these issues helps them more deeply understand the impact of technology in their lives.

CONCLUSION

Concerns of distraction motivated this section, yet distraction is not best addressed from a technological standpoint. Students have always been distracted in school. Students are not distracted because of a new device; pencils have distracted students for years. Students are distracted because of decontextualized instruction, disconnected curriculum, and pointless assignments. Yet, this thinking does not mean technology is without shortcomings. The trade-offs, biases, and limits of technology ought to be carefully considered.

Some might say I choose to see the negative side of technology. They might be right. Of course, for every point there is a counterpoint. This fact is what makes education so wonderfully nuanced and paradoxical. However, if educators do not consider the negative side of technology, then they have not made a decision; instead, they have blindly accepted the tyranny of technology.

FURTHER READINGS AND RESOURCES

Bell, V. (2010). Don't touch that dial! A history of media technology scares, from the printing press to Facebook. *Slate.* Retrieved from http://www.slate.com/id/2244198/pagenum/all

Keen, A. (2008). *The cult of the amateur.* New York: Doubleday.

Klopfer, E., & Squire, K. (2008). Environmental detectives: The development of an augmented reality platform for environmental simulations. *Educational Technology Research and Development, 56*(2), 203–228.

Kukulska-Hulme, A. (2007). Mobile usability in educational context: What have we learnt? *International Review of Research in Open and Distance Learning, 8*(2), 1–16.

Park, Y. (2011). A pedagogical framework for mobile learning: Categorizing educational applications of mobile technologies into four types. *International Review of Research in Open and Distance Learning, 12*(2), 78–102.

PBS, & Grunwald Associates LLC. (2011). *Deepening connections: Teachers increasingly rely on media and technology.* Retrieved from http://www.pbs.org/about/media/about/cms_page_media/182/PBS-Grunwald-2011e.pdf

Pea, R., & Maldonado, H. (2006). WILD for learning: Interacting through new computing devices anytime, anywhere. In R. K. Sawyer (Ed.), *The Cambridge handbook of the learning sciences* (pp. 427–441). Cambridge, UK: Cambridge University Press.

Peters, K. (2007). m-learning: Positioning educators for a mobile, connected future. *International Journal of Research in Open and Distance Learning, 8*(2), 1–17.

Project Tomorrow. (2010). *Creating our future: Students speak up about their vision for 21st century learning.* Retrieved from http://tomorrow.org/speakup/pdfs/SU09natio nalfindingsstudents&parents.pdf

Schmoker, M. (2006). *Results now: How we can achieve unprecedented improvements in teaching and learning.* Alexandria, VA: ASCD.

Wagner, T. (2008). *The global achievement gap: Why even our best schools don't teach the new survival skills our children need—and what we can do about it.* New York: Basic Books.

Are today's policies and procedures governing online student course offerings in the K–12 school environment appropriate to fully realize the unique policy and technology advantages of these online classes?

POINT: Leanna Matchett Archambault, *Arizona State University*
COUNTERPOINT: Anne F. Thorp, *Ottawa Area Intermediate School District*

OVERVIEW

The existing research on K–12 online student learning environments dates back to the mid-1990s. While it is clear that K–12 online learning environments have considerably expanded and improved over the past decade, the amount of published, peer-reviewed research specifically covering K–12 online or virtual schooling environments is relatively limited. For example, during the 2007 to 2008 school year, K–12 online student enrollments surpassed 1 million students, and approximately 25% of the K–12 school districts surveyed across the country anticipated adding online courses to their current course offerings in the next 3 years. In this chapter, the authors debate the major policy and technology advantages to online courses in K–12 school environments. The literature detailing the policy and technology advantages of K–12 online courses tends to fall into two categories. The first category is research address-ing the effectiveness of K–12 online courses. The second category is research addressing issues related to student readiness and retention.

In her point essay, author Leanna Matchett Archambault (Arizona State University) presents evidence that an increasing number of K–12 school dis-tricts across the country are offering at least some form of online learning initia-tive to their students. Based on the existing research, Archambault argues studies have shown that there is no significant difference between the academic performance of students in traditional, face-to-face courses compared to stu-dents in online courses. Instead, the most frequently cited advantage of online courses for students in K–12 school environments is that they provide the ability to offer students additional courses that would not otherwise be available at a traditional, face-to-face school. For example, some traditional brick-and-mortar schools are unable to offer certain Advanced Placement courses because they do not have teachers with the appropriate credentials to teach the course. Additionally, some K–12 brick-and-mortar schools are limited in the number of credit recovery courses they are able to offer. Credit recovery courses are those that allow students to earn credit for classes they previously took and failed. The ability to retake classes and earn academic credit allows students to potentially graduate on time or with minimal delays. In addition to helping students meet graduation requirements, the ability to take credit recovery courses allows stu-dents who have previously dropped out of school to regain entry back into school, provides educational equity for all students, and meets budgetary con-cerns while simultaneously attempting to serve all students.

Furthermore, Archambault contends that, given the current need for a skilled and diversified workforce, online courses provide the necessary access to Advanced Placement or credit recovery courses that are not uniformly avail-able throughout all K–12 brick-and-mortar student learning environments. Since the current research reveals that there are no significant differences in the academic performance between students who took traditional, face-to-face courses compared to online or distance education courses, researchers should expand on the access to learning opportunities that online student learning provides. For instance, current research on the K–12 student learning environment demonstrates that online courses enhance learning opportunities for a wider range of student populations compared to traditional, face-to-face course offerings. By offering student courses in both face-to-face and online learning environments, school officials are extending vital educational opportunities to a wider student audience.

In her counterpoint essay, author Anne F. Thorp (Ottawa Area Intermediate School District) argues that online education is misunderstood by many in the educational community. According to Thorp, effective online courses developed for the K–12 student population have the potential to increase educational opportunities for students in a flexible learning environment. However, Thorp argues, a majority of the existing policies and procedures used for online courses are still written for traditional brick-and-mortar school environments. Thorp contends that without adopting rules and regulations that are unique to the online student learning environment, school officials, students, teachers, and parents will be unable to realize the major policy and technology benefits associated with online courses in K–12 school environments.

While both authors agree that online courses provide students with greater access to certain courses, including Advanced Placement and credit recovery courses, Thorp maintains that inefficient and irrelevant policies and procedures for online courses interfere with their policy and technological effectiveness. For instance, Thorp maintains that online educational policies and mandates differ widely by both state and district. Most district-level policies and procedures governing online student course offerings in the K–12 school environment do not allow students to participate in online course offerings outside of the district. This limitation, Thorp argues, negatively impacts a student's ability to interact with other students and teachers outside of their local culture, region, or locale. Today's online tools, such as Facebook, Skype, and Twitter, coincide well with the "anytime, anywhere" notion of student learning in a modern, digital age.

While Archambault maintains that existing research demonstrates that online course offerings in the K–12 school environment enhance student equity by offering courses otherwise unavailable in traditional brick-and-mortar school settings, Thorp's major argument is that the majority of policies and procedures applied to online course offerings fail to recognize the unique policy and technology advantages of online, or distance education, student course offerings. Most of the current policies and procedures directed at online courses, Thorp argues, were originally developed for and applied to traditional, face-to-face student course offerings. Policies and procedures for online student course offerings should be seen more as a process to allow for the flexibility inherent in online or virtual school environments. While this chapter clearly demonstrates the growth of online course offerings for today's K–12 students, the authors differ on the issue of whether today's policies and procedures governing online student course offerings are appropriate to fully realize the unique policy and technology advantages of these online classes.

Kevin P. Brady
North Carolina State University

POINT: Leanna Matchett Archambault
Arizona State University

Online courses at the K–12 level have begun to grow at an astounding pace. Virtual learning opportunities are more extensive than ever before, expanding to include 45 states with either a state-led virtual school, an online initiative, or both (Watson, Gemin, Ryan, & Wicks, 2009). In a national survey of 2,305 public school districts in the 50 states as well as the District of Columbia, J. Carl Setzer and Laurie Lewis (2005) found approximately one-third of public elementary through secondary school districts (36%) had students enrolled in online education courses. In fact, more recent national data indicate that in a survey of 366 school districts, 57.9% had at least one student enrolled who took at least one online course during the 2005 to 2006 school year, with an additional 24.5% more school districts planning to add online courses to their offerings in the next 3 years (Picciano & Seaman, 2007). According to these statistics, an increasing number of school districts in the United States are offering some form of online learning for their students, and more school districts plan to do so within the next three years.

The number of online student enrollments grew to an estimated 1,030,000 students during the 2007 to 2008 school year (Picciano & Seaman, 2009). This represented a 47% increase in only 2 years, and these figures are expected to increase as more school districts explore the potential policy and technology advantages of offering online classes, including addressing growing student populations, dealing with the challenges of limited space, geographical location, scheduling conflicts, failed courses, and meeting the needs of specific groups of students by allowing them to take courses for credit recovery or Advanced Placement. The most frequently cited reason for the importance of online courses was the ability to offer classes that would not otherwise be available at a particular school (80% of student respondents reported this as being very important). Other reasons ranking high on the "very important" category included meeting the needs of specific groups of students (59%) and being able to offer Advanced Placement or college-level courses (50%). As a whole, 72% of districts with online education programs planned to expand them in the future (Setzer & Lewis, 2005).

Online education opportunities have continued to proliferate because of the potential benefits they provide to students. Online classes present potential advantages when compared with traditional schools due to the inherent flexibility that comes to those students who attend a class offered in an online environment. One of the major positive aspects of online education is "any-time, anyplace" learning, in addition to the ability of the technology to tailor the curriculum to meet the needs of individual students. Fulfilling each child's specific educational requirements has long been a goal of the modern educational system, but unfortunately it has often acquiesced to offering the same general curriculum due to convenience. Traditionally, schools have been organized by an industrial model that specifies structure in terms of time, space, and modes and places of learning. Online education challenges this industrial model, and technology makes it possible for different students at various levels to engage with the course content at their own pace and speed. According to the National Educational Technology Plan (2010),

> With online learning, learners can gain access to resources regardless of time of day, geography, or ability; receive personalized instruction from educators and experts anywhere in the world; and learn at their own pace and in ways tailored to their own styles and interests. Moreover, it enables our education system to leverage the talents and expertise of our best educators by making their knowledge and skills available to many more learners. In addition, all these benefits can be realized through online learning at considerably less cost compared to providing students with additional in-person, classroom-based instruction by extending the school day or year. (p. 69)

Prior to considering the benefits of offering online education, it is helpful to examine the literature that focuses on its effectiveness. In a landmark meta-analysis of online distance education programs, Cathy Cavanaugh and colleagues (2004) synthesized findings from 14 controlled, systematic, and empirically based studies, representing 116 scientific findings concerning K–12 online distance education programs from 1999 to 2004. These studies compared the performance of a group of online students to those in a nondistance environment in online distance education programs in which students' participation was at least 50% web-based. The major focus of the studies was the academic achievement of K–12 students; student satisfaction; student achievement, attitude, and retention; and networked and online learning. These studies found that after examining 11 variables that may affect student performance, including the duration of the program, frequency of use of distance learning, instructional role of the program, number of distance learning sessions, pacing of the instruction, role of the instructor, timing of the interactions, type of interactions, amount of teacher preparation for distance instruction, and level of teacher experience in distance instruction, there was no significant difference between the performances of students in distance education programs compared with performance in traditional, face-to-face programs.

Because the effectiveness of K–12 online distance education is a growing field of study, much of the literature concentrates on aspects of student achievement. With no significant difference found in a number of studies, researchers have begun concluding that online distance education in a K–12 environment results in similar outcomes as traditional instruction (Cavanaugh, Gillan, Kromrey, Hess, & Blomeyer, 2004; Smith, Clark, & Blomeyer, 2005). With significant meta-analyses in place that confirm the viability of K–12 online distance education, recent literature has begun to delve into other areas of consideration, including the benefits of offering courses online, such as the ability to offer varying types of classes to meet the needs of diverse student populations, the ability to extend the school day, the ability to offer quality courses across physical boundaries, and the ability to prepare students for 21st-century job skills.

One of the primary advantages of offering online classes in K–12 school environments is that it extends the types of courses that are able to be offered beyond that of a single school building. This includes Advanced Placement courses in addition to classes that are geared for credit recovery.

ADVANCED PLACEMENT

The need for a skilled and diversified workforce is well documented. A widening skills gap is developing in which the vast majority of future jobs will require, minimally, a 2- or 4-year college degree. Courses that go beyond the basic core to challenge students intellectually, adding to their ability to reason, think critically, consider and evaluate differing viewpoints, and develop a sense of self-regulation are desperately needed. One of the ways that this can be addressed is through the expansion of Advanced Placement (AP)–level classes. Despite this need, the access to advanced coursework is not uniform or equitable in all areas. The National Center for Educational Statistics (2007) reported that more than 25% of high schools across the United States did not offer AP classes, and small schools with less than 150 students and schools in rural areas were the least likely to offer AP courses to their students. Schools that do offer AP courses are often limited to one section per day, and students often encounter schedule conflicts as well as problems with student enrollment that can stem from strict prerequisite requirements and a limited number of available slots. To address this gap, many traditional brick-and-mortar schools are turning to online classes that can offer advanced-level coursework for students. As a result, more and more school districts are turning to online course delivery as a practical and effective means of expanding student access to AP courses.

Online courses are offering additional options to students who may not otherwise have access to advanced-level classes. These types of classes can be classified in a number of ways: dual enrollment courses that allow students to earn college and high school credit simultaneously; honors classes that require students to complete assignments that are greater in difficulty and that are often measured against higher standards; AP courses that offer preparation in content areas with the goals of having students pass a standardized exam and then earning college credit as a result of their high performance; and International Baccalaureate (IB) classes that provide a 2-year sequence of rigorous, college-preparatory coursework that then lead to an internationally recognized diploma. As with research confirming no significant difference in outcomes between online and face-to-face classes, student tracking of AP test performance shows that the percentage of students passing the AP exam by taking the class in an online format has exceeded the overall passing rate of traditional AP student test-takers, which was 59% for 2009 (College Board, 2009). Traditional brick-and-mortar schools that add the option of access to online advanced courses will extend this opportunity to a wider student population and, by doing so, will work toward adding challenging curricula to help students reason and think critically as well as prepare them with the essential skills necessary for success in the 21st-century workforce.

CREDIT RECOVERY

In addition to offering advanced coursework, schools also have a responsibility to assist students who are struggling to meet high school credit requirements. Credit recovery refers to the process of taking and passing a class that a student has previously attempted but was not successful in earning academic credit toward graduation requirements. Typically, these students have failed a traditional class and need to make up the credits to stay on track for graduation, and often, students who need to take advantage of credit-recovery opportunities can be designated as *at-risk students*. An at-risk student is defined as one who is likely to fail at school due to variables associated with demographic characteristics, including family and personal background characteristics, the amount of parental involvement in the student's education, the student's academic history, student behavioral factors, teacher perceptions of the student, and the characteristics of the student's school (Kaufman, Bradby, & National Center for Education Statistics, 1992).

Nationally, approximately 1.2 million students in the United States, representing almost 9% of the total student population, do not complete their high school education (U.S. Department of Education, 2009). This is a major epidemic, as not only do students who drop out emerge into the workforce without adequate academic preparation, they also run a higher risk of being unemployed, suffering from poor health, living in poverty, depending on public assistance, and being incarcerated. Online credit recovery classes provide schools a viable alternative to seek ways to reach out to struggling students to help ensure their success, and this delivery model can be well suited to directly address the needs of at-risk learners. Goals related to credit recovery and at-risk students vary with each online program; often they include one or more of the following:

- help students make up credits to meet graduation requirements
- help students meet graduation deadlines
- prepare students for state exams
- get dropout students back in school
- provide educational equity for all students
- meet budgetary concerns while trying to serve all students

Through the use of online education, specific instructional strategies that support achievement are possible. These include the implementation of individualizing instruction, being able to offer a flexible schedule, increasing contact and communication between teachers/support staff and students/families, implementing specific online curricula, and training teachers and support staff regarding successful strategies for working with at-risk students. By focusing on these elements, schools implementing online classes that are geared toward helping students meet high school graduation requirements have had positive outcomes, such as an increase in course completion rates, standardized test scores, and graduation rates, as well as a decrease in course drop rates, student truancy, and other behavioral issues.

STUDENT LEARNING IN THE 21ST CENTURY

The Internet and World Wide Web have profoundly shifted the ways in which we interact with new information and knowledge. As advances in technology move forward and the Internet becomes an ever-increasing part of our everyday lives, learning and our concept of education are changing. In modern students' views, learning does not only occur within the confines of the classroom. Expanding beyond the boundaries of their classrooms and communities, students see the world as their classroom and view technological devices and online learning as integral elements to creating a 21st-century learning environment. Students cite a variety of reasons for wanting to engage in online education, primarily saying it allows them additional freedom, flexibility, and choice when it comes to education. Specifically, this includes the ability to earn college credit, work at their own pace, take a class that was not offered at their school, complete high school requirements they may have missed, get additional help in a particular subject, fit additional classes into their own schedule, and engage in a format that makes it easier for them to learn.

Because of the expanded opportunities that online student learning provides, brick-and-mortar school districts are beginning to recognize the advantages to offering their own online classes to students and the multiple benefits these classes provide their students. This is being driven by a strong demand for online learning due to the increasing acceptance of online learning for a wide range of student populations. Without offering these opportunities, districts are susceptible to losing students to districts that do provide online student course options. Schools need to offer online education opportunities, as an ever-increasing student population and their parents are seeking out these options. High school students who have a parent who has taken an online class are twice as likely to take an online class themselves (Project Tomorrow, 2010). This expectation for schools to offer online education as an additional means of learning for students is one that schools must address to stay competitive, especially in the current economic and global climate. By extending online class options to students, traditional schools can assist their students by offering classes to meet their needs, including the addition of AP and credit recovery courses. These vital opportunities extend the student learning environment beyond the constraints of a traditional 7-hour school day that has to occur in the traditional brick-and-mortar school environment. Both the policy and technological benefits of online courses in a K–12 school environment include greater flexibility for students, allowing them the ability to engage with challenging curricula to help prepare students with the necessary skill sets for success in a technologically rich and global 21st-century workplace.

COUNTERPOINT: Anne F. Thorp
Ottawa Area Intermediate School District

Education is radically changing. Teachers and students are no longer bound by rigid geographical barriers. Or are they? Are they bound by outdated school and district-level policies that inhibit opportunities to learn with, from, and through worldwide partnerships to enhance learning, collaboration, and communication? This counterpoint essay addresses the concern that many of today's K–12 school environments currently lack the proper policies and procedures for understanding the educational benefits of online courses.

ONLINE LEARNING

Online learning is growing as a means to meet many student learning goals as well as learner needs. Examples of these goals and needs include meeting the technologically savvy students where they are, using the technology tools they use on a frequent basis, expanding course availability to students beyond school offerings, providing courses with highly qualified teachers in areas where qualification levels may be deficient, and overcoming scheduling conflicts for students. Additionally, meeting the multiple needs of students who may be at risk of dropping out or being incarcerated, expelled, or homebound allows them to continue their own learning outside of the traditional brick-and-mortar school building from which they would usually be assigned.

Online education is still relatively new and misunderstood by many parents, teachers, school administrators, and legislators. Ask any 25 people what "online learning" is and there will more than likely be 25 different definitions. The online learning of today involves collaboration, communication, interactivity, engaging materials, and opportunities to interact with participants from all over the world. Effectively written and developed online student courses are successful in educating participants through both highly challenging and interactive topics offered exclusively in an online environment.

Effectively developed online courses provide remarkable opportunities for students to access learning in a flexible environment that has only recently become prevalent and widely available. However, many of the policies and procedures used are still school rules written for the traditional brick-and-mortar school environment. Uninhibited learning opportunities through online courses lead students toward self-actualized lifelong learning with skills for collaboration, connection, and continued learning so as to be active participants in 21st-century opportunities.

Considerations need to be made so that all students have access to online courses and the advantages that come with them. Creating processes that allow districts, schools, and teachers to understand the benefits and advantages of online courses, guiding decisionmakers to make informed decisions about implementing online courses to meet the multiple learning needs of all students, is a necessity in today's educational environment. Without proper rules and procedures, local school officials, students, and parents will be unable to understand the major policy and technology benefits of online courses in K–12 school environments.

IMPLEMENTING ONLINE COURSES

The end result of implementing successful processes and procedures for the implementation of online courses will be flexible learning environments in which districts, schools, teachers, and students are empowered to apply modifications as needed to successfully meet the educational needs of diverse student learners. Employing effective processes and procedures is critical to not only educating, but also reaching today's learners, as well as future generations of student learners.

When it comes to offering quality education for students, initiatives change almost as quickly as existing technologies. Creating procedures and processes for students, teachers, and districts to follow will lead all student learners to a clear understanding of the implementation of online courses and sessions available. Flexibility needs to be included in these processes for students to be able to access learning materials at any time, from any place, and with any technology-assisted device they may have in their possession, as the governor of Michigan, Rick Snyder, stated in his special message on education reform, "Any Time, Any Place, Any Way, Any Pace." Many students today are far more proficient with technology than their parents or their teachers could ever hope to be. The increased opportunity for learning, the flexibility of anytime, anywhere learning, as well as the convenience of "at your fingertips" learning allows new ways of reaching learners, some of whom have not previously experienced success in traditional learning environments, yet will benefit with great success using technology tools that allow for a much more flexible learning environment.

Creating procedures and processes for online course access allows learners and teachers opportunities for the exploration of ways to offer a wider range of courses to students, as well as more effective and greater opportunities for teachers to meet professional development needs and goals. With the emergence of online tools, collaborations, and online providers, as well as teachers integrating more online tools into the classroom environment, greater numbers of courses available for completion online are surfacing for K–12 students.

Offering and supporting a wider range of online courses that are equally accessible to all students everywhere opens doors to student learning opportunities as well as opportunities for teachers, parents, policymakers, and administrators to support and guide students toward learning that supports them from where they are in their academics rather than from a strict, structured, and inflexible curriculum based on outdated policies written years ago and not yet revised to meet current student learning goals and needs through online courses.

While it is important for schools to provide information to all involved, including parents, students, staff, and policymakers, regarding online course options and opportunities, an inflexible policy can be a disadvantage to the growth of any program. Creating processes and procedures rather than strict policy is definitely preferable so that as technology changes and grows, the coordination of these processes can be applied to meeting the needs of all student learners through the effective use of online courses. While policy generally includes student access to programs, eligibility principles, types of courses available, student technology access, course credit granting, and teacher expectations, implementing process over policy can generate fluidity in access and use, rather than strict rules with little flexibility in meeting student needs.

Online education policy and mandates differ for each state, yet there are a number of similarities that exist regarding the student learning goals each state is striving to achieve. Many school policies do not allow online course participation to take place outside of their district or state, thus prohibiting the opportunity for participants to interact with others outside of their own culture, region, or locale. Students today are interacting with other students from across the world through the online tools that allow for connection and communication, such as Facebook, Skype, Twitter, and so on, connecting on levels and in ways unimaginable to previous generations. Students today use technology as their primary means of entertainment, as evidenced by the worldwide closings of brick-and-mortar entertainment rental stores, such as Blockbuster Video. The use of these technologies can be incorporated into educational settings and implemented for anytime, anywhere student learning, which can take place at the student's individual learning pace.

21ST-CENTURY LEARNING

Learning across boundaries takes students to new levels of understanding and propels them into college and work readiness for the 21st-century level of success needed in business and learning. A picture of today's student would show him or her surrounded by a variety of technologies, which may include a cell phone, MP3 player, a computer, and possibly a handheld device, such as an Apple iPad. Today's technologies create a bridge to information that is easily accessible and timely, as well as varied in presentation, and provide digital learning tools not available through traditional print.

Today, student learning can happen through connections with laptops, iPods, smartphones, tablet computers, and online tools at anytime from anywhere there is an Internet connection. Learning is no longer confined to a 50-minute classroom session or the reading of a text and answering the questions at the end of the chapter. It's time to embrace the experiences of online courses in our classrooms and reconfigure strict, inflexible policy into processes and procedures to enable and lead to successful learning opportunities for all learners, regardless of age, location, or learning needs.

Technologies change quickly, the tools that bring learning to our fingertips change quickly. While there is an overabundance of online tools, open source programs, and free downloads available for teaching and learning, these also change quickly, thus outpacing the ability to keep up with them, as well as their power for effective teaching and learning for filling curriculum holes left by outdated textbooks and encyclopedias all but forgotten on library shelves. The rate of these changes makes it extremely difficult to keep up the policies that shape their use. Many strict policies prohibit the use of these tools in schools, yet expect participants to access them outside of the school day to complete research, collaboration, or other connections to learning. Alternately, policy may allow only teachers to access these sites and materials in a "sit and get" session, such as a lecture format where the student is the recipient of information with little interaction between the instructor and participants, forcing the learner to participate as a passive observer. Yet, students figure out how to get around these filters through alternative means, such as proxies, which they share with each other and, in some cases, with their teacher so all can be active participants during the learning day. It's time for change in technology policy in education.

CHALLENGES TO IMPLEMENTING ONLINE COURSES

While implementing online courses faces many challenges, such as effective design, student and teacher schedules, and teacher and student skill levels, these are issues that are more clearly adapted to fit the needs of the school, teacher, and learner. One enormous challenge for districts, schools, teachers, students, and parents includes ways of fitting this emerging, yet still somewhat unconventional, learning model into the existing educational structure. When reviewing current education policy, there is very little room for expansion and implementation of online courses and the flexibility these can bring to teaching and learning due to outdated policies written with traditional learning in mind. Many of the creators of current policy have little understanding of online learning as a whole and base the upholding of these policies on fear or on outdated, preconceived notions of education in the traditional sense. Changing policy to procedure and process must include changing the perspectives of students, parents, teachers, administrators, and even legislators.

Scheduling needs to be addressed as a process rather than policy so that the flexibility students and teachers need is built in and available as an element of suppleness as needs will vary, as will times for connection and collaboration. For example, in the 8:00 to 3:30 traditional scenario, schedules are pretty well set in stone. In the online course, however, students will be working all hours of the day and night and teachers will need to adapt their schedules to meet their students' most effective learning times and needs. Teachers may need to connect with their students remotely as a group or individually, and that connection may understandably take place outside of the traditional school hours. Building flexible hours into teachers' schedules, especially those teaching full time, will aid in teacher planning without taking chunks out of their personal time to work with students in the online course.

Teacher skills and student skills are also to be considered when it comes to introducing and implementing online courses. The skills each groups needs are quite varied and will need to be updated on a regular basis. Policy mandating certain skills or specific training will need to change as often as the technologies change and as the learning management systems are updated. Fluidity needs to be built in so that as changes occur, updates to processes and procedures can take place quickly, rather than needing a large policy committee and review group to gather and comb research, review other policies, and make determinations for updates, which by then may be outdated.

Student use of technology is almost intuitive, and they will intuitively learn to navigate the course or learning management system rather quickly, even through their own exploration. It is the academic application in which they may need direct instruction. Regarding student skills, prerequisites may prevent students from participating in an online course, when an orientation can simply be built into the initial course introduction.

Teachers, on the other hand, will need to learn the learning management system, as well as any outside collaboration or connection tools, such as Skype or Google Docs, in addition to learning to be effective online course instructors. Professional development for teachers will need to start long before the online course opens and will need to be continuous as technologies, content, and services shift. Online learning is also an effective method to meet the multiple learning needs of teachers through providing online professional development, from mentoring to learning community membership, and from content expansion to technology implementation.

Access can be approached from many directions, from ownership to right to use technologies in the community. At minimum, participants need to have Internet access to participate in an online course. No longer is a computer the only means of access.

Many students today carry access in their own pocket or backpack, in the form of a smartphone, an iPad, an iTouch, a laptop, and so on. Yet, predominantly, school policy forbids students from using these tools during the school day, thus forcing them to forego many learning opportunities that could be incorporated into their daily learning. Policy forces shut down. Processes and procedures create opportunity: opportunity to incorporate that which is already in the hands of participants, and opportunity for extended learning within classroom walls when the computer lab is not available. Creating processes to include the use of outside devices will bring learning to real time. Imagine being a teacher in a classroom and discussing the history of a worldwide event and having only one computer in a classroom of 30 or so. Therefore, students getting out their devices to research the event or to locate digital resources for learning will create engagement, opportunity, and ignite an excitement for learning that may not be present in the "sit and get" environment of a one-computer classroom. Allowing students to interact with members of communities from that era in real time will increase the learning as well as the recall of that learning due to digital opportunities that allow and encourage them to go outside the walls from within which they are sitting.

Students without home access may be shut out from online course opportunities due to lack-of-ownership issues. To address this, school procedures can be changed to include longer school library hours before and after school for students to work on their online pieces and remain caught up in their work. Some schools accommodate learners with loaner equipment to meet the learning goals of the courses.

When considering adding online course opportunities to student schedules, one must remember that these courses must also be available to all students, including those with disabilities, whether physical or learning disability. While brokered courses are generally created with this mandate in mind, teacher-created courses must include provisions for meeting the needs of all learners, thus adding this element to their professional development skills.

CONCLUSION

Policy governing regulation and insurance of high-quality online education must be examined to determine if there are areas stifling student opportunities or areas that are roadblocks to allowing the use of common technologies and available tools, whether it is hardware, software, or online. Too often, student online learning policies are still written with the traditional school model in mind. Moving away from "policy" in investigating and creating opportunities allows for the exploration and addition of new and upcoming technologies and tools as they prove value as effective implementation into online education.

Today's learners do not think of technology as a separate entity in their daily lives. To them, it is as commonplace as a pencil and paper was to previous generations of students, yet the implementation of technology and online tools into their daily education is not regularly taking place. Much of this is due to outdated and irrelevant policies based on fear, as well as not taking into account new and emerging technologies, hardware, software, and online tools commonly used in today's online K–12 school environments.

The roles of today's teachers and students are changing. It is time to examine policy and determine where the stifling, inflexible pieces can be eliminated and processes and procedures can be created that are adaptable, adjustable, and easily modifiable as technologies used in the online student learning environment continue to grow and change.

FURTHER READINGS AND RESOURCES

Arora, R. (2009, November 1). The K–12 online evolution: 21st-century solutions for 21st-century learning. *Internet @ Schools.* Retrieved from http://www.internetat schools.com/Articles/Editorial/Features/The-Ke2809312-Online-Evolution-21st-Century-Solutions-for-21st-Century-Learning-60015.aspx

Brown, M. (n.d.). *Online high schools as possible solution to America's education problem.* Retrieved from HubPages: http://hubpages.com/hub/Online-High-Schools-As-Possible-Solution-to-Americas-Education-Problem

Cavanaugh, C., Gillan, K. J., Kromrey, J., Hess, M., & Blomeyer, R. (2004). *The effects of distance education on K–12 student outcomes: A meta-analysis.* Naperville, IL: Learning Point Associates.

College Board. (2009). *Summary reports: 2009.* Retrieved August 27, 2010, from http://www.collegeboard.com/student/testing/ap/exgrd_sum/2009.html

Institute for Interactive Technologies. (2006). *E-learning concepts and techniques.* Retrieved from http://iit.bloomu.edu/Spring2006_eBook_files/chapter1.htm

Kaufman, P., Bradby, D., & National Center for Education Statistics. (1992). *National Education Longitudinal Study of 1988: Characteristics of at-risk students in NELS:88.* Washington, DC: U.S. Department of Education.

Lips, D. (2010, January 12). *How online learning is revolutionizing K-12 education and benefiting students.* Retrieved June 29, 2011, from the Heritage Foundation website: http://www.heritage.org/research/reports/2010/01/how-online-learning-is-revolutionizing-k12-education-and-benefiting-students

National Center for Educational Statistics. (2007). *High school coursetaking: Findings from the condition of education.* Washington, DC: Author.

National Educational Technology Plan. (2010). *Transforming American education: Learning powered by technology.* Washington, DC: U.S. Department of Education, Office of Educational Technology.

Picciano, A. G., & Seaman, J. (2009). *K–12 online learning: A 2008 follow-up of the survey of U.S. school district administrators.* Needham, MA: Sloan Consortium.

Project Tomorrow. (2010). *Learning in the 21st century: 2010 trends update.* Irvine, CA: Author.

Setzer, J. C., & Lewis, L. (2005). *Distance education courses for public elementary and secondary school students: 2002–03.* Washington, DC: U.S. Department of Education, National Center for Education Statistics.

Smith, R., Clark, T., & Blomeyer, R. (2005, November). *A synthesis of new research on K–12 online learning.* Naperville, IL: North Central Regional Educational Laboratory. Retrieved from http://www.ncrel.org/tech/synthesis/synthesis.pdf

U.S. Department of Education, National Center for Education Statistics. (2009). *The condition of education.* Washington, DC: Author.

Watson, J., Gemin, B., Ryan, J., & Wicks, M. (2009). *Keeping pace with K-12 online learning: An annual review of state-level policy and practice.* Evergreen, CO: Evergreen Education Group.

5

Are today's virtual schools effective student learning environments?

POINT: Kathryn Kennedy, *Georgia Southern University*

COUNTERPOINT: Abigail Hawkins, *Adobe Systems Incorporated*

OVERVIEW

In this chapter, authors Kathryn Kennedy (Georgia Southern University) and Abigail Hawkins (Adobe Systems Incorporated) debate the controversial issue of whether K–12 virtual schools are effective student learning environments. Virtual, or online, schools first began in the mid-1990s when the Internet increasingly became an additional method of communication in educational environments. In 1997, for example, Florida became the first state to establish a fully online public high school, Florida Virtual School. Nationwide, 24 states currently have K–12 virtual school programs. Similar to traditional brick-and-mortar schools, K–12 virtual schools strive to become successful learning environments for students. Unlike traditional brick-and-mortar schools, how-ever, virtual schools provide instruction exclusively in online environments and allow students access to curriculum 24 hours a day, 7 days a week. Virtual schools provide today's K–12 and higher education students with the flexibility of anytime, anywhere access to a specific educational curriculum.

In her point essay, Kennedy contends that initial empirical evidence sug-gests that students in virtual school environments benefit from online learning, and the online environment itself represents an effective student learning envi-ronment. More specifically, Kennedy contends that today's K–12 virtual schools are effective student learning environments based on two factors: first, the effectiveness of student-learning outcomes, such as student achievement on test scores; and second, the effectiveness based on certain characteristics of students' learning environments.

In addition to being effective student learning environments, Kennedy maintains that K–12 virtual schools offer additional and heightened benefits compared to conventional, brick-and-mortar, or face-to-face classroom instruction. K–12 virtual schools can meet the academic performance needs of students who have previously struggled academically in traditional, face-to-face classrooms, including students with disabilities or special needs. K–12 virtual schools also provide students access to specific classes, such as Advanced Placement (AP) classes and credit recovery classes, that might not otherwise be available to them in their local school environments. Kennedy specifically points to students in rural school communities, who often do not have comparable access to AP classes compared to students in either urban or suburban school communities.

In her counterpoint essay, Hawkins cautions that there is currently not enough rigorous and methodologically sound empirical research being done on K–12 virtual schools, specifically as it relates to whether or not they are effective student learning environments compared to traditional, face-to-face school environments. According to Hawkins, there is a limited amount of empirical research as it relates to K–12 virtual schooling effectiveness. More important, a closer examination of the existing research on K–12 virtual schools as effective student learning environments reveals several noteworthy methodological research problems, including whether the students often sampled in K–12 virtual school studies are actually representative of the larger and accurate student virtual school population. In addition to nonrepresentative samples of today's virtual school student populations, Hawkins contends that K–12 virtual schools, as a whole, have higher student attrition rates, which demonstrate that virtual schooling may not be as effective a learning environment for all students. According to Hawkins, high student attrition rates are often concealed by the lengthy trial periods that virtual schools adopt.

While Kennedy argues in her point essay that K–12 virtual school environments can be deemed successful student learning environments by focusing on students' learning outcomes as well as specific characteristics of the students' learning environment, Hawkins disagrees, saying that inconsistent metrics for measuring student success make it extremely difficult to make valid comparisons between virtual and traditional, face-to-face student populations. For example, Hawkins makes the point that there is currently no consistency regarding how virtual schools define successful course completion by a student. Presently, successful course completion in virtual schools ranges from simply remaining in the course until its completion to passing a particular course with a relatively high grade.

Kennedy and Hawkins ultimately agree that K–12 virtual schooling continues to experience tremendous student growth. It is unquestionable that at least a part of that student growth is fueled by the perception that K–12 virtual schools are effective student learning environments. Both authors also agree that K–12 virtual schools, despite having existed for nearly 2 decades, deserve more research attention and have been studied relatively little in terms of assessing their effectiveness as student learning environments. Nevertheless, 45 states and the District of Columbia have presently adopted state virtual schools at both the K–12 and postsecondary levels, full-time online schools, or both. Therefore, it is critically important that educators, parents, and policymakers have the necessary and rigorous research to make informed decisions regarding the viability of K–12 virtual schools as effective student learning environments.

Kevin P. Brady
North Carolina State University

POINT: Kathryn Kennedy
Georgia Southern University

D espite their existence for nearly 20 years, K–12 virtual schools have only recently become a high profile and fairly controversial issue in American education. Virtual schools are defined as state approved and/or regionally accredited schools that offer instructional courses through distance learning methods delivered through the Internet. A topic frequently discussed during the 2008 presidential campaign in terms of its impact on educational reform, K–12 virtual schooling was recently ushered into the limelight of educational reform and politics. Virtual, or online, education at the K–12 educational level has become an increasingly popular method of delivering educational instruction in the United States, and it is continuing to grow exponentially. For example, recent statistics indicate that today's K–12 virtual schools enroll more than 1 million students nationwide, and in 2011, more than 8 million students encounter some form of online learning during their K–12 schooling period (Greaves Group & Hayes Connection, 2006). However, an important question regarding K–12 virtual schools remains: Are today's K–12 virtual schools really effective student learning environments? In other words, can today's students learn as much or more in an online learning environment compared to a traditional, face-to-face classroom?

Indeed, this is a weighted question that can be answered only by first defining the word *effective*. For the purposes of this point essay, *effective* will be defined in two distinct ways:

- effectiveness based on students' learning outcomes

- effectiveness based on characteristics of students' learning environment

EFFECTIVENESS BASED ON STUDENTS' LEARNING OUTCOMES

Today's K–12 virtual schools can be effective student learning environments based on recent and quality research from existing studies involving student learning outcomes. A majority of studies detailing the effectiveness of K–12 virtual schooling and online learning have focused specifically on student learning outcomes, including student achievement as a measure of both test scores and grades (Gallagher & McCormick, 1999). For instance, a meta-analysis study examined 14 studies that explored student achievement in K–12 online learning and the combined results demonstrated that online learning is as effective in terms of student learning as traditional brick-and-mortar education (Cavanaugh, Gillan, Kromrey, Hess, & Blomeyer, 2004).

Aside from this particular meta-analysis study, some comparative studies at the high school level have found that online learning students have outperformed their traditional counterparts (Aivazidis, Lazaridou, & Hellden, 2006). Additionally, many studies have shown that online learning in the K–12 school environment can be as effective as the traditional brick-and-mortar classroom. Specifically, students in K–12 virtual schools have been recently shown to outperform their traditional classroom student counterparts in such skills as conducting research, making decisions, solving problems, learning independently, and thinking critically. For instance, students taking Advanced Placement (AP) courses in three virtual schools—Apex Learning, Florida Virtual School, and Virtual High School—were found to outscore the national student average for the end-of-year AP exams.

K–12 virtual schools providing increased student access to these AP and other courses is crucial because many traditional brick-and-mortar schools do not have enough qualified teachers to teach all of the necessary subjects students often request or even are required to take. In particular, many rural schools throughout the United States have neither enough teachers nor appropriately qualified teachers to support such classes. As a result, many K–12 virtual schools reach out to all students to enrich the curriculum by offering courses such as AP courses in various fields, including mathematics and the sciences. In addition to ensuring teacher quality, K–12 virtual schools routinely hire professional consultants to ensure quality online courses by performing evaluations of their online learning programs. For instance, one particular performance evaluation performed on the Illinois Virtual High School (IVHS) found that all stakeholders, including students, instructors, and school administrators, were satisfied with the online school's progress. A similar evaluation was published about Virtual High School (VHS), which was established in 1997 as one of the very first K–12 virtual, or online, student learning programs. This evaluation included AP exam scores as well as credit recovery information. This VHS evaluation showed that most of the students completed their courses successfully. All stakeholders were supportive of the student courses and teachers' professional development opportunities. Many other evaluations of virtual schools exist.

A study spanning 2001 to 2006 was published that looked at the students' course grades in the subject areas of mathematics, science, fine arts, English language arts, French, general studies, technology, and social studies (Barbour, 2010). Students were completing their course in one of the following ways: fully online in a rural setting, fully online in an urban setting, fully face-to-face in a rural setting, or fully face-to-face in an urban setting. Findings showed that the final course grades were consistent for the most part, except that the students taking online mathematics outperformed those who were in a face-to-face setting. In addition, it was found that the students completing their courses face-to-face in science and social studies were outperforming their online counterparts. Overall, the researchers found that there was no significant difference when it came to student academic performance in face-to-face versus online environments and regarding the students' geographic location.

EFFECTIVENESS BASED ON MEETING STUDENTS' LEARNING NEEDS

When examining K–12 online learning environments, effectiveness should be demonstrated by meeting students' learning needs based on the characteristics of the learning environment and what those environments afford their students when it comes to learning. K–12 virtual schools have been found to offer students multiple benefits to enhance their learning needs. Praised by school administrators in a 2008 public school district survey, online learning is serving the individual needs of students and providing a lifeline of education to those students who are not able to partake in courses not offered at their traditional school (Picciano & Seaman, 2009). As previously mentioned, AP courses and other advanced courses are provided to students. In addition, K–12 virtual schools have been known to work for students who are at risk of not graduating by offering credit recovery courses. Virtual schools have also proven effective for other learner groups, including students with dusabilities and English language learners. Virtual schools have also been noted to extend students' learning time and reach underserved populations, especially since distance learning is not affected by geographic boundaries.

K–12 virtual schools also allow for students' differing learning styles by offering individualized instruction to their students. It has been found that learners' satisfaction will be greater when their learning environment matches their own learning style. Students and parents have the option to choose what format of learning best suits their needs. Students who are falling behind are offered remedial courses to catch up to their peers and earn additional credits. Students who are excelling and need a challenge are enriched through AP courses in varying subjects. Students who are homeschooled have additional opportunities to engage in topics that are beyond their parents' knowledge or beyond their family resources.

K–12 virtual schools offer students flexibility in their learning options. In one study, students were asked to create, edit, and design digital artifacts, which subsequently increased student motivation and positive influence on the students' achievement. When it comes to teaching online, because online instructors do not have the luxury of reading student cues (both verbal and nonverbal) in an online learning environment, K–12 online instructors typically have to check in with their students either by phone or via online communications to make sure the student is understanding the material and succeeding in the learning environment. This communication is an important part of the students' academic achievement in the online learning environment. In addition to communicating with students, the learning management or course management system typically has a way of tracking students' activities in the learning environment to see what they are doing in the classroom and to ensure their road to success.

CONCLUSION

Despite over more than two decades of being in existence, K–12 virtual, or online, learning is still in its infancy, and more research is needed in this area, especially as it relates to the viability of K–12 virtual schools as effective student learning environments. However, initial research findings examining the effectiveness of K–12 virtual schools reveal the potential of these schools to be just as effective learning environments for students compared to the traditional brick-and-mortar classroom. Additionally, K–12 virtual schools provide some additional benefits of increased access to AP and credit recovery courses that some students might not otherwise have access to. While today's researchers and educators continue to study virtual schooling as actively as current funds and other resources will allow them, the advancement and use of emerging online technologies for teaching and learning as well as the continued exploration and understanding of online learning pedagogy and design principles will continue to enable virtual schools, either fully or partially online, to reach many more students who are in dire need of diverse as well as effective learning opportunities that work effectively for them in the educational process. As the emerging research is beginning to reveal, K–12 virtual schools not only increase student access to certain courses but they can provide students with a quality and effective learning environment. The time is now to see K–12 virtual schools as credible learning environments for today's students.

COUNTERPOINT: Abigail Hawkins
Adobe Systems Incorporated

K–12 virtual schools have experienced explosive student growth. Since their inception in 1994 with the creation of Utah's Electronic High

School, K–12 virtual school programs in the United States are now available in all but five states (Watson, Gemin, Ryan, & Wicks, 2009). The first national survey of K–12 student online learning estimated that between 40,000 and 50,000 K–12 students were enrolled in online courses. Today, researchers estimate that slightly more than 1 million K–12 students are enrolled in at least one online course. As evidenced by student growth, K–12 virtual schooling is becoming an acceptable alternative to the traditional brick-and-mortar classrooms in many K–12 schools across the United States.

One major factor contributing to the growth of K–12 virtual schooling is the increasing number of research studies reporting positive student academic performance related to K–12 online learning environments. Unfortunately, there is presently a limited amount of research on the subject of K–12 virtual schools as effective student learning environments, and a closer examination of existing research highlights many methodological problems associated with the research of K–12 online learning. In addition to the research-based methodological shortcomings, the ways in which existing research has been interpreted and used by advocates of K–12 online learning is misleading. Despite the rhetoric of many virtual school proponents that K–12 virtual schools are unquestionably effective student learning environments, the leading current research reveals it is actually uncertain whether K–12 virtual schools provide as effective student learning environments as traditional, face-to-face classrooms.

This counterpoint essay highlights the lack of current and quality research focusing on K–12 online learning, the methodological shortcomings in existing research, the difficulty of making comparisons due to inconsistent student success metrics, and the misinterpretation of study results from several seminal studies—factors which, to date, make it difficult to definitively state one way or the other whether K–12 virtual schools are, in fact, effective student learning environments.

LACK OF RESEARCH

To credibly claim that K–12 virtual schools are effective student learning environments, there needs to be a substantial body of evidence to support such claims. Since K–12 virtual schooling is a relatively recent, but growing, phenomenon in K–12 education, research in K–12 online learning is lagging behind research in student online learning at the college and university environments. To date, there is a limited amount of current research published in peer-reviewed, refereed journals in the field of K–12 online learning. There is an even greater absence of empirical research in K–12 online student learning.

An examination of current research studies finds that the majority of these studies focused on two general areas: the benefits of virtual schooling and student readiness/retention issues. The rapid, widespread adoption of K–12 virtual schooling, paired with the limited body of research, indicates that the practice is outpacing the availability of useful research. The majority of research on student performance indicates that students do as well or better than their classroom-based counterparts. To date, there have been four meta-analysis studies, which included data from K–12 distance education studies (Bernard, Abrami, Low, Borokhovski, Wade, & Wozney, 2004; Cavanaugh, 2001; Cavanaugh, Gillan, Kromrey, Hess, & Blomeyer, 2004; Means, Toyama, Murphy, Bakia, & Jones, 2009). All of these studies found either no significant difference in student performance or small positive effect sizes in online student performance compared to classroom-based students.

METHODOLOGICAL ISSUES

A closer examination of the research, however, indicates potential methodological problems that may call into question the studies' positive results about student learning environments. First, there may be a problem with the research samples. It is possible that the research samples of students in the online programs were not equivalent to the samples of traditional, face-to-face classroom students. In other words, students in the online and classroom programs may have been too dissimilar from the outset to attribute differences in performance to the actual delivery medium. Thus, lower-performing students may have self-selected out of the virtual school sample (and many likely ended up back in their traditional classroom environments). Similarly, some researchers speculate that the higher performance by students in the virtual courses was due to the high dropout rate and not necessarily the online learning experience. Essentially, these results in favor of the virtual school samples may have been due to the fact that the students were simply better students and not due at all to the virtual school environment.

Second, researchers' descriptions of online students are also evidence that, to date, online students in comparative studies may not necessarily be representative of the overall classroom student population. Students in the virtual school environments were frequently described as highly motivated, self-directed learners, strong readers and writers, college bound, predominately honors or Advanced Placement students, and typically A or B students. These characteristics are not representative of the average or the majority of classroom-based students. Yet these characteristics accurately describe students included in the virtual school samples in the body of research comparing student performance between online and traditional, face-to-face classroom environments.

The third problem regarding sampling methods in the current research body is whether students participating in these studies are even representative of the larger virtual student school population. Today, a broader range of students are choosing virtual schooling for the purpose of credit recovery or to fulfill a graduation requirement. As most states require that students have at least one year of math to complete high school, many of these students were likely enrolled for the second or third time to pass the course to graduate. Thus, credit recovery students likely constitute large enrollment numbers for these basic math courses.

Additionally, the largest growth in K–12 student online learning enrollment were full-time online programs, such as cyber charter schools, which typically have a higher percentage of students classified as *at risk*, a label frequently given to students who are likely to drop out, flunk out, be pushed out, or "age out" before successfully completing their course or schooling. This further lends weight to the fact that the larger population in K–12 online learning may not be representative of the highly motivated, self-directed, higher ability students frequently sampled and cited in the K–12 online literature. Thus far, the populations examined by researchers have not been representative of the entirety or possibly even the majority of students attending virtual schools. Thus, results from studies with the highly selective sample likely do not generalize to the larger K–12 online student population.

Some researchers even question the effectiveness of online learning for struggling, underperforming student populations. Unfortunately, few studies have examined the experience of lower-performing students in an online environment to draw any conclusive answers, and many researchers call for an examination of the quality of the learning experience for this struggling student population. The lack of research on this group of students, coupled with the sampling problems present in existing studies, leads to the conclusion that there is not enough evidence to definitively claim that virtual schooling serves all students equally.

Additionally, high student attrition rates among virtual schools can be another indicator that virtual schooling may not be an effective learning environment for all students. According to John Watson, Butch Gemin, Jennifer Ryan, and Mathew Wicks (2009), completion rates are a key quality measure for virtual schools. Though no exact figure exists for completion rates, attrition is believed to be a significant problem among virtual schools. While student attrition rates vary greatly due to a lack of common metrics used among virtual schools, actual attrition figures may be masked due to course completion policies such as trial periods and definitions of a successful course completion. Two-thirds of respondents had a trial period policy, where students could withdraw from a course before a specified amount of time or activity without penalty. The length of the trial periods ranged from 1 day to 185 days, with 2- and 4-week trial periods accounting for more than half of the trial period policies. Essentially, students could drop out during that period and not be counted in the schools' attrition statistics. Consequently, high student attrition rates may actually be masked by the presence and length of trial period policies the school adopts.

Another policy that muddies the student attrition metric is how K–12 virtual schools define a successful course completion. In other words, so long as the students remained enrolled, they were counted as a successful completion. The researchers argued that the inconsistency in how and when students were counted in the completion metric render it useless for comparative purposes among virtual schools and with traditional brick-and-mortar schools. Therefore, making a judgment on the effectiveness of virtual schools using completion and attrition metrics is highly questionable.

Advocates of K–12 online learning often cite the four meta-analysis studies conducted on K–12 online learning thus far. These studies point to either no significant differences or small positive effect sizes in favor of online learning.

CONCLUSION

This counterpoint essay has outlined how there is limited empirical research in the area of K–12 online learning. Of the existing research on K–12 virtual schools, the samples studied are skewed toward those students who are academically advanced and fail to represent all or even most K–12 online student learners. Furthermore, inconsistent metrics for measuring student success make it difficult to make performance comparisons between virtual and traditional brick-and-mortar schools. Even ignoring these methodological and measurement challenges, to date, studies show that academic performance is no better or even worse than classroom practices. While virtual schooling has promise and its practice continues to grow, it is time for academics to conduct more methodologically sound research studies. Only when studies address these limitations can we claim with confidence that virtual schools are as effective a learning environment as their traditional brick-and-mortar counterparts.

FURTHER READINGS AND RESOURCES

Aivazidis, C., Lazaridou, M., & Hellden, G. F. (2006). A comparison between a traditional and online environmental educational program. *The Journal of Environmental Education, 37*(4), 45–54.

Barbour, M. K. (2010). Researching K-12 online learning: What do we know and what should we examine? *Distance Education, 7*(2), 7–12.

Bernard, R. M., Abrami, P.C., Low, Y., Borokhovski, E., Wade, A., & Wozney, L. (2004). How does distance education compare with classroom instruction? A meta-analysis of the empirical research. *Review of Educational Research, 74*(3), 379–439.

Cavanaugh, C. (2001). The effectiveness of interactive distance education technologies in K-12 learning: A meta-analysis. *International Journal of Educational Telecommunications, 7*(1), 73–88.

Cavanaugh, C., Barbour, M. K., & Clark, T. (2009). Research and practice in K-12 online learning: A review of open access literature. *The International Review of Research in Open and Distance Learning, 10*(1).

Cavanaugh, C., Gillan, K. J., Kromrey, J., Hess, M., & Blomeyer, R. (2004). *The effects of distance education on K–12 student outcomes: A meta-analysis.* Naperville, IL: Learning Point Associates. Retrieved from http://www.ncrel.org/tech/distance/k12distance.pdf

Gallagher, P., & McCormick, K. (1999). Student satisfaction with two-way interactive distance education for delivery of early childhood special education coursework. *Journal of Special Education Technology, 14*(1), 32–47.

Greaves Group, & Hayes Connection. (2006). *America's digital schools 2006: A five-year forecast: Mobilizing the curriculum.* Retrieved August 22, 2010, from http://www.ads2006.net/ads2006/pdf/ADS2006KF.pdf

Means, B., Toyama, Y., Murphy, R., Bakia, M., & Jones, K. (2009). *Evaluation of evidence-based practices in online learning: A meta-analysis and review of online learning studies.* Washington, DC: U.S. Department of Education. Retrieved August 22, 2010, from http://www2.ed.gov/rschstat/eval/tech/evidence-based-practices/finalreport.pdf

Picciano, A. G., & Seaman, J. (2009). *K-12 online learning: A 2008 follow-up of the survey of U.S. school district administrators.* Needham, MA: Sloan-C.

Watson, J., Gemin, B., Ryan, J., & Wicks, M. (2009). *Keeping pace with K-12 online learning: An annual review of state-level policy and practice.* Vienna, VA: North American Council for Online Learning.

6

Are virtual schools more cost-effective compared to traditional brick-and-mortar schools?

POINT: Michael Barbour, *Wayne State University*

COUNTERPOINT: Allison Powell, *International Association for K-12 Online Learning (iNACOL)*

OVERVIEW

Virtual schools and cyberschools are public (including charter) or private accredited schools where all or most courses are taught via the Internet. Virtual schools are the modern-day version of correspondence or distance learning schools and essentially are an outgrowth of those institutions. There are two types of virtual schools: *synchronous,* where all students are online at the same time, and *asynchronous,* where students access course content according to their own schedules. According to the U.S. Department of Education, 48 states and the District of Columbia currently support online learning opportunities, ranging from classroom supplementation to full-time enrollment in virtual schools. Twenty-seven states and the District of Columbia offered full-time online schooling to students statewide as of the end of the 2010 school year. The International Association for K-12 Online Learning (iNACOL) estimated that more than 1.5 million K–12 students were involved in some type of online learning in the 2009 to 2010 school year.

In this chapter, authors Michael Barbour (Wayne State University) and Allison Powell (iNACOL) debate whether virtual schools are more cost-effective compared to traditional brick-and-mortar schools. As of 2010, 48 states offer at least some form of online instruction to K–12 students. Both authors agree that there is presently very little research detailing how today's virtual schools are funded. The issue of funding is complicated by the fact that virtual schools are considered supplemental programs in which a student is simultaneously enrolled in a traditional brick-and-mortar school as well as enrolled in at least one virtual course as a means to supplement his or her curriculum. In contrast, cyberschools are defined as those online programs in which students complete all of their courses online and are considered full-time student programs. As a result, whether a student attends a supplemental, virtual school or a full-time cyberschool program impacts the relative level of funding they receive.

In his point essay arguing that virtual schools are more cost-effective compared to traditional brick-and-mortar schools, Barbour highlights the fact that determining the costs associated with full-time cyberschools is extremely difficult, mainly due to the fact that many cyberschools in the United States are owned and operated by private, for-profit companies not required to release their schools' budgetary information to the public. As more public school districts across the country form cyberschools, however, these budgets will become more readily available to the public. Furthermore, Barbour points out that the most common method of funding supplemental, virtual schools is through a combination of governmental block grants and student per course fees paid by the school district.

Barbour argues the few existing studies analyzing the costs associated with funding virtual or cyberschools conclude that their costs are in line with those of traditional brick-and-mortar schools. However, Barbour points out that the current cost studies of virtual and cyberschools do not include costs associated with either capital expenses or transportation. If capital expenses or transportation-related expenses were included, Barbour contends, the costs associated with funding virtual or cyberschools would be much lower on a per-pupil basis compared to traditional brick-and-mortar schools. Since capital expenses such as building-related construction and maintenance expenses as well as transportation costs are minimal or nonexistent for most virtual and cyberschools, these cost savings advance Barbour's primary argument that virtual and cyberschools are, on average, more cost-effective compared to traditional brick-and-mortar schools.

In her counterpoint essay, Powell agrees that the majority of operating costs for student online-related programs are fairly similar to traditional, brick-and-mortal schools. For example, Powell argues that virtual schools share many of the identical costs compared to traditional brick-and-mortar schools, including administrators, teachers, staff, curriculum, course materials, professional development, and data systems. Unlike traditional brick-and-mortar schools, however, Powell argues, virtual and cyberschools do not incur the same related costs associated with instructional facilities or transportation-related expenses. Despite these cost savings, virtual schools, Powell contends, have unique and substantial costs that most traditional brick-and-mortar schools do not have, including increased technological infrastructure-related costs, including course and learning management systems (LMS) and staff for technical maintenance and support. According to Powell, some of these technological infrastructure-related and training costs can be substantial and often exceed the level of costs experienced by traditional brick-and-mortar schools.

In his point essay, Barbour acknowledges the unique costs associated with online schools when he cites research that indicates that both virtual and cyberschools need to be initially funded at a higher rate when first developed as a means to build an efficient and effective instructional capacity. Yet, Barbour argues that these initial funding increases for funding virtual and cyberschools often steadily decrease after several years as the virtual or cyberschool builds institutional capacity.

According to Powell, there are often additional costs associated with funding effective virtual or cyberschools. For example, Powell argues, virtual schools are required to provide appropriate and updated professional development, training teachers for student instruction in an online environment. Additionally, course development is a major expense category for today's virtual and cyberschools since these schools often must purchase online courses from a private content provider.

In this chapter, detailing the cost-effectiveness of today's virtual schools, both authors reference the same existing studies, concluding that the operating costs of virtual and cyberschools are fairly comparable to traditional brick-and-mortar schools. However, Barbour contends that virtual and cyberschools are more cost-effective compared to traditional brick-and-mortar schools largely due to the cost savings they provide in the areas of building and transportation-related expenses. Capital and transportation expenses are a significant and increasing expense for today's traditional brick-and-mortar schools.

While Powell acknowledges certain cost savings associated with capital and transportation-related expenses for virtual and cyberschools, she contends that the unique and increased costs of funding today's virtual and cyberschools, including teacher professional development in online settings, course development for virtual and cyberschools, technology set-up expenses, and personnel for technology maintenance, substantially minimize or completely cancel out any existing cost savings provided by virtual and cyberschools. While Barbour does not agree that the unique costs associated with virtual and cyberschools make them significantly less cost-effective compared to traditional brick-and-mortar schools, he does agree that virtual and cyber-schools are more expensive to operate on a per-student basis when they are first started as they begin to develop an effective institutional capacity. Clearly, more studies are necessary to examine the specific costs of funding virtual and cyberschools, and whether today's virtual and cyberschools can simulta-neously provide a high-quality education at a more cost-effective funding level compared to existing traditional brick-and-mortar classrooms remains a pressing question for education researchers.

Kevin P. Brady
North Carolina State University

POINT: Michael Barbour
Wayne State University

In the United States, public K–12 education is funded primarily through local property taxes, along with a variety of federal and state-level funding. These various sources of money result in a base per student amount that schools receive primarily based on student enrollment. Schools generally receive additional funding to support students who require services beyond that of a regular student (e.g., students with special needs and disabilities). Some schools also qualify for additional funding based on their location or the unique demographic characteristics of their students.

To date, there has been little published on how virtual or online schools are funded. There are, however, specific budgetary items that policymakers, researchers, practitioners, and other educational stakeholders have been able to identify that apply specifically to traditional brick-and-mortar schools, virtual schools, or both. Based on research conducted by John Adsit (2004); Amy Berk Anderson, John Augenblick, Dale DeCescre, and Jill Conrad (2006); Florida TaxWatch Center for Educational Performance and Accountability (2007); and the Southern Regional Education Board (2006), Rob Darrow (2008) created a comparison of the cost factors associated with the operation of traditional brick-and-mortar schools and virtual schools (see Table 6.1).

Unfortunately, the actual costs associated with K–12 online learning, particularly the full-time costs of cyberschools, are difficult to determine. One of the reasons for this difficulty is due to the fact that many cyberschools are operated by private, for-profit companies. For example, the largest cyberschool operator in the United States is K12 Inc., a publicly traded company that offers proprietary curriculum and educational services created for online delivery to students in kindergarten through 12th grade. In September 2010, for example, K12 Inc. opened the Michigan Virtual Charter Academy (MVCA) with an initial enrollment of 400 students. Regulations in the state require that MVCA release its annual operating budget on its website.

Based on the student enrollment cap, the budget reports expected revenue of $2,881,830 or $7,205 per student. The budget calls for expenditures of $1,812,256 on basic instruction and additional needs instruction (presumably access to the online course content, textbooks, and other instructional materials), and $1,069,574 on support services, such as the cost of the administration, teachers, learning coaches, the capital costs of the office (it is unclear in which category access to K12 Inc.'s proprietary course management system is included). Assuming the course management system costs are included in the instructional expenditures, it would mean that the MVCA has entered into an

Table 6.1

A comparison of brick-and-mortar school and virtual school cost items

Brick-and-Mortar Schools	Virtual Schools	Brick-and-Mortar and Virtual Schools
Buildings and ground maintenance	Space for offices	Administration
Transportation	Course management system	Teachers
Security	Course content	Professional development
Energy	Mobile communication devices for teachers and network	Computer lab and/or computer access for students
Athletics	Technology support	Computer and Internet access for teachers
Music program	Marketing and advertizing	Courses and course outlines approved by governing bodies
Substitute teacher costs (for professional development and sick days)	Home computers or laptops and Internet access for students	Students
Medical services (e.g., nursing office, first aid)		Student information systems
		State testing system
		Textbooks
		Special education services
		Student support (e.g., counseling, library)
		Network infrastructure
		Telephone and network

Source: Darrow, R. (2008). *Review of literature: Cost items for implementing and maintaining a K-12 online school* (p. 9). Unpublished manuscript. Fresno: California State University, Fresno.

annual contract with K12 Inc. for access to their course management system and online content for $1,812,256. Even without understanding the exact amount of the cyberschool's budget going to its parent company, such as MVCA and K12 Inc., clearly the cyberschool business is a lucrative business.

However, in recent years there has been an increase in the number of public school districts that have been creating full-time cyberschool programs. These programs have been increasingly more transparent with their financial data. Additionally, as various state governments demand greater oversight over their cyber charter schools, these schools have become more forthcoming in their release of their budgetary information.

COST-EFFECTIVENESS OF VIRTUAL SCHOOLS

The issue of cost-effectiveness can be approached in a variety of ways. With reference to virtual schools or supplemental programs, students enrolled in these programs attend a traditional brick-and-mortar school and are enrolled in one or more online courses to supplement their education. This form of K–12 student online learning is more common in rural and inner-city schools, where it may be difficult to attract teachers who have specialized subject matter expertise or enrollment in a specific course may not warrant the allocation of a teacher (Barbour, 2009). The most common method for funding these supplemental virtual schools is a combination of block grants from the government, along with the use of per course fees ranging from $100 to $500 paid for by the school or school district. There are some virtual schools that do receive per-student funding in a similar manner to their traditional brick-and-mortar counterparts, however, this represents very few virtual schools in the United States.

In 2007, the Florida TaxWatch Center for Educational Performance and Accountability conducted an audit of the Florida Virtual School (FLVS) "as a credible alternative to traditional schooling as regards both student achievement outcomes and cost-effectiveness" (p. 1). The FLVS is one of the few virtual schools that receive per student funding at levels similar to those of traditional brick-and-mortar schools. Based on its examination of only the funds provided by the Florida Education Finance Program over the previous 4 years, the Florida TaxWatch Center (2007) concluded that the FLVS was $284 more cost-effective in 2003 than 2004, and this rose to $1,048 more cost-effective in 2006 to 2007. The authors reported that "capital outlay expenses make those savings even bigger" (p. 79). Simply put, "FLVS gets solid student achievement results at a reduced cost to the State" (p. 79).

This is not to suggest that supplemental virtual school funding has not been without controversy. For example, in 2010, the governor of Idaho proposed phasing out the direct per-student funding for the Idaho Digital Learning Academy (IDLA) altogether, as school districts also received funding for their students enrolled in the IDLA, resulting in double funding for each IDLA. This proposal was met with strong resistance—both in Idaho and nationally—however, cuts to the IDLA funding did occur, and, for the first time in its history, the virtual school has had to implement enrollment caps. Further, the fact that the FLVS spends $1,000 per student less than its traditional brick-and-mortar counterparts has allowed that program to devote additional funding to other aspects of its business model (e.g., its course development process, which is known to be one of the more comprehensive, allowing it to be one of the few statewide virtual schools able to operate as a course content provider and lease that content to other programs). Like most aspects of K–12 online learning, both of these examples are unique to the individual funding model used in that particular state.

COST-EFFECTIVENESS OF CYBERSCHOOLS

The question of how cyberschools are funded has consistently been a political issue. For example, in 2009, Ohio Governor Ted Strickland proposed that the state's cyber charter schools be funded at a rate that was approximately 25% of the funding that traditional brick-and-mortar schools received (Candisky, 2009). More recently, two cyberschool providers that had been granted charters to begin operating in the state of Georgia for the 2010 to 2011 school year announced that they were delaying their opening because the funding model proposed by the state was insufficient. The state had proposed a funding model of $3,200 per student, or approximately 60% of the funds provided to traditional brick-and-mortar schools (Dodd, 2010). Interestingly, the Georgia Cyber Academy, another cyber charter school in the state that received $3,500 per student in funding, has been able to meet Adequate Yearly Progress (AYP) based on their students' performance on the state's standardized exams (Dodd, 2010).

While many cyber charter schools have been reluctant to provide their actual per-student cost, there are some specific examples we can draw on. In a recent webinar hosted as a part of Learn Central and *Elluminate*'s Classroom 2.0 series, Lisa Gillis from Insight Schools Inc. (a cyber charter school provider), spoke on the topic of virtual schooling. During the 2008 to 2009 school year, the average expenditure per student in the state was $9,760, yet the per-student cost to Insight Schools was only $6,480. In this instance, Insight Schools was able to provide students with an online education $3,000 cheaper than its traditional brick-and-mortar counterparts. This was consistent with an earlier study conducted by the Ohio legislature, which determined that the per-student cost for its five cyber charter schools was $5,382 per student, compared to $7,452 per student in traditional brick-and-mortar charter schools, and $8,437 per student in public brick-and-mortar schools (Ohio Legislative Committee on Education Oversight, 2005).

Additionally, Michigan has seen an increase in the number of school districts that have created their own full-time cyberschools in the past 3 years (e.g., Dearborn Heights Virtual Academy, St. Clair County Regional Education Service Agency's [RESA] Virtual Learning Academy, and Westwood Cyber High School). Over the past 2 years, the St. Clair Virtual Learning Academy has posted its budgets on its website. According to both documents it is more cost-effective to provide an education to the group of at-risk students they serve in an online environment (with students using laptops, but also being required to spend five hours in the school's distance education lab) than it would be to provide that education in the traditional brick-and-mortar environment. In fact, it cost 16% less in 2009 to 2010 and was projected to cost 7% less in 2010 to 2011.

THE CASE FOR EQUAL FUNDING

Beyond the individual virtual school and cyberschool programs, along with the school choice movement, the two main sources that have argued online schools should be funded at levels equal to traditional brick-and-mortar schools have been proponents of cyberschooling in Colorado, the authors of a report prepared to the BellSouth Foundation, and the professional association representing practitioners of K–12 online learning (International Association of K-12 Online Learning [iNACOL]). In 2004, the joint budget committee of the Colorado state legislature began examining its funding of full-time cyberschools in the state. Various groups made reports to the committee, including Lucy Hausner (2004), who prepared a report on behalf of the Colorado Cyberschool Association—the professional organization representing cyber charter schools in the state. Not surprisingly, the report concluded that the "cost per student [of cyberschooling] is not enormously higher than for in-class students. Over time, cybereducation will become substantially more cost-efficient" (p. 10)—essentially arguing that, at the time, cyberschooling cost more than traditional brick-and-mortar school.

In 2006, the BellSouth Foundation funded Augenblick, Palaich, and Associates to conduct a study on the *Costs and Funding of Virtual Schools.* The report concluded, "the operating costs of online programs are about the same as the operating costs of a regular brick-and-mortar program" (Anderson, Augenblick, DeCescre, & Conrad, 2006, p. 4). To reach this conclusion, the study used a professional judgment methodology, which relies on the expertise of experienced individuals to pass opinions on a particular issue. The experienced individuals who formed the sample for this study included a group of representatives from supplemental virtual schools and a group of representatives from full-time cyberschools. Even if the opinions of these individuals were not based on the best interest of the online programs they all represented, immediately following the conclusion quoted earlier the authors indicated that the study did not include costs associated with capital expenses or transportation and, if it had, "the costs of operating virtual schools would have been less per pupil than brick-and-mortar schools" (p. 5).

Based on this report, along with the work conducted as a part of iNACOL's *Promising Practices in Online Learning* series, this professional association has regularly called for the full or equal funding of K–12 online learning programs. In the *Promising Practices in Online Learning* report focused on the funding of online learning, John Watson and Butch Gemin (2009) argued, "online schools should be funded within the range of brick-and-mortar school operating costs" (p. 10). They support this assertion with the Anderson and colleagues report, but at no point in the report do they mention the obviously methodological bias in favor of online learning or the caveat Anderson and colleagues offer to their overall conclusion. It is also worth noting that iNACOL is the professional association representing practitioners of online learning.

MAKING THE CASE THAT VIRTUAL SCHOOLS ARE MORE COST-EFFECTIVE

Given the scope of K–12 student online learning in the United States, the amount of information available associated with funding virtual and cyberschools is extremely limited. However, as the evidence clearly shows, online learning—both supplemental and full-time—is more cost-effective compared to traditional brick-and-mortar schooling. The only sources that argued the need for equal funding have either methodological questions or questionable motives. This is not to say that virtual- and cyberschools would not put additional funding to good use, in the same way that any traditional brick-and-mortar school with additional funding would be able to increase programming or decrease class size or any number of positive improvements to the student learning environment. The limited research available tends to demonstrate that it is more cost-effective to provide students with opportunities in supplemental virtual schools and full-time cyberschools than it is to educate a student entirely in a traditional brick-and-mortar school environment.

Unfortunately, the issue isn't quite that simple. The general lack of information does indicate that this conclusion is based on a selective amount of data. If cyber charter schools were more forthcoming with their financial information, and particularly their profit margins, we would be better able to determine if this initial conclusion would hold true. Additionally, in many instances the previous examples are based on established programs. For example, there is potentially a high investment required to start a virtual or cyberschool (e.g., the cost of training of teachers to use the course management system and to teach in an online environment, along with the cost of online course content development, to name just a few). After these initial start-up costs, as Watson (2004) concluded in his presentation to the Colorado joint budget committee, "over time, as programs evolve, grow, and achieve some economies of scale, Colorado can fund online programs for less than the state's minimum per pupil revenue" (p. 3).

Linda Cavalluzzo and Michael Higgins (2001) described a model where virtual- or cyberschools need to be funded at a higher level in those initial years but that funding should be decreased as the online learning program builds capacity. This would indicate the answer to the question may be based on at what point in a virtual- or cyberschool's development the question is being asked.

COUNTERPOINT: Allison Powell
International Association for K-12 Online Learning (iNACOL)

Online learning provides new opportunities for students—in rural schools without licensed teachers, for diverse students with a range of needs, with specialized faculty to offer honors and Advanced Placement courses, serving homebound students, providing credit recovery to struggling learners, and reducing scheduling conflicts through flexibility. These are just a few of the reasons students are asking for the expansion of online offerings and virtual schools. Outdated policies and a lack of funding are preventing all children from accessing an equal, world-class education.

Virtual schools are providing individual online instruction and increasing access to courses by providing flexibility in time, place, and pace of instruction. Today's virtual schools present exciting promise to students, which many teachers and administrators now understand and support. However, some policymakers may still not understand the value of and the costs to fund these schools and programs.

Funding is the single most important policy issue for today's virtual schools. Full-time virtual schools are full-service public schools with many of the same costs compared to their brick-and-mortar, or traditional physical classroom counterparts, including salaries, benefits, initial training, and ongoing staff development. Online programs do not incur the same level of facilities and transportation costs as traditional districts, but they have significant technological components, with associated costs for hardware, bandwidth, and the like, which are critical to supporting the teaching and learning process (International Association of K-12 Online Learning [iNACOL], 2009). Questions have been raised about how the costs of educating students in virtual schools compare to those of traditional brick-and-mortar public schools. The best available information on virtual schools' revenue and expenditures will be used to address these important questions.

FINANCIAL COSTS OF VIRTUAL SCHOOLS

The financial costs associated with starting a virtual school are comparable to those of opening and operating a traditional brick-and-mortar school. Many of the costs associated with virtual schools parallel those of traditional brick-and-mortar schools: administrators, teachers, staff, curriculum and course materials, professional development, assessments and evaluations, and data systems. However, virtual schools have little and, in some cases, no cost for instructional facilities, transportation, and related staff, but they do incur other substantial costs, such as a technology infrastructure, including a course and learning management system (LMS) and staff to support this, as well as staff to support course and curriculum design in some cases.

A virtual school that develops its own online courses takes on all of these costs and functions. A school that provides online courses to its students that are developed and taught by a "virtual school takes responsibility for students' access to the site-based technology devices, infrastructure, and learning facilitators needed for student success" (Cavanaugh, 2009, p. 16).

Over the past few years, educational policymakers in several states have struggled with how to fund both full-time and supplemental virtual schools. As there are several types of virtual schools across the country, there are also various funding models for these schools. Because the student is taking the course online, many policymakers who are unfamiliar with online learning tend to think there are considerable cost savings to educating students in this environment because it does not require an actual physical building and teachers. However, in a quality virtual school, teachers are key to the success of students, as are other personnel, their training, and the curriculum, which are also some of the largest costs associated with a traditional brick-and-mortar school.

MAIN COSTS

The five main categories of costs for today's virtual schools include the following: management, instruction, course development, technology setup, and technology personnel, which should also be broken down into start-up and ongoing costs and vary based on different factors of how the school is set up, which are described in the following pages (Anderson, Augenblick, DeCescre, & Conrad, 2006).

Management

The costs of managing virtual schools are very similar to those of traditional brick-and-mortar schools. These costs include administrators, such as a principal/executive director and administrators over content and technology and clerical support for them, as well as other administrative personnel, such as counselors, school psychologists, and registrars. This set of personnel tends to work from a common office, which adds the costs of office furniture and equipment, supplies, facilities, insurance, legal, postage, travel, marketing, public relations, recruitment, and strategic planning (Anderson, Augenblick, DeCescre, & Conrad, 2006). The facilities costs will vary depending on the amount of time students are required to meet face-to-face with school personnel based on state and federal policy. Full-time schools must complete all state and national testing face-to-face throughout the year, adding transportation and additional meeting space to the costs of running these schools. All of these costs are common to a traditional brick-and-mortar school and should be considered when funding virtual schools, whether they are full time or part time.

Instruction

Instruction is the next key category in running all types of virtual schools. Policymakers and those unfamiliar with online learning often assume the student is reading and answering questions on the computer in an online class and does not have a teacher to work with or that one teacher can teach thousands of students in one class because the students can learn on their own. However, online learning allows for the individualization of instruction for each student, allowing the teacher to work one-on-one with each student to customize his or her learning, and often the student communicates with a teacher on an ongoing basis. Because of this individualized instruction, it is common to have the same student-teacher ratios as seen in traditional brick-and-mortar schools. Teachers in full-time virtual schools and larger supplemental programs are often hired as full-time positions. In hard-to-staff courses and several supplemental programs, teachers are hired on a part-time contract to teach one or two courses in addition to their face-to-face teaching load.

The costs under instruction also include professional development for the teachers. Across the United States, virtual schools are required to train their new teachers to teach online and the schools must develop ongoing professional development for them, as there is a lack of programs at the university level both in pre-service and graduate education programs. This is an additional cost that is higher than a traditional school, as universities are focused on preparing teachers for the face-to-face classroom.

Instructional supplies and materials, assessments, contracted services, and software licenses (Anderson, Augenblick, DeCescre, & Conrad, 2006) for online instruction are also included in this category, which are similar costs to those in a traditional school. Some online courses still require a textbook and consumables for the student and teacher. Textbook publishers are now starting to put more of these online, but in some cases, the virtual school must still purchase and send, via the mail, a textbook to each student and teacher, incurring additional costs. As publishers create online versions of their textbooks, these costs will be cut, but at the present time, this can still be a rather large expense for virtual schools.

Course Development

Course development is another major expense for several virtual schools. This cost can vary school by school. When virtual schools began operating in the mid-1990s, they were forced to develop their own online courses as publishers and education vendors did not offer full online academic courses; however, as the field grows, more and more publishers and online course providers are developing high-quality courses for virtual schools. Because of this new service, this cost will vary greatly by individual school, but still remains a cost for all virtual schools.

If a virtual school chooses to purchase online courses from a content provider, it is usually ready out of the box. Some professional development will be required to navigate through the course and LMS, but overall, if the teacher is familiar with the content of the course, he or she should be able to teach it. Most content providers will update the course as needed, so the cost of maintaining the course is included in the price. Purchasing content allows virtual schools to access a wide variety of high-quality, interactive courses without the expense of full-time personnel to design, develop, create, and update the course. Content providers have varying models of purchasing their courses—ranging from a per-student annual fee to purchasing their entire curriculum and adding costs of maintenance and professional development to the contracts, but the schools never own the course—so they incur annual curriculum costs if they choose to purchase online content.

Virtual schools that choose to develop their own content will not have the annual costs of purchasing content from a provider; however, they can build and customize their own courses to meet their schools' specific goals and needs. The development of a high-quality online course requires more initial investment, but the ongoing costs of maintaining them can save money over time, as the school then owns them. Course development usually occurs in teams, which can include subject matter experts, instructional designers, web developers/ programmers/designers, and so on. These can be full-time or part-time personnel, depending on the course needs of the school. They must ensure a course meets the state standards; has a variety of lessons, activities, and assessments to meet various student learning needs; is easy to navigate; and is engaging for both the student and teacher. Once a course is developed by a school, they can use it over and over again, but they also need to maintain it as the world changes. In some schools, the course teacher does this, while in other schools, the course development team maintains and recreates existing courses on an ongoing basis or as needed, adding to the costs of operating a virtual school.

Technology Setup

The costs of technology in a virtual school are not always required in a traditional brick-and-mortar school. While traditional schools have transportation costs, such as buses to get students to school and home, students in a virtual school use the Internet and a computer, and sometimes a telephone, to "travel" to school. For this to happen, several pieces of technology need to be set up and maintained to ensure students are able to attend their courses.

An LMS can be compared to a traditional school building. The LMS houses the online courses, and students, teachers, and administration learn and communicate through this tool. To get to the school, each student, teacher, and personnel needs access to the Internet and a computer. In some cases, mostly seen in the full-time virtual schools, the school will provide a computer and Internet stipend for students to participate; however, in most supplemental programs, the student can access the course from their traditional brick-and-mortar school or from home.

According to iNACOL (2010), "A Student Information System (SIS) stores and manages all the basic information about students such as demographic information, student schedule, and student performance data. A SIS is a familiar administrative component for brick-and-mortar schools and is also critical for an online program." The LMS, SIS, computers, and Internet access are essential to the virtual school; however, other systems must also be in place to ensure the use of these systems, such as servers, networking hardware, licensing fees, and other software. These are also essential for virtual schools, which are costs for which not all traditional brick-and-mortar schools have to budget.

Technology Personnel

Because of all the technology requirements, technology personnel are also a need for virtual schools. These people install and manage all of the technology, as well as assist the school's students, administration, faculty, and staff with tech support and manage software licenses and technology updates. Virtual schools can either hire the technology personnel as part of the staff or contract for these services, depending on their size, setup, and needs.

ADDITIONAL COSTS

The aforementioned five main categories describe the common costs to all virtual schools. In addition to these, sometimes other costs can occur on an ongoing basis, similar to those in the traditional brick-and-mortar schools. As in traditional schools, sometimes a substitute teacher needs to step in if the teacher of record cannot teach the class for an extended period of time. Several virtual schools operate on a year-round basis, and their teachers are located across the state or country, making it difficult to bring them together face-to-face for professional development. Some schools will have face-to-face professional development days, while others will blend their training (combination of face-to-face and online) or offer it fully online. Whichever model they choose, their teachers need initial and ongoing professional development, which adds to the costs of operating a virtual school.

As virtual schools are still a new idea in a lot of places around the country, marketing and recruitment are a necessity for educating and enrolling families and students in these programs. This cost is not required of a public brick-and-mortar school, as students are assigned to attend their neighborhood school.

Other costs can include the costs of travel for administrators and teachers to attend face-to-face meetings, meet with students, and engage in recruiting, extracurricular activities, field trips, and educational conferences. Full-time virtual schools often plan field trips and extracurricular activities for students so they can connect with other students enrolled in their class and school and still participate in clubs and sports like a traditional school offers, which can add to the expenses for traveling to common locations and renting facilities to house these events.

CONCLUSION

According to iNACOL (2009), "Few studies have compared the cost of online schools to traditional schools; those that have been done suggest that the cost of educating a student in an online environment is about the same as educating the same student in a brick-and-mortar school." While per-pupil funding for students varies among states for face-to-face students, it also varies among virtual schools. Among the few studies completed, the *20/20 Costs and Funding of Virtual Schools* study found ranges of $3,650 to $7,500 per full-time equivalent (FTE) in a supplemental online program depending on various levels of quality assurance, instruction, professional development, and continuous research, development, and planning (2006). The same study found that "costs ranged from $7,200 to about $8,300 per FTE for full-time virtual schools, again dependent on the variables discussed above" (Anderson, Augenblick, DeCescre, & Conrad, 2006). Full-time programs have additional state and federal requirements and are also responsible for special needs students, which supplemental programs are not always responsible for and can result in higher costs.

This study and others have concluded that, "the operating costs of online programs are about the same as the operating costs of a regular brick-and-mortar school" (Anderson, Augenblick, DeCescre, & Conrad, 2006). According to iNACOL (2009), "Funding for online schools and, indeed for all learning, should facilitate quality learning while allowing for ongoing investment in research and innovation." As the studies have shown, virtual schools have similar costs to those of traditional brick-and-mortar schools, as well as unique costs that average out to the costs of running traditional schools. The cost of providing a high-quality education for all students remains the same, no matter whether students are in traditional brick-and-mortar or virtual school environments.

FURTHER READINGS AND RESOURCES

Adsit, J. (2004). *Estimated cost of operating a cyberschool in Colorado.* Denver, CO: Donnell-Kay Foundation. Retrieved from http://www.dkfoundation.org/pdf/ CyberschoolCostReportFeb2004CCA.pdf

Anderson, A., Augenblick, J., DeCescre, D., & Conrad, J. (2006). *20/20 costs and funding of virtual schools.* Atlanta, GA: BellSouth Foundation. Retrieved from http://www .apaconsulting.net/uploads/reports/9.pdf

Barbour, M. K. (2009). Today's student and virtual schooling: The reality, the challenges, the promise. . . . *Journal of Distance Learning, 13*(1), 5–25.

Candisky, C. (2009, March 1). Strickland plan would slash online-school funding: Roughly 75 percent cut a death blow, charters' backers say. *The Columbus Dispatch.* Retrieved from http://www.dispatch.com/live/content/local_news/stories/2009/ 03/01/charter.ART_ART_03-01-09_B3_UDD2SLF.html?sid=101

Cavalluzzo, L., & Higgins, M. (2001). *Policy and planning series #102: Who should fund virtual schools?* Alexandria, VA: Appalachian Technology in Education Consortium. Retrieved from http://citeseerx.ist.psu.edu/viewdoc/download?doi=10.1.1.102.478 &rep=rep1&type=pdf

Cavanaugh, C. (2009). *Getting students more learning time online: Distance education in support of expanded learning time in K-12 schools.* Washington, DC: Center for American Progress. Retrieved from http://www.americanprogress.org/issues/2009/ 05/pdf/distancelearning.pdf

Darrow, R. (2008). *Review of literature: Cost items for implementing and maintaining a K-12 online school.* Unpublished manuscript, California State University, Fresno. Retrieved from http://robsdoc.wikispaces.com/file/view/DarrowReviewof%20Lit%20OnlineSchoolCostsMay12008.pdf

Dodd, D. A. (2010, August 19). Cyber charter schools celebrate two state victories, may get more funds. *Atlanta Journal-Constitution.* Retrieved from http://www.ajc.com/news/cyber-charter-schools-celebrate-595707.html

Florida TaxWatch Center for Educational Performance and Accountability. (2007). *Final report: A comprehensive assessment of Florida Virtual School.* Tallahassee, FL: Author. Retrieved from http://www.floridataxwatch.org/resources/pdf/110507FinalReportFLVS.pdf

Hausner, L. (2004). *Estimated cost of operating a cyberschool in Colorado.* Denver: Colorado Cyberschool Association. Retrieved from http://www.dkfoundation.org/pdf/CyberschoolCostReportFeb2004CCA.pdf

International Association for K-12 Online Learning (iNACOL). (2009). *Promising practices in online learning: Policy and funding frameworks for online learning.* Vienna, VA: Author.

International Association for K-12 Online Learning (iNACOL). (2010). *How to start an online program: A practical guide to key issues and policies.* Retrieved from http://www.onlineprogramhowto.org

International Association for K-12 Online Learning (iNACOL). (2010). *A national primer on K-12 online learning, version 2.* Retrieved from http://www.inacol.org/research/docs/iNCL_NationalPrimerv22010-web.pdf

Ohio Legislative Committee on Education Oversight. (2005). *The operating costs of Ohio's eCommunity schools.* Columbia, OH: Author.

Southern Regional Education Board. (2006). *Cost guidelines for state virtual schools: Development, implementation and sustainability.* Atlanta, GA: Author. Retrieved from http://publications.sreb.org/2006/06T03_Virtual_School_Costs.pdf

U.S. Department of Education. (n.d.). *Use of technology in teaching and learning.* Retrieved from http://www.ed.gov/oii-news/use-technology-teaching-and-learning

Watson, J. (2004). *Report to the joint budget committee on the Colorado state legislature on the cost of online education.* Evergreen, CO: Evergreen Education Group.

Watson, J., & Gemin, B. (2009). *Promising practices in online learning: Policy and funding frameworks for online learning.* Vienna, VA: International Association for K-12 Online Learning. Retrieved from http://www.inacol.org/research/promisingpractices/NACOL_PP-FundPolicy-lr.pdf

Is the use of video surveillance cameras in schools an invasion of student privacy?

POINT: Kevin P. Brady, *North Carolina State University*
COUNTERPOINT: Justin M. Bathon, *University of Kentucky*

OVERVIEW

Public opinion polls taken since September 11, 2001, reveal that the American public is extremely divided on the issue of using video cameras for surveillance purposes, as it is perceived to be an intrusion to an individual's right to privacy. Yet, the debate involving the same issue of video camera surveillance in schools is considerably more divided in terms of public opinion. Unquestionably, video camera surveillance has become one of the fastest-growing industries, with sales approaching nearly $20 billion in 2010. Additionally, evidence indicates that the use of video camera surveillance is growing in today's schools. In 2002, for example, nearly 1,000 new public schools were opened, and approximately three-fourths of those schools were found to have been equipped with some form of video camera surveillance. The first uses of video camera surveillance devices by school officials can be traced back to the late 1980s, when school buses were initially equipped with video cameras as a means to improve student discipline, prevent vandalism, and avoid litigation with parents. In 2003, the Biloxi Public School District in Biloxi, Mississippi, received national media attention by being the first public school district in the nation to install video surveillance cameras in every classroom.

In this chapter, point essay author Kevin P. Brady (North Carolina State University) and counterpoint essay author Justin M. Bathon (University of

Kentucky) wrestle with the question of whether video surveillance cameras in schools constitute an invasion of student privacy rights. In his point essay, Brady argues that schools represent special environments that warrant school officials to heighten attention to student safety and security concerns in lieu of student privacy. However, Brady believes that video camera surveillance in schools exceeds the current legal boundaries of what constitutes a reasonable and acceptance search technique. Additionally, Brady cautions school officials not to abuse surveillance technologies and provides six guidelines for legally compliant use of video cameras.

In his counterpoint essay, Bathon argues that video camera surveillance is "the lesser of multiple evils." Bathon contends that the current media's reporting of school shootings, possession of drugs and weapons, and a multitude of other daily safety issues in schools justify the need for school officials to take greater control over school safety and security on school premises. Unlike Brady, who argues that there is a lack of empirical evidence to support the fact that today's schools are generally unsafe, Bathon argues that when it comes to implementing video surveillance cameras in a school, local school officials should have the legal flexibility and discretion they need to address any potential threats to student safety or security.

Another point made by Bathon in his counterpoint essay is the notion that local school officials should have more control over the technological aspects of video camera surveillance. While both authors agree that local school officials' excessive control over their video surveillance programs can result in unreasonable student searches that violate student privacy, Bathon contends that violations of student privacy are unlikely to occur when data from video camera surveillance are properly protected. Additionally, Bathon makes the point that video camera surveillance programs frequently benefit students in terms of making the overall student learning environment safer. While Brady's point essay argues that video camera surveillance exceeds the boundaries of a reasonable search, Bathon counters by arguing that video surveillance results in many benefits to students, including not only safety but educational benefits.

Brady's point essay stresses the fact that the video camera surveillance of adults in school settings is radically different compared to minor, school-age children. Brady highlights several court cases that have legally upheld the use of video camera surveillance as a method of evaluating employee performance or as providing evidence of an employee's inappropriate behavior in the workplace. However, Brady argues, the current reasonable suspicion legal standard for students is enough for school officials to address most student safety and security considerations. Bathon's counterpoint essay steadfastly maintains that the relative benefits of using video camera surveillance far outweigh the potential violations of student privacy.

While both authors agree that local school officials should always consider potential abuses to student privacy when using video camera surveillance, the authors differ markedly in whether the general use of video camera surveillance violates student privacy. On the one hand, Brady's point essay clearly argues that the daily use of video camera surveillance violates student privacy. Bathon's counterpoint essay maintains that local school officials should largely have the authority to ascertain whether video camera surveillance in necessary in a particular school or not. Additionally, it is only when school officials get careless and do not follow basic procedural guidelines when using video camera surveillance that violations to student privacy are much more likely to occur. Despite this range of noticeable disagreement on the topic of whether video camera surveillance practices in schools are an invasion of student privacy, both authors agree that emerging and constantly changing surveillance techniques used in schools will only make this topic more divided and controversial.

Kevin P. Brady
North Carolina State University

POINT: Kevin P. Brady
North Carolina State University

It is clear that the use of video surveillance cameras in today's schools has become increasingly more commonplace. It is equally true that the use of video surveillance cameras in schools is one of the more controversial trends being used as a measure to safeguard school safety and security. In a modern technological society where constantly advancing surveillance technologies, including video camera surveillance, can monitor a person's every movement, do these surveillance technologies run afoul of an individual's right to privacy under the Fourth Amendment of the U.S. Constitution? This legal question is especially interesting in the context of schools where the majority of inhabitants are legal minors and school officials are entrusted with their care and safety. In the school environment, the U.S. Supreme Court held in *New Jersey v. T.L.O.* (1985) that searches are deemed legally reasonable only if the search is both justified at its inception and reasonable in scope. This point essay argues that the use of video camera surveillance clearly violates the boundaries of a reasonable search method or technique, especially involving school-age children. Moreover, the use of video surveillance cameras in schools run counter to the reasonable searches the Fourth Amendment was originally intended to protect. Many legal scholars predict that many of the future Fourth Amendment legal challenges in this technological age will involve balancing constantly changing surveillance technologies with issues of protecting student privacy.

THE USE OF VIDEO CAMERA SURVEILLANCE IN TODAY'S PUBLIC SCHOOLS

A major source of the controversy surrounding the use of video camera surveillance in schools is whether it is actually effective at reducing incidents of school violence as well as improving overall school safety. In other words, is the use of video camera surveillance a significant deterrent to school-related crimes and violence? Despite perceptions by some school officials and parents who argue that the placement of video cameras in schools significantly reduces incidents of school violence, there is no credible empirical evidence to date demonstrating the direct effectiveness of video camera surveillance as a means of effectively decreasing school crime and violence levels (Brady, 2007). Despite national media attention given to instances of school-related violence, existing research reveals that, overall, the nation's schools are relatively safe places. Consequently, some of the general public's perceptions of today's schools as unsafe environments serve as both an inaccurate and misguided catalyst justifying the increased use of surveillance technologies, including video cameras, by local school officials. This mismatch between the public's perception of safety and security in schools with the reality of school safety is both unfortunate and problematic.

To date, the vast majority of legal cases involving video surveillance have actually taken place outside school settings. It is unfair to compare an adult's expectation of privacy compared to students who are legal minors. While the Fourth Amendment of the U.S. Constitution does protect all individuals against unreasonable searches and seizures as well as invasions against their personal privacy, this legal standard only until recently applied exclusively to adults. It was not until the 1985 *New Jersey v. T.L.O.* decision that a search-and-seizure legal standard was created that was specific to school-age legal minors. The fact that school officials only require reasonable suspicion to justify the search of a student, compared to the usual probable cause standard required by law enforcement officials to conduct searches of adults, demonstrates that the courts recognize the unique and special situation of today's school environment. The reasonable suspicion legal search standard for today's school officials provides educators inherently more flexibility to initiate student searches. School officials' increased flexibility to conduct student searches minimizes the need for today's school officials to use more intrusive student search methods, such as video camera surveillance, and greatly increases the probability of violating a particular student's privacy rights.

The general public's perception of unsafe schools has definitely served as a catalyst for the increased use of video camera surveillance in today's schools. However, an examination of the limited legal cases involving video camera surveillance in school environments reveals that video cameras are routinely used in today's schools for both security- as well as nonsecurity-oriented tasks, such as assisting with teacher evaluations or local school staff performance evaluations. For instance, in *Roberts v. Houston Independent School District* (1990), a Texas appellate court held that a terminated teacher's reasonable expectation of privacy was not violated by the videotaping of her classroom. The videotaping was used as a measure of the teacher's performance. In another court case, *Crist v. Alpine Union School District* (2005), a court ruled that there was no invasion of school employee's privacy when a school district placed hidden cameras in a shared office space as a way to gain evidence that a specific school employee was gaining unauthorized computer access after school hours. In a third case, *Brannen v. Kings Local School District Board of Education* (2001), a court ruled that a school district's installation of hidden video cameras in a school custodian's break room did not violate the employees' right to be free from unlawful searches guaranteed by both the Fourth and Fourteenth Amendments to the U.S. Constitution. In this case, a school custodian was suspected of not working his assigned shift and video camera surveillance was used as evidence to demonstrate that the custodian was not working during that shift period. In all of these cases, the video camera surveillance was used to monitor adults in school settings. This point argues that the video camera surveillance of adults is much different compared to school-age children. The potential, negative impacts on children are much more severe in terms of privacy violations.

One troubling example that demonstrates how video camera surveillance in schools can severely damage student privacy occurred at Livingston Middle School in Overton County, Tennessee. At this middle school, local school board members placed video surveillance cameras in the doorway of the gym's locker rooms. Unfortunately, the wide-angle lens of the video camera was able to film middle-school-aged students undressing in the gym's shower area. What was more troubling was the fact that the video surveillance camera was linked to an unsecure website created by the school to allow parents to view the video camera at any time. Images of naked, middle-school-aged students were accessed over the Internet. Both the inappropriate video camera location and the school district's lack of computer security protections compromised student privacy.

THREE LEGAL TESTS FOR ANALYZING SURVEILLANCE TECHNOLOGIES ON INDIVIDUAL PRIVACY
The Reasonable Expectation of Privacy Test

The U.S. Supreme Court first dealt with the issue of video surveillance and individual privacy in the landmark case of *Katz v. United States* (1967). In the *Katz* decision, the Court held that the Fourth Amendment of the Constitution requires a warrant when a person exhibited an expectation of privacy and that expectation of privacy is one that society recognizes as reasonable. The *Katz* case involved an investigation into an illegal betting scheme where Federal Bureau of Investigation (FBI) officials taped a microphone to the roof of a public phone booth used by the defendant, Charles Katz. As soon as Katz used the public phone booth, the microphone turned on and recorded Katz's conversations. The FBI used the recordings as evidence to implicate Katz in the illegal betting scheme. Writing for the majority, Justice Potter Stewart held that defendant Katz's privacy was violated because when someone enters a public telephone booth and closes the door behind them, they do not expect that their conversations will be broadcast to the world. The *Katz* ruling basically expanded the scope of legal protection under the Fourth Amendment because it protects an individual's reasonable expectation of privacy in any location where circumstances might potentially present such an expectation. Unfortunately, the *Katz* reasonable expectation of privacy test provides little guidance to the specific techniques used in video camera surveillance nor does it apply to the special nature of schools.

The General Public Use Test

More recently in *Kyllo v. United States* (2001), the U.S. Supreme Court developed a second legal test for analyzing surveillance technologies, named the general public use test. In the *Kyllo* case, law enforcement officials used the surveillance technology of a thermal imaging device to observe large heating lamps used in a private residence to grow marijuana. In this case, the Court ruled that the thermal imaging device was not used in the general public use and the search was an unreasonable invasion of privacy without a warrant. A major shortcoming of the *Kyllo* decision is that the general public use test applies only to searches of people's homes. Therefore, the general public use test could not be applied to a school environment.

The Legitimate Governmental Interests Test

The third and most recent legal test applied to surveillance technologies and whether they violate privacy is the legitimate governmental interests test. Unlike the two previous legal tests for analyzing surveillance technologies and their impact on privacy, the *Board of Education of Independent School District No. 92 of Pottawatomie County v. Earls* (2002) directly involved a school setting. The *Earls* case addressed the legal question of whether the random drug testing of students involved in school-sponsored, extracurricular activities constitutes a violation of their individual privacy. It is important to note that the U.S. Supreme Court has defined the public school environment as a unique place for Fourth Amendment analysis purposes. The *Earls* decision and the legitimate governmental interests test provide an exception to the traditional Fourth Amendment warrant requirement for searches that are not conducted for law enforcement purposes but are for special governmental reasons. Based on the legitimate governmental interests test, searches do not need to be supported by a warrant or probable cause. In the *Earls* case, the Court held that local school officials may randomly drug test students who are members of school-sponsored, extracurricular activities such as student athletes. Three modern-day examples of searches that reflect the legitimate governmental interests test would be random drug testing, checkpoints on public highways, and searches of closely regulated spaces.

Due to the special nature of the school environment, the legitimate governmental interests test is the most relevant and applicable to analyzing the use of video camera surveillance in school settings. However, as the *Earls* decision demonstrates, the case involved the use of random drug testing of a student involved in extracurricular activities, not surveillance technologies, such as video cameras. Quite simply, the use of video cameras for monitoring student safety and security is too intrusive a search tactic for school officials.

GUIDELINES FOR A LEGALLY COMPLIANT VIDEO CAMERA SURVEILLANCE SYSTEM IN SCHOOLS

While this point essay argues that the general use of video camera surveillance in schools does often violate student privacy, the following six guidelines for school officials will increase the likelihood that abuses of student privacy will be minimized. If unmonitored, video camera surveillance programs at schools will inevitably abuse fundamental student rights to privacy. These guidelines for school officials address areas of concern for abusing student privacy rights when implementing video camera surveillance programs in individual schools.

1. *School officials need to properly determine the costs, rationales, and limitations of a video camera surveillance system at their specific school.* Quite simply, school officials must be able to justify the use of video camera surveillance at their school. Adopting a video camera surveillance system solely as a symbolic effort to address the security and safety of students is not enough. School officials must have valid reasons for developing a video camera surveillance system, such as evidence of increasing student safety and security problems at the school.

2. *Video surveillance cameras must be clearly placed in "common" public places throughout the school environment.* School officials may not place video surveillance cameras in areas of the school where students have a reasonable expectation of privacy. For example, school officials should not place video surveillance cameras in school bathrooms, gym locker rooms, student lockers, or private offices. Examples of common areas of the school where video surveillance cameras may be placed include school hallways, school parking lots, cafeterias, and libraries.

3. *If video surveillance cameras are used, school officials should strongly consider not recording audio conversations.* Given the current legal climate of

surveillance technologies, school officials should avoid recording audio conversations in conjunction with video camera surveillance because it increases the possibility of violating a student's Fourth Amendment right to privacy.

4. *School officials need to legally comply with the Family Educational Rights and Privacy Act (FERPA).* Local school officials must be aware of FERPA legal guidelines in relation to video camera surveillance. Under FERPA guidelines, an education record is defined as one that includes any document, photograph, data, or image-processed document that is maintained by an educational agency or individual(s) acting on behalf of the educational agency. Under FERPA guidelines, parents of students are usually legally entitled to access to videotapes of their children unless these videotapes are necessary to protect the health or safety of a particular student in the school environment.

5. *School officials need to provide adequate signage of the location(s) of video surveillance cameras and notify students that they are being videotaped.* School officials need to explicitly notify students as well as the general public of the location of video cameras.

6. *School officials need to develop a detailed video camera surveillance policy when they place video cameras in their school.* When school officials develop formal policies concerning video camera surveillance policies, they inform students, parents, and school staff members of how the cameras will be used and encourage both compliance and familiarity with these policies.

CONCLUSION

Today, video surveillance cameras are used in schools for a variety of reasons, ranging from maintaining student safety and security to facilitating the process of evaluating teachers and school staff. While adults working in public places, such as the workplace, require intrusive searches usually to be conducted with the legal search standard of probable cause and a warrant, the courts have recognized that legal minor students in schools are a unique and special community of individuals. Under the U.S. Supreme Court's *New Jersey v. T.L.O.* (1985) landmark decision, school officials may successfully search students as long as they satisfy the lower legal standard of reasonable suspicion. Under the reasonable suspicion standard, a student search must be both justified at its inception and reasonable in its scope.

Emerging surveillance technologies, such as video surveillance cameras, represent an increasingly popular method of monitoring student safety and security levels in today's schools. The U.S. Supreme Court's recent articulation of the legitimate governmental interests test represents a legal test for analyzing whether traditional student search techniques and measures violate student privacy. Video camera surveillance is outside the scope of an acceptable search technique for searching students. First, existing evidence does not substantiate that video camera surveillance is an effective deterrent to reducing student crime and violence.

While it is clear that emerging technologies, including video camera surveillance, challenge the existing delicate balance between student privacy and safety, the unique nature of the school environment should direct the legal tipping scales in favor of protecting student privacy while maintaining student safety and security over privacy considerations. The current legal search standard of reasonable suspicion does a good job of balancing student safety with students' privacy rights. Most emerging surveillance techniques, such as video camera surveillance, are not only too intrusive but often unnecessary given the current student safety and security climates of most schools.

COUNTERPOINT: Justin M. Bathon
University of Kentucky

Currently, it is unquestionably legal for the government to place video surveillance cameras in public places, such as public schools, and to record the happenings therein. Numerous court cases have firmly established that citizens do not have a legal expectation of privacy in these public spaces and, therefore, there is no reasonable argument from which to claim an invasion of privacy violation. Thus, from a legal perspective, the use of at least some forms of video camera surveillance in schools is currently permissible. Where there is room for debate, however, is the extent to which video surveillance cameras should infiltrate the school and impact the daily lives of today's students. The current level of video camera surveillance intrusion into the lives of students is high and will only increase with technological advances in video camera surveillance. While attempting to improve student safety is a noble goal, many feel that the increased video camera surveillance may not be the best method to achieve this goal and today's public school officials should not take on the role of Big Brother as they attempt to improve student safety and security. However, as this counterpoint essay will illustrate, the government has multiple opportunities to regulate against such video surveillance, and cases in the federal courts and newspapers have provided ample notification of possible concerns. Thus, the inaction of multiple governmental bodies regarding video surveillance as well as audio recordings in schools can and should be interpreted as a democratic affirmation of the practice.

OPPORTUNITIES FOR ACTION

First, the Constitution of the United States does not specifically address privacy. While courts have historically interpreted the Fourth, Ninth, and Fourteenth Amendments as containing some measure of privacy protection, the lack of a specific provision addressing privacy in the Constitution has left a great deal of uncertainty concerning exactly how much privacy the public-at-large, and especially legal minors such as schoolchildren, is entitled. This uncertainty creates a multitude of expectations regarding the extent to which we expect the government and other citizens stay out of our lives. Courts have filled this gap in constitutional law by imposing standards of reasonableness, as determined by both judges and juries. The cumulative effect of these reasonableness interpretations forms the backbone of the law of privacy in the United States. In today's public schools, for example, a school official must have individualized reasonable suspicion before invading the privacy of a student with a search (*New Jersey v. T.L.O.*, 1985).

In addition to this common-law-created protection of privacy interests, individual states can add other statutory privacy protections. Congress has seen fit on multiple occasions to create statutes specifically protecting the privacy of individuals or corporations. Broadly, these statutes include laws protecting health records, identity theft, social security and telephone numbers, voter privacy, and more. Some of these statutes apply directly to education, such as the Family Educational Rights and Privacy Act (FERPA, 2006) that protects student records. Further, other federal statutes apply tangentially, such as Title II of the Health Insurance Portability and Accountability Act (HIPAA, 2011) regarding student health information records. These statutes permit Congress to provide privacy in specific circumstances where problems with open information may arise.

States may add their own privacy protections for their citizens. In some states, such as California, a privacy provision has been added to the state constitution. Other states allude to privacy rights, such as Kentucky's right to obtain and protect property. These state constitutional privacy rights frequently provide more protection and are thus the basis of claims utilized in local lawsuits. State legislatures can also pass privacy-related statutes on specific privacy issues within their state. These too can provide some additional privacy protection to students.

Finally, within this broad legislative framework, the executive branch, consisting of federal and state regulatory authorities, such as Departments of Education, can issue regulations and guidance providing some protection. For instance, although the federal FERPA statute is quite broad in nature, the U.S. Department of Education implementing regulations are very specific and provide schools with detailed guidance on implementation.

Understanding all the ways the federal and state governments can formally protect privacy rights is important in this discussion because, although there is currently no constitutional provision concerning privacy, multiple outlets are available to legislators to protect specific rights of privacy when they arise. Yet, no such specific prohibition against the use of video camera surveillance of students in schools has been passed. Therefore, it seems reasonable given the current absence of a constitutional provision for privacy to assume that the decision of whether or not to install video cameras in schools should be left to the discretion of local school officials.

PUBLIC NOTIFICATION

In addition to the multitude of legal avenues available to governmental officials to regulate, several cases and news events have arisen in the past decade to put the public on notice of potential issues. For instance, recent news articles have documented partnerships between urban school districts and urban police forces to install thousands of video cameras in schools and on buses, which send their live feed to police or 911 headquarters (Kelly, 2009). In recent years, the use of video cameras in schools and on buses has also expanded beyond solely urban schools (Kennedy, 2011). The expansion of video camera surveillance technology into schools has been well documented in the media, with little public policy outcry against its general practice.

Further, the court system has also heard several cases regarding video camera surveillance of both teachers and students. The courts have found surveillance permissible in most cases, ruling that it has only been impermissible in special circumstances where the expectation of student privacy is much higher. For instance, a school district in Tennessee was using video camera surveillance in the physical education locker rooms of students. The federal district court found unconstitutional the use of video cameras where students were changing clothes, because of their heightened expectation of privacy (*Brannum v. Overton County School Board*, 2008). However, courts have found that classrooms, break rooms, school libraries, and even school employee workstations are places where the school's interest in gaining information in the operation of the school outweighs any expectation of privacy, at least for school employees

(Brady, 2007). With increases in video camera surveillance, school officials do need to be careful that the cameras do not unintentionally video areas of the school, including bathrooms, shower areas, and other private areas, where a student's privacy is protected in the school setting.

These news articles and court cases demonstrate that the public has at least been made aware of the issue of video camera surveillance in today's schools. While there is sparse academic literature researching the subject, debate has taken place both in the media and in the courts concerning the relative merits and legality of school video camera surveillance. Much less attention has been paid to the issue of the extent to which local school officials should be able to implement video camera surveillance. At the district or school level, who knows more about the present school safety level than local school officials?

PUBLIC SUPPORT FOR VIDEO CAMERA SURVEILLANCE IN SCHOOLS

Admittedly, video camera surveillance of public school children does initially strike the conscience as particularly distasteful. Governmental surveillance of any kind, but especially of young children, implies a certain level of distrust that the American libertarian notion of freedom reactively rejects. However, on closer examination, such video camera surveillance may be the lesser of multiple evils.

Within the present context of school shootings and possession of drugs and weapons on school grounds, coupled with the various other daily safety issues encountered at schools, the general public has clearly voiced support for school officials taking greater control of school safety and security on school premises. While Brady's point essay indicates that the prevalence of violence in today's schools is not empirically supported, it should be emphasized that any surveillance technique, such as video surveillance, which would reduce the likelihood of a school shooting is worth adopting.

Moreover, it seems likely, given the current economic and personnel limitations of schools, video surveillance cameras serve as a significantly more affordable "second set of eyes" in locations throughout the school that do not receive constant supervision by school-related staff. This second set of eyes permits local school officials or school resource officers to supervise larger parts of the school environment to ensure the safety and security of students. For instance, the school parking lot is part of school premises that is not typically under constant human supervision but where much contraband and misbehavior has often occurred. Thus, the school parking lot is an ideal candidate for video camera surveillance. Additionally, school buses have historically been a growing haven of student disciplinary problems, as supervision of that environment presents a physical, and mobile, challenge. But a mounted video camera in the front of the bus permits school officials to properly discipline student incidents that occur on the bus and, thus, the video camera has had a deterrent effect on student misbehavior.

From a technological standpoint, school officials have increasing control over the technical aspects of the surveillance. New video recording technology permits recording from low-quality, low-frame-rate, black-and-white to high-definition color images. Further, the data can be stored and accessed from a diverse range of locations, including limiting access exclusively to local law enforcement officials. This increasing control over the technological aspects of video surveillance further strengthens the school administrator's ability to customize the technology to support the ongoing safety and security of the school. The technological variability also permits school officials to adjust the elements of video recording to fit the specific needs of the local school community, including local perceptions and expectations of privacy. This technological progress can be used for unreasonable intrusions, as occurred in the *Robbins v. Lower Merion School District* case where the school used laptop webcams to watch students, even in the privacy of their homes. However, the public outcry, combined with the $610,000 settlement by the school, in this case shows that the legal system can provide not only quick remedies, but also public precedent to ward off similar unreasonable intrusions by schools in the future (Martin, 2010). Given the adaptability of the technology, a use of video camera surveillance to record only the hallways of the school building during school opening and closing may make the practice palatable to even the most libertarian local school boards.

Further, student privacy, while certainly something to be cherished and protected, is impacted little through the use of video camera surveillance when data is properly protected. First, video cameras should not be placed in locations where there is a heightened expectation of privacy, such as bathrooms or changing rooms. In those areas with a lower expectation of privacy, though, such as hallways and other public spaces in the building, students are used to being watched by other students and school officials. Their behavior should not be affected by this additional set of eyes. If the behavior is within expected norms, the student will never even know whether anyone viewed the video. It is only when the student's behavior deviates from expected standards of conduct that the video will even come into play. And, even then, it is only one piece of evidence that could potentially be used against a student. The simple fact is that students do not have a right to misbehave in a school building when they think no one is watching.

Finally, one element not frequently considered is that the potential benefit to the student may outweigh the detriment to the school. Not only are the video surveillance cameras likely to make the student learning environment safer, but the video surveillance cameras could also potentially increase the student learning opportunities through the better administration of the school. For example, video cameras are increasingly used as a means to supplement the teacher evaluation process. In addition to written teacher observations, video cameras are being used to help improve instruction and the overall student learning environment. The video surveillance cameras, once installed, treat school employees in the same way they treat students. The videos will capture mistreatment of students by employees, but the additional supervision can also lead school employees to improve their own behavior and teaching. Thus, while there are legitimate privacy concerns for employees and students, a multitude of benefits, including student safety and security, might improve with their implementation.

For all of these reasons, policy dictates flexibility for different situations. In situations where school safety is threatened, heightened video camera surveillance is warranted. However, in safer school communities that value student privacy, schools should have the flexibility to meet those needs, as determined by the local school board. Thus, as long as public outcry and the courts continue to overrule the outlandish implementations of video surveillance, the legal environment should reflect this need for flexibility. Inasmuch as the current combination of rules does provide this flexibility to meet local needs, the law is currently well construed in this area.

CONCLUSION

While there are legitimate concerns about the use of video surveillance cameras in our public schools, when properly used, they do not invade the privacy of students. The law concerning video camera surveillance in schools currently strikes a good balance between permitting schools to increase the safety and security of the school building while simultaneously providing local communities the ability to protect student privacy. Since legislatures and regulatory agencies have not broadly addressed video camera surveillance at a national or state level, local schools have the flexibility they need to address local situations. This local flexibility is both critical to ensure student safety within the norms of communities and also an appropriate democratic solution of shared governance to meet the demands of a very complex problem.

A central premise in this counterpoint essay is that local school leaders should have the administrative discretion to determine whether or not to have video surveillance cameras at their school. While in his point essay Brady argues that the use of video camera surveillance clearly violates the current reasonable suspicion standard under the Fourth Amendment, the delicate balance between video surveillance as a means to increase student safety with protecting individual student privacy is largely a local issue. Both federal and state governmental agencies have had numerous opportunities to regulate video surveillance in schools, but they have often chosen inaction. This relative inaction indicates that the issue of video surveillance in schools and the potential threats to student privacy need to be addressed locally by individual schools and districts.

The decision to implement video camera surveillance in today's schools by local school officials does not generally interfere with the privacy rights of students. While school officials need to be wary of the limited areas within a school where a student's expectation of privacy is high, the vast majority of locations in schools are public areas where video camera surveillance is permissible. Local school officials need to be given administrative discretion in determining whether a particular school would or would not benefit from the use of video camera surveillance as a means to improve student safety and security. It is primarily the legal community that needs to recognize the right of local school officials to determine the methods and techniques most suited to improve student safety and security at any particular school.

FURTHER READINGS AND RESOURCES

Blitz, M. J. (2004). Video surveillance and the constitution of public space: Fitting the Fourth Amendment to a world that tracks image and identity. *Texas Law Review, 82*(6), 1349–1389.

Brady, K. P. (2005, November). Video surveillance in public schools: The delicate balance between security and privacy. *School Business Affairs, 71*(10), 24–27.

Brady, K. P. (2007). Big brother is watching, but can he hear too? Legal issues surrounding video camera surveillance and electronic eavesdropping in public schools. *West's Education Law Reporter, 218*, 1–6.

Kelly, R. (2009, February 6). School security cameras provide live video feeds to Missouri deputies. *St. Louis Post-Dispatch.*

Kennedy, K. (2011, January 31). Cameras in busses, schools growing more common. *Chicago Daily Herald*, p. 1.

Martin, J. P. (2010, October 12). Lower Merion district's laptop saga ends with $610,000 settlement. *The Philadelphia Inquirer.* Retrieved August 12, 2011, from http://articles.philly.com/2010-10-12/news/24981536_1_laptop-students-district-several-million-dollars

Nilsson, F. (2004). Surveillance 101: Leveraging network video to enhance school security, student learning and teacher standards. *T.H.E. Journal, 32*(1), 12–14.

Van Dyke, J. M. (2010). The privacy rights of public school students. *University of Hawaii Law Review, 32,* 305–322.

Warnick, B. R. (2007). Surveillance cameras in schools: An ethical analysis. *Harvard Educational Review, 77*(3), 317–343.

COURT CASES AND STATUTES

Board of Education of Independent School District No. 92 of Pottawatomie County v. Earls, 536 U.S. 822 (2002).

Brannen v. Kings Local School District Board of Education, 144 Ohio App. 3d 620 (Ohio Ct. App. 2001).

Brannum v. Overton County School Board, 516 F.3d 489 (6th Cir. 2008).

Crist v. Alpine Union School District, Cal.Rptr.3d (Cal. App. 4th Dist. 2005).

Family Educational Rights and Privacy Act, 20 U.S.C. § 1232g (2006).

Health Insurance Portability and Accountability Act, 29 U.S.C. § 1181 (2011).

Katz v. United States, 389 U.S. 347 (1967).

Kyllo v. United States, 533 U.S. 27 (2001).

New Jersey v. T.L.O., 469 U.S. 325 (1985).

Robbins v. Lower Merion School District, 2010 WL 3421026, 2010 WL 1957103, 2010 WL 1976869 (E.D. Pa.).

Roberts v. Houston Independent School District, 788 S.W.2d 107 (Tex. Ct. App. 1990).

8

Should national and/or state-level technology standards be required for today's teachers?

POINT: Kevin M. Oliver, North Carolina State University
COUNTERPOINT: Raymond Rose, Rose & Smith Associates

OVERVIEW

The old classroom model of educators teaching in a traditional, brick-and-mortar building to a limited group of students is quickly disappearing. Beginning in the early 1980s, advances in technology have radically changed the nature of the classroom. More specifically, the new and constantly evolving "digital classroom" has dramatically altered the ways students learn and teachers teach. In their 2008 book, *Disrupting Class,* authors Clayton Christensen, Michael Horn, and Curtis Johnson speculate that by the year 2019, nearly half of all high school courses in the United States will be delivered online. As evidence of the technology revolution in the classroom, a recent survey reported that more than 90% of teachers responded that the use of technology tools must increase and that the use of technology in the classroom is very important (Tech & Learning, 2010). Additionally, today's educators are using new educational technologies to help improve student performance by enhancing content and research through the use of the Internet, using powerful learning management systems, such as Blackboards and Moodle, to track student performance and analyze online assessment to help identify student academic deficiencies and increase student test scores. This chapter detailing whether national and/or state-level technology standards should be required for today's teachers focuses on the pedagogical aspects rather than the classroom management aspects associated with the use of technology in the classroom.

A central question discussed in the debate in this chapter is whether national and/or state-level technology standards actually help teachers use technology properly to improve instruction. In the point essay, Kevin M. Oliver (North Carolina State University) argues that the use of national or state-level technology standards should be adopted by today's teachers and would improve teacher instruction and student learning through the use of technology. Counterpoint essay author Raymond Rose (Rose & Smith Associates), on the other hand, contends that national and state-level technology standards for today's teachers would be too nuanced and are too political to actually improve teacher instruction and student learning through the implementation of technology.

As Oliver notes in his point essay, there are several professional organizations that have currently proposed the mandatory use of technology standards for teachers. While these professional technology standards do not represent national or state-level technology standards for teachers, Oliver suggests that the movement for mandatory technology standards for the nation's teachers is growing and provides applications of technology in the classroom that can be used to guide teachers.

As emphasized in Oliver's point essay, another equally compelling benefit associated with national or state-level technology standards for teachers is that the implementation of these standards will greatly assist schools and colleges of education across the country in the training of preservice teachers. Mandatory national or state-level technology standards for teachers, Oliver insists, will encourage schools and colleges of education to reflect and improve on existing courses in the curriculum and identify gaps or approaches that would increase the likelihood that teacher candidates would be able to more effectively integrate technology in the support of student learning.

One of the primary arguments for requiring technology standards for teachers, Oliver argues, is that they would create systematic and uniform goals and objectives for teachers that will inform students of their academic expectations. Mandatory national or state-level technology standards for students would increase the leverage necessary to increase technology integration by teachers across the country using common expectations. Moreover, Oliver argues that without national or state-level technology standards, teacher preparation in colleges and schools of education is extremely divergent and inconsistent involving how teachers use technology in the classroom.

Another benefit of incorporating national or state-level technology standards for teachers, Oliver points out, is that the use of required national or state standards provides useful assessment data for identifying teachers that are not meeting accepted proficiency standards in the area of technology integration for learning. More important, Oliver maintains, the assessment data can be used by school officials to plan and implement professional development to address teacher deficiencies in the use of technology for student learning.

According to Oliver, the best justification for the mandatory use of national or state-level technology standards for teachers is that the process would facilitate greater collaboration among teachers with technology-oriented lesson plans to actively interact with their peers. Without national or state-level technology standards, Oliver argues, today's teachers do not have much of an incentive to collaborate with other teachers in the development of lesson plans that incorporate technology in the student learning process.

In his counterpoint essay, Rose takes exception to Oliver's contention that national and state-level standards should be required for today's teachers. Instead, Rose argues that the national and state experts that would comprise a technology standards committee would be forced to make compromises to reach a consensus. The end result, Rose contends, would be that the creation of national or state-level technology standards for teachers that are too general to allow for interpretation. Therefore, the technology standards for teachers would not be useful. Rose points to some of the existing professional technology standards for teachers as evidence of the fact that the developed standards are too general.

In the counterpoint essay, a major source of Rose's opposition to the imposition of mandatory national or state-level technology standards for teachers is that today's influential policymakers, especially in the wake of No Child Left Behind (NCLB) legislation, have connected the national and state-level standards movement with high-stakes testing. According to Rose, the problem with linking national or state-level teacher technology standards with the high-stakes testing movement is that it is possible to create multiple-choice tests where teachers prove their proficiency in using technology to improve instruction by paper-and-pencil tests that are easily scored by machines. Rose argues that requiring teachers to learn technology standards through required testing will not assist teachers in creating a technology vision. Curriculum standards should be the domain of school and district committees, not national or state-level policymakers.

The major dividing line between the authors of the essays in this chapter is in the proper approach necessary to most effectively improve the teaching of technology and its impact on student learning. In his point essay, Oliver maintains that mandatory national or state-level technology standards for teachers would most certainly improve teacher instruction using technology and student learning. Oliver argues that national or state-level technology standards for teachers improve teacher collaboration, provide useful assessment data for evaluating teacher instruction incorporating technology, and provide uniform guidelines for teachers across the country in terms of their expectations involving the proper uses of technology in their instruction. In direct contrast to Oliver's advocacy of national or state-level technology standards for teachers, counterpoint essay author Rose argues that the politicized process associated with the policymakers who ultimately create national or state-level technology standards for teachers is inherently flawed. The need to create consensus to approve national or state-level technology standards results in technology standards that are too general to allow for viable teacher improvement in the use of technology in the instructional process. Moreover, the passage of NCLB has resulted in the high-stakes testing movement nationwide. Rose argues that the national and state-level teacher technology standards movement has been linked with the high-stakes testing movement with negative consequences, namely resulting in the inability of teachers to create an accurate vision for the integration of technology in teacher instruction.

Kevin P. Brady
North Carolina State University

POINT: Kevin M. Oliver
North Carolina State University

While investments in classroom technology have increased steadily over the past decade, it is still unclear whether teachers are making consistent and effective use of technology throughout the school year as well as across curricular disciplines. If one assumes that students in the modern digital age should be learning to learn with technology, national teacher technology standards are important to inform technology integration practices toward this ultimate goal.

SAMPLE TECHNOLOGY STANDARDS APPLICABLE TO TEACHERS

Numerous groups have proposed teacher technology standards. Technology standards are available to guide general educators (e.g., International Society for Technology in Education [ISTE]; National Educational Technology Standards for Teachers [NETS-T]; UNESCO Information, Communication, Technology [ICT] competency framework for teachers), specific subject areas (e.g., technology standards embedded in the National Council of Teachers of Mathematics [NCTM] math standards), and specific delivery modes (e.g., Southern Regional Education Board [SREB] standards for quality online teaching, adopted by the International Association for K-12 Online Learning [iNACOL]). Furthermore, technology standards are available for accrediting college and university programs that prepare technology leaders (e.g., Association for Educational Communications and Technology [AECT] standards for accrediting school media and educational technology specialist programs; ISTE standards for accrediting educational computing and technology programs). While professional technology standards are not teacher technology standards per se, they do recommend applications of technology in the classroom that can be used to guide teachers. In fact, ISTE's technology facilitator/leader standards cover the same six categories as the 2000 NETS-T, with supplemental standards for program planning, budgeting, and leadership/vision for facilitators/leaders.

Many arguments for and against national teacher technology standards stem from the content of what is in the standards, thus it is important to briefly consider what technology competencies they generally represent. If the NETS-T and UNESCO-ICT technology standards are taken as a national and international sample of teacher technology standards, some similarities emerge. The key teacher expectations from the 2008 NETS-T include the following: an understanding of basic technology skills; an ability to model legal and ethical use of resources; an understanding of the relationship between content, pedagogy, and technology with the ability to integrate relevant technology resources in lessons; an understanding of student-centered teaching strategies to promote creative and innovative thinking, including using technology in support of real-world and authentic problems, collaborative and global activities, and alternative assessments; and the ability to employ technology to communicate with students and parents and collaborate with teacher communities that reflect on practice. UNESCO-ICT promotes three different standards "modules," each with different overall goals and emphases for teachers. The first emphasis is "technology literacy," where teachers integrate commercial software, such as games and tutorials, as well as web-based content in support of the existing curriculum and teaching methods. A second area of emphasis is "knowledge deepening," where teachers design and facilitate more student-centered, real-world problems and group projects to convey complex concepts, as well as integrate open-ended, subject-specific tools in support of problem solving and inquiry (e.g., spreadsheets in math). The final emphasis is "knowledge creation," where teachers design reflective learning environments and communities and model learning processes in support of critical and creative thinking in students.

While acknowledging that these summaries are oversimplifications of larger frameworks, it is evident both sets of standards encourage basic teacher technology literacy that can be modeled for students as well as an understanding of subject-specific tools that represent appropriate intersections of technology with curriculum content. Further, both frameworks suggest teachers should understand the intersections of technology and pedagogy by recommending student-centered learning environments and communities that engage authentic problems. Finally, both frameworks recommend uses of technology that foster the ideal student outcomes of critical and creative thinking among self-directed learners who develop the capability to respond to future problems.

It is noteworthy that neither framework recommends teachers learn to use specific technology software or hardware. The rationale for such generality is not that discussions of new and emerging technology tools that will likely influence education do not exist. Indeed, the New Media Consortium and the EDUCAUSE Learning Initiative have released their Horizon Report on emerging trends in higher education annually since 2004. One reason teacher technology standards trend toward the general is likely related to the rapid rate of change in educational technologies and the difficulty educational institutions and schools would face adopting technology standards if they were updated every two to three years to incorporate emerging technology-based tools. Since technology standards for educators take a long time to propose and even longer to adopt into teacher education courses and teacher-created lessons, it can be argued technology standards should remain primarily technology tool–neutral while emphasizing the pedagogy, or teaching practices, technologies are known to support well (e.g., problem solving, inquiry, community) and the related outcomes that are desirable in the working world (e.g., ability to parse vast amounts of data and extract/summarize that which is relevant to an assigned topic, ability to communicate and collaborate globally).

Another reason teacher technology standards trend toward the general is likely related to the considerable research that has demonstrated instructional strategies, rather than technology, are key elements to student learning. Since any number of technology-related tools can generally be applied to support the same strategy, technology standards for educators should focus on the effective and desirable strategies and outcomes that we know digital-age technology tools can support very well (e.g., teachers should demonstrate an ability to support student–student collaboration and knowledge construction with technology, which we know can be fostered by many new web 2.0 tools). Technology standards for teachers then provide a rationale and direction for integration while simultaneously permitting the flexible incorporation of technologies available in a given teacher's skill set or classroom environment.

RATIONALE FOR REQUIRING TECHNOLOGY STANDARDS FOR TEACHERS

One of the first steps in a systematic instructional design process is to create goals and objectives that will inform learners of academic expectations. For teachers, technology standards can serve a similar role, setting expectations for technology use. When educators with a strong understanding of technology set common expectations at national and/or state levels, educational stakeholders benefit by understanding what exactly to teach and assess to ensure teachers appropriately leverage school technology. The United States has made significant progress in linking virtually every school to the Internet with considerable recent funding going toward one-to-one laptop computing and mobile computing programs. While investments in infrastructure are supportive of technology integration, today's technology standards help provide the vision for how best to leverage increased computing power in support of student learning.

Pre-service teachers are among the stakeholders who potentially benefit the most from teacher technology standards. Technology standards can help colleges and schools of education reflect on existing courses to identify voids and create new activities that ensure teacher candidates are able to effectively integrate technology in support of student learning. Further, when technology standards for teachers exist, authors of textbooks and online teaching resources can provide illustrations of technology standards in use to help teachers apply standards to teaching practices. Without some specific vision for technology use established by standards, teacher preparation would be highly divergent and inconsistent, with schools unable to determine whether or not new teacher hires were adequately prepared to teach with technology in the classroom.

Those involved in assessing teachers to ensure they are technologically proficient are also among the educational stakeholders who benefit from national teacher technology standards. Some states require new teachers to demonstrate basic technology proficiency as part of licensing, and some states have aligned technology endorsements for previously licensed teachers with technology standards, allowing teachers to serve as computer teachers, technology facilitators, or technology professional developers. Colleges and universities preparing teachers for these teaching licenses and endorsements can use assessment data to determine if teachers meet technology standards and, if not, revise the courses to address deficiencies. National accrediting bodies can use assessment data to determine if programs are teaching to important technology standards with existing teacher candidates capable of performing desired skills. School districts and individual schools can also benefit from assessment data to assist with teacher hiring and annual reviews. Human resource officers can use assessment data to determine teacher candidate eligibility for positions, and having common national technology standards would facilitate hiring from different colleges or states with the expectation that all teacher candidates would have similar capabilities. School administrators can use assessment data as part of annual reviews of teachers as well as to help justify expensive equipment and professional development inputs based on increases in teacher integration of standards. If assessment data demonstrate that teachers are not meeting standards, school administrators can better argue for increased resources from grants or districts to bridge a potential digital divide and provide equivalent experiences for their students. Technology facilitators and professional developers in schools can also use assessment data to determine if teachers meet standards and, if they are not, plan professional development to address deficiencies.

Can technology proficiency be assessed on the basis of national technology standards for today's teachers? Some technology standards are more easily assessed than others, such as technology standards that recommend knowledge of copyright issues and legal and ethical use of resources, or standards that recommend teachers participate in continuing professional development or reflective communities. Technology standards related to teaching practice are more challenging to assess and probably best documented by exhibits or portfolios demonstrating how different standards have been addressed in one's individual teaching. Many researchers have relied on teacher self-reports to evaluate how well standards are being met in general across a group of teachers. Scales based on the 2000 NETS-T have demonstrated strong reliability, suggesting self-reporting can be used to measure the NETS-T in teachers. In one international study by Ahmet Naci Coklar and Hatice Ferhan Odabasi (2009), five of the six NETS-T categories fit a factor model with the addition of one new culturally specific factor pertaining to the use of technology for differentiating course content. In a study with U.S. teachers by Kristen A. Corbell, Jason W. Osborne, and Lisa Leonor Grable (2008), all six NETS-T categories fit a factor model.

Perhaps the best rationale for requiring national teacher technology standards is related to the opportunities that national technology standards would foster for teachers to collaboratively plan technology-enhanced lessons with other mentors and peers with reflection on ways to improve teaching through the use of technology. Without the need to address national technology standards, such teacher collaborations might not take place at all and certainly not to the same level as they would with national technology standards for all teachers. The following section addresses this specific point in further detail.

FOSTERING ADOPTION OF NATIONAL TECHNOLOGY STANDARDS FOR TEACHERS

While a rationale for national teacher technology standards has been provided, it is clear that simply providing technology standards will not by itself promote better technology integration. Further steps must be taken to encourage teacher understanding, adoption, and application of the technology standards. The NETS-T were written with a list of essential conditions that are recommended to facilitate the integration of standards and include such items as continuing professional development, technical assistance, access to technology, and leadership.

No one has argued that national technology standards are a quick fix to improved technology integration in the classroom, but rather, will require investments of both time and cost. Terri Teal Bucci and Anthony J. Petrosino (2004) provide a glimpse of the work that is required to adopt teacher technology standards in their summary of six teacher education programs that won ISTE awards for implementing strategies to integrate NETS-T standards. Some of the recurring strategies across programs included the following: explicating connections between college course work and NETS-T, so there is agreement about which courses will address which standards to avoid any gaps; connecting teacher candidates with expert technology-using teachers who can model appropriate application of technology standards; providing teacher candidates with technology to use in field placements; and providing teacher candidates with opportunities to develop their own lessons and portfolios connected to standards with feedback from mentor teachers, faculty, and fellow candidates.

Technology standards can be a helpful impetus to engage faculty and teachers in collaborations and reflections on their technology integration plans. Wayne A. Nelson and Melissa Thomeczek (2007), for example, describe the use of two design studios implemented at one institution among faculty and teacher candidates creating technology activities aligned to new state technology standards. Participants were able to share their projects and receive feedback from peers. Additionally, Belinda Gimbert and colleagues (2003) describe a school–university partnership, whereby in-service teachers tackled inquiry projects with the support of university faculty, many of which allowed teachers to test and reflect on technology integrations.

Not every school can take advantage of formal collaborations with colleges and universities, but standard professional development can also provide teachers with opportunities to align standards with their curricular goals, educational strategies, and available tools. Punya Mishra and Matthew J. Koehler's model of technological pedagogical content knowledge (TPCK) is helpful for interpreting the role of standards in a more systematic or comprehensive framework of instructional planning. When developing lessons, for example, teachers must have knowledge of their content or curriculum, knowledge of appropriate pedagogy or teaching strategies for conveying that material (e.g., lecture, small group discussion, questioning, inquiry, project-based learning), and knowledge of appropriate technologies that align with and can help to support the strategies. General technology standards such as NETS-T and UNESCO-ICT can aid planning by recommending pedagogical practices that technologies should support. Some content-specific standards, such as those by NCTM, may aid planning by specifying actual tools that are helpful to the teaching of specific curricular concepts.

ADDRESSING ISSUES WITH TECHNOLOGY STANDARDS

One common criticism of national technology standards for teachers relates to the generality or specificity of a given set of standards. Some suggest standards are too general to communicate what teachers need to do. On the other hand, Bob Hughes (2004) warns if technology standards are too specific in their focus on given tools or skills (e.g., expertise with word processing), they may lead teachers to focus on a limited set of technologies when other technologies may be excluded that are just as applicable and sometimes more readily available in a given setting. Examples of both general and specific teacher technology standards are available, although most lean toward the general. In subject-specific technology standards, such as those from NCTM for math, specific software programs and tools are suggested in reference to the teaching of math content (e.g., spreadsheets, geometry software, calculators). The online teaching standards proposed by SREB recommend proficiency with specific online teaching tools, such as discussion boards, email, chat, and electronic whiteboards, but also recommend teachers know how to support effective online teaching strategies, such as group interaction, collaboration, and regular feedback, without specifying any tools.

The NETS-T and UNESCO-ICT do not specify software or hardware to be mastered, focusing instead on the types of activities and experiences teachers should be fostering via technology (e.g., authentic problems, collaborations) and the types of skills or outcomes that are desired (e.g., creative thinking, critical thinking, self-directed learning). The flexibility afforded by more open standards helps to address the criticisms many have made regarding standards that impose specifics regarding what must be taught. Standards presented in a few general categories such as NETS-T and UNESCO-ICT also address a common criticism that standards documents are too lengthy and promote selective use.

A second common criticism of technology standards for teachers relates to their being out of touch with local educational contexts. Many have argued top-down standards are inflexible and restrictive such that local goals cannot be met. The alternative is bottom-up standards defined locally that may increase flexibility but may not promote the highest standards when left to teachers who may have had limited opportunities to work with technology. A compromise is afforded by many of the current teacher technology standards that provide a vision and set a bar, yet remain general enough to allow customization. Erring toward more general standards when dealing with technology may be the preferred option, given differences in technology available to different sites, and also given the more flexible opportunity afforded stakeholders to collaborate and reflect on how to best address standards in their context. When technology standards are more general, it can help to have performance indicators, criteria, rubrics, and lesson examples that can help to clarify by example what the standard can represent. And both ISTE and UNESCO have provided such elaborations to accompany their standards.

A third common criticism of technology standards for teachers relates to their alleged inability to address the developmental nature of teacher technology integration. Hughes (2004) highlights that teachers progress in developmental stages from novice adopters to expert innovators. He suggests standards that promote specific technology skills (e.g., spreadsheets) only prepare teachers for the earliest developmental stages where technology is used in support of traditional classroom practice. This is a valid argument when technology standards focus only on productivity with specific tools, but NETS-T and UNESCO-ICT both emphasize pedagogy beyond tools. Further, they both address the developmental nature of teacher change. NETS-T, for example, includes a standard for professional growth whereby teachers are expected to continue their education and collaborate with other educators and researchers to improve their practice. Further, the performance profiles provided by the NETS-T outline increased expectations along four stages of teacher preparation, including student teaching and first-year teaching. Likewise, UNESCO-ICT hints at a progression from basic technology literacy with productivity tools to knowledge-deepening approaches with projects and collaborations, to knowledge-creation approaches with problem solving, experimentation, and critical thinking.

CONCLUSION

National teacher technology standards are important to provide a vision for technology use in the classroom and to assist education stakeholders in preparing and assessing teachers to ensure they can meet the vision and ultimately positively impact student learning. Today's technology standards for teachers largely emphasize pedagogy over technology applications and provide opportunities for educators to plan and reflect on appropriate applications of technology that are appropriate for divergent teaching contexts. The continued use of teacher technology standards is important to both guide and foster technology integration practice for today's teachers educating students in both a global and technological age.

COUNTERPOINT: Raymond Rose
Rose & Smith Associates

What is the purpose of technology standards, be they national, state-level, or local? That question needs to be answered first before even considering if they should be required for today's teachers. And then, what does "required for today's teachers" actually mean?

PURPOSE OF STANDARDS

Teacher standards help focus attention on specific issues. The standards movement for teachers came about in this country as a vehicle for setting an absolute floor on instruction. Curriculum standards were meant to specify the minimum level of content knowledge students should attain at any particular grade level. They were meant to solve the problem of different levels of instruction and student achievement that were taking place among different school districts. The expectation was, by creating standards for teachers, schools would know the minimum level of student knowledge expected, and then schools would arrange instruction and curriculum to ensure that all students achieved or exceeded those standards. In the beginning, teacher standards were seen as a school improvement effort.

National teacher curriculum organizations, such as the National Council of Teachers of Mathematics (NCTM), the National Council of Teachers of English (NCTE), and others, created teacher standards to help support their membership and to provide a context and definition of what they considered important content in their particular curriculum area. The standards created by the various national organizations were only recommendations but did begin to have an impact on textbooks. However, as state departments of education began to adopt more rigid curriculum standards, some schools adopted the standards of the national organizations, others adapted the state standards, and a few opted to create their own, starting from scratch. It became clear one way to impact schools was through the creation and promulgation of curriculum and program standards. More national organizations joined the standards movement by creating standards of their own.

The International Society for Technology in Education (ISTE) created their first set of standards for technology and use for students in 1998, and then added standards for teachers and school administrators, periodically revising these standards. In 2004, ISTE reported that 48 states had used at least one set of standards in their state technology plans, certification or licensure requirements, curriculum plans, assessment plans, or other official state documents.

The use of standards as a way to ensure consistency in and across schools is not a bad notion. And, if consistency is seen as a necessary step in school improvement, then the use of standards can be thought of as a school improvement strategy. The problem with this idea, however, is that standards identify the minimum level of student achievement. The recent push for high-stakes testing, which flowed from the passage of the federal No Child Left Behind Act, has used national standards as the student testing target. As a result, the expectation is that tests only strive to measure student progress toward the minimum.

And, because teachers and schools are judged by student performance on those tests, the schools focus on ensuring students reach, rather than exceed, the minimum level of learning as defined by the standards.

Standards have also shifted in granularity over time. Some policy-making groups have established very granular standards. This approach resulted in large sets of standards that, rather than painting the big picture of student learning, are a laundry list of narrowly defined and specific skills that can be more easily tested on traditional multiple-choice, paper-and-pencil tests. There are school jurisdictions where classroom teachers are expected to identify in each daily lesson plan the standards they address, and since the requirement is to identify every standard and subset, national standards can potentially double the size of the teacher's lesson plan.

ARGUMENTS OPPOSING REQUIRING TECHNOLOGY STANDARDS

The primary focus of this counterpoint essay is to argue that national technology standards should not be required for today's teachers. The current ISTE National Educational Technology Standards for Teachers (NETS-T) are a far better iteration than the earlier versions, with just five major headings: (1) facilitate and inspire student learning and creativity, (2) design and develop digital-age learning experiences and assessments, (3) model digital-age work and learning, (4) promote and model digital citizenship and responsibility, and (5) engage in professional growth and leadership.

The questions to ask about these standards are numerous. Do these really help teachers use appropriate technology as part of instruction? Do they help a teacher who is in a technology-poor school? Do they or the National Educational Technology Standards for School Administrators (NETS-A) provide guidance for the purchase and allocation of technology in schools? The answer to all of these questions is no.

Standards are typically much too highly nuanced. The people who put the standards together are experts in the field and have a very clear vision of what the ideal implementation of those standards would look like. In some cases, the standards committee is forced to make compromises to reach consensus. To fit within the current educational structure, to not appear too radical, and to ensure broad acceptance of the standards, the language of standards sometimes become too general to allow for broad interpretation. Then there are the political statements that come from the policy-making structures they opt to include in their standards.

The International Association for K-12 Online Learning (iNACOL) endorsed a set of standards for quality online learning. Susan Patrick, the current president and CEO of iNACOL and former director of the Office of Technology at the U.S. Department of Education, stated,

> Standards help ensure the quality and consistency of online learning in K–12. *The National Standards of Quality for Online Courses* offers an important measuring tool to help policy leaders, schools, and parents across the nation evaluate course quality and implement best practices. (International Association for K-12 Online Learning [iNACOL], 2007)

One of the iNACOL standards is "The course meets universal design principles, Section 508 standards, and W3C guidelines to ensure access for all students." This is an important issue and one most people would support. As the primary author of the iNACOL Research Brief, *Access and Equity in Online Courses and Virtual Schools,* this is an issue I take personal interest in, and I have had the opportunity to review courses from both online course vendors and those produced in school programs. Vendors will readily identify their courses as meeting all the iNACOL standards. A number of state and local online programs have adopted the iNACOL standards and, in at least one state, courses are required to be reviewed to ensure they meet all iNACOL standards. When reviewed by an independent expert, it becomes clear even those that have been reviewed and are designated as in full compliance with the iNACOL standards are often not. The definition of what standards mean is so widely interpreted that they give a feeling of compliance when it is not the case. It is clear that reviewers have different levels of understanding.

Just to focus on one component of the NETS-T standards, the second standard includes the following:

> **Design and Develop Digital-Age Learning Experiences and Assessments**
> Teachers design, develop, and evaluate authentic learning experiences and assessments incorporating contemporary tools and resources to maximize content learning in context and to develop the knowledge, skills, and attitudes identified in the NETS-S [National Educational Technology Standards for Students]. Teachers:
> a. design or adapt relevant learning experiences that incorporate digital tools and resources to promote student learning and creativity. . . .

It sounds good. How can anyone object? But what does it mean? Do we all have the same definition of "authentic learning experiences?" Aren't all learning experiences authentic, or are there also fake learning experiences? Is a 1980s computer-based instruction-module digital tool acceptable in this context, or are there only specific web 2.0 digital tools that meet this standard?

The ISTE standards are ultimately trying to ensure that students are adequately prepared to be effective participants in the 21st century, and that they have an appropriate 21st-century education. Everyone would agree that technology is ubiquitous today, and that both the near and distant future only appear to hold increased integration of digital technology, so students should be well prepared to enter a technology-filled 21st century.

Then the question to ask of the national standards is: Do they identify the best way to adequately prepare students for the 21st century? As the U.S. Department of Education's 2010 National Educational Technology Plan (NETP) points out, our current educational model is based on the thinking of the late 1800s, and thus far, we've only seen evolutionary tinkering. The standards movement has been the result of a general unhappiness with the current state of education and the need of policymakers to say they have a simple solution. There is no simple fix. Creating standards hasn't brought about the fundamental changes in American education that improve our education to the point policymakers wanted to take credit for it.

Policymakers connected the national technology standards movement and high-stakes student testing. After all, if there are standards, it is important to ensure that they are being met. But the policymakers have, with content standards, limited themselves to traditional measures of student learning, and generally focused on measuring progress toward the standards with traditional paper-and-pencil tests that are easily machine scored.

Where does this leave the technology standards and performance indicators? It's possible to create a multiple-choice test of the ISTE standards where teachers prove they understand the standards by parroting the correct statement (as in the following fictional test example):

> NETS-T standard 2: Design and Develop Digital-Age Learning Experiences and Assessments is best demonstrated by:
>
> a. promote, support, and model creative and innovative thinking and inventiveness
>
> b. collaborate with students, peers, parents, and community members using digital tools and resources to support student success and innovation
>
> c. promote and model digital etiquette and responsible social interactions related to the use of technology and information
>
> d. design or adapt relevant learning experiences that incorporate digital tools and resources to promote student learning and creativity

(The correct answer is *d*. The other responses are from other NETS-T standards.)

But is that really what the creators of the NETS wanted? It was not what I had in mind as one of those who participated in the process. We will not see a significant movement toward real 21st-century education simply by preparing teachers to prove their knowledge of the standards on a test. Requiring teachers to learn the standards will not help teachers create a vision for the use of digital technology in the 21st century. Rather, national technology standards for teachers could serve as the basis for a more nuanced discussion to help teachers create and understand the vision for the use of digital technology as part of 21st-century education.

Appropriate technology should be used as part of student learning across the full curriculum spectrum. Students should be prepared to be productive participants in the 21st century, to understand how and where technology is used, and how it impacts their lives. That's not going to be done through the simple process of requiring teachers to learn a set of technology standards. This situation is reminiscent of the concern with educational equity in the 1980s. One of the major concerns was how to address educational equity issues in education. While many believed that equity issues should be integrated into the fabric of our education, there were two distinct camps about the process. Both sides believed race, gender, and national origin topics should ultimately be integrated into instruction, but the struggle was over the best way to achieve that end. One camp felt that, at least at the start, it was better to have specific chapters in textbooks and separate courses on African American history and women's issues to ensure that students would be exposed to that content. There was also concern that the integration of those issues would result in their being so watered down as to make the issues invisible. Gradually, as more people have become aware of these issues, more of the separate content has been integrated into and has changed the fabric of curriculum and instruction.

The issue of teaching and learning with technology should follow a similar trajectory. Early on in the application of digital technologies in learning, it was important to help teachers and administrators have descriptions of how to include technology as part of instruction. The decision to do that, given the educational climate at the time, was by developing a set of standards that helped to provide direction.

If we must have standards, then the use of digital technology ought to be integrated into the specific curriculum content areas. It is not something that new teachers should be tested on. They should know there are standards, and that state policymakers have required adherence to those as a quality control issue. In some states, standard-setting can be fraught with politics. Curriculum standards should be the purview of the school and district curriculum committees. They are the ones who should ensure the textbooks purchased match the standards that are being assessed, and not just some of the standards, but all the standards. If there is not a textbook that does an adequate job, then the curriculum experts, not classroom teachers, should be responsible for finding or creating the supplementary necessary materials. And, in the case of digital technology, they can also find the appropriate technology applications and make the case for their use in the student learning process. They would also have the responsibility to ensure that the classroom teachers receive the high-quality professional development to ensure they know how to use and manage the technology to maximize student learning. There is no reason for today's classroom teachers to become technology standards experts. Teachers need to focus on student learning.

However, there is another and better reason for not requiring teachers to know national technology standards. The U.S. Department of Education's NETP does not present a set of technology standards for our schools. The NETP calls for revolutionary transformation of U.S. education and an end to the history of evolutionary tinkering that has resulted in minor changes in our educational policies and practices for the past half-century. The NETP starts by identifying a set of real 21st-century competencies: critical thinking, complex problem solving, collaboration, data literacy, and multimedia communications. It presents an additional five goals focused on learning, assessment, teaching, infrastructure, and productivity.

NEW MODELS OF EDUCATION

Rather than advocating for a set of national standards, we need to create a set of transformative educational models that reflect a 21st-century education. We need to help policymakers rethink their basic educational assumptions and expectations about what schools need to look like—how they should function.

Virtual, or online, education has provided today's educational leaders with the opportunity to rethink certain basic premises of education. Seat-time as a measure of student learning, while still operational in most educational policies today, is also clearly recognized as an ineffective strategy for ensuring student learning. But what policymakers do not yet have is a clear vision of what to move to as a replacement that is more than just another attempt at evolutionary tinkering.

The same process that was used to create the technology standards can be used to create a model of a real 21st-century student learning environment, one that is not mired in late 1800s thinking, or in the industrial era design of the mid-1900s. As long as we continue to use the existing models of schooling as the basis for our educational change, we will continue to lag behind the rest of the world in education. There needs to be a different approach to the use of technology as it relates to student learning. We need to take what is known about how students learn and what is known about how technology can facilitate student learning, and design a new model of education around that.

For years, people have proclaimed that technology would revolutionize education, and that promise has yet to be seen, but every new technology that has been introduced into education has tried to fit within the existing educational structure. National technology standards for teachers set a minimum bar for schools and maintain the status quo for today's schools. We have proof, in the form of our abysmal school drop-out rates and the academic achievement gap, that the existing model of education is flawed. It is time to stop focusing on national teacher standards and use that effort to develop new models of education. We need a model of education for the 21st century that reflects the revolutionary transformation called for in the NETP.

FURTHER READINGS AND RESOURCES

Bucci, T. T., & Petrosino, A. J. (2004). Meeting the ISTE challenge in the field: An overview of the first six distinguished award winning programs. *Journal of Computing in Teacher Education, 21*(4), 11–21.

Christensen, C., Horn, M., & Johnson, C. (2008). *Disrupting class: How disruptive innovation will change how the world learns.* New York: McGraw-Hill.

Coklar, A. N., & Odabasi, H. F. (2009). Educational Technology Standards Scale (ETSS): A study of reliability and validity for Turkish preservice teachers. *Journal of Computing in Teacher Education, 25*(4), 135–142.

Corbell, K. A., Osborne, J. W., & Grable, L. L. (2008). Examining the performance standards for in-service teachers: A confirmatory factor analysis of the assessment of teachers' NETS-T experience. *Computers in the Schools, 25*(1–2), 10–24.

Gimbert, B., Zembal-Saul, C., & Abruzzo, S. (2003). Infusing technology through teacher inquiry in a school-university partnership. *Teacher Education and Practice, 16*(1), 13–31.

Hughes, B. (2004). The opposite intended effect: A case study of how over-standardization can reduce efficacy of teacher education. *Teacher Education Quarterly, 31*(3), 43–52.

International Association for K-12 Online Learning (iNACOL). (2007). *iNACOL National Standards of Quality for Online Courses.* Retrieved September 29, 2010, from http://www.inacol.org/research/nationalstandards

Nelson, W. A., & Thomeczek, M. (2007). Design as a focus for technology integration. *Computers in the Schools, 23*(3), 93–104.

Tech & Learning. (2010). *Are schools prepared for the digital classroom?* Retrieved from http://techlearning.com/article/28318

U.S. Department of Education. (2010). *National Educational Technology Plan 2010.* Washington, DC: Author. Retrieved from http://www.ed.gov/sites/default/files/NETP-2010-final-report.pdf

Court Cases and Statutes

No Child Left Behind Act, 20 U.S.C. §§ 6301–7941 (2006).

9

Should teachers have the right to create and post online content about their school on social networking sites, when such posts are made on their own time and without the use of school resources?

POINT: Jayson W. Richardson, *University of Kentucky*
COUNTERPOINT: Bruce Umpstead, *Michigan Department of Education*

OVERVIEW

Social networking sites are defined as web-based tools that allow their users to create an online profile and electronically communicate with others who share a common, online connection based on interests, including education, profession, or professional development interests. The first social networking websites were created in the mid-1990s; the two most popular being Geocities, created in 1994, and Tripod.com, created in 1995. The social networking website Facebook, developed in 2004, is currently the most popular social networking website, boasting 500 million–plus registered users. Recent usage statistics on Facebook reveal exactly how significant and widespread social networking websites have become in our society. Recent statistics on how extensively individuals use Facebook, as reported by Facebook, include

- 50 percent of active users log on to Facebook in any given day;
- the average user has 130 friends;
- people spend more than 700 billion minutes per month on Facebook;
- users interact with over 900 million objects (i.e., pages, groups, events, and community pages);
- the average user is connected to 80 community pages, groups, and events;
- the average user creates 90 pieces of content each month;
- more than 30 billion pieces of content (web links, news stories, blog posts, notes, photo albums, etc.) are shared each month.

Twitter is the most recent social networking website to gain worldwide notoriety. Users create a webpage on which to post short, online comments limited to 140 characters in length. Users attract "followers" by posting these "microblog" comments and build their own list of users that they follow online. The combination of posts and reposts can make for a rich dialogue on an individual user's page. In January 2011, officials at Twitter announced it had broken the 200 million user account mark. In January 2011, Twitter had more than 175 million registered users with 370,000 new accounts being added each day. Every day, 95 million tweets, or brief online messages, are sent via Twitter. These numbers indicate there has been and continues to be a mass adoption of these social networking technologies by individuals of every age group, gender, race and ethnicity, and socioeconomic status. Today's educators, quick to adopt new technology, are beginning to use the social networking website Twitter to connect and communicate with colleagues, students, and parents.

In 2011, some of the most popular social networking sites in the United States are Facebook, Twitter, LinkedIn, Ning, Tagged, Myspace, Classmates .com, Friendster, and Orkut. Globally, the most popular social networking sites differ by region and country. For example, Bebo is common in the United Kingdom, Tuenti is popular in Spain, Kaixin001 is popular in China, and Millat is popular in Muslim-oriented societies. What we see globally is that online-based social networking is culture-specific and that a single platform rarely fits the social networking wants and needs of everyone.

In this chapter, point author Jayson W. Richardson (University of Kentucky) and counterpoint author Bruce Umpstead (Michigan Department of Education) debate the issue of whether teachers have the right to create and post online content about their schools on popular social networking sites, when these online posts are made on the teacher's own time and without the use of any school resources. In his point essay, Richardson provides three primary reasons why teachers should have the right to post online content about school matters on social networking websites, especially if such online postings are done on a teacher's own time and without the use of school resources.

First, restricting or disciplining teachers from posting online content regarding school matters on social networking websites significantly interferes with a teacher's lifelong learning process. Not allowing teachers to engage in online communications with other educators regarding education-related issues, Richardson argues, interferes with a teacher's personal learning network, which can be easily found on today's social networking websites. Second, Richardson maintains that today's social networking websites provide new and struggling teachers a constructive online venue to discuss, vent, brainstorm, and seek creative appropriate solutions to their questions and concerns. Third, restricting teachers from posting online content on social networking websites significantly reduces trust between school leaders and their teachers. More specifically, banning teachers from posting online content on school or education-related issues sends a clear message that school administrators do not respect their teachers' ability to exercise proper discretion and responsibility when posting online content to social networking websites. Overall, Richardson contends, school districts that presently have policies and procedures restricting teachers from posting online content on school matters using social networking websites result in multiple negative outcomes for teachers, ranging from facilitating low teacher esteem and morale to leaving today's teachers unprepared to educate technologically literate students in an increasingly global and digital society.

Umpstead's counterpoint essay, however, argues that today's teachers have special ethical and moral obligations to both their own students and society at-large. While both Richardson and Umpstead agree that teachers need to be responsible users of technology, Umpstead cautions that teachers need to be especially mindful of the implications of how they use technology, noting the unique speed and permanence of online communications. Even when an educator engages in online social networking on their own time and without the use of school resources, lasting negative outcomes can result that not only negatively impact the individual teacher and students but the overall school community as well. As Umpstead notes, the dark side of online social networking activities, such as cyberbullying and sexting (taking and transmitting sexually suggestive or explicit photos using a mobile device), are becoming increasingly more common among today's teachers.

According to Umpstead, district- and school-level social networking safety policies in school employee manuals are just a necessary first step in protecting schools from the negative consequences of online teacher posts involving school matters. Ultimately, the ethical and moral standards that should be applied to today's teachers and that are found in many state-level teacher codes of ethics, as well as professional responsibility, justify both the restrictions as well as disciplinary actions taken against teachers who post online content involving school matters on social networking websites, even on their own time and without the use of school resources. Both authors, however, agree that with the inevitable growth of social networking sites, the issue of whether or not school officials can restrict teacher online postings on school matters on social networking sites, even when those online posts are made on a teacher's own time and without school resources, will only escalate.

Kevin P. Brady
North Carolina State University

POINT: Jayson W. Richardson
University of Kentucky

By definition, a social network consists of individuals who are connected to one another by a common bond. This common bond could potentially be based on friendship, kinship, common interests, core beliefs, or any other type of social connection. Prior to the mass adoption of digital technologies, social networks were developed slowly and were commonly created and maintained in person. As the Internet became increasingly more ubiquitous, or common-place, the development of social networking websites, such as Facebook and Myspace, has shifted into a digital world where connections are made and maintained quickly, in a much more fluid manner. One of the major differences between today's digital social networks compared to the face-to-face social networks of the past is that modern virtual social networks are considerably more temporary but the lasting impact and evidence of these relationships are considerably more permanent.

The diffusion of innovations theory contends that for any innovation, there are innovators, early adopters, majority adopters, and late adopters. The adoption of the diffusion of innovations theory usually tends to follow a normal bell curve distribution. The diffusion of innovations theory adoption curve is quite applicable for the adoption of most technology-based innovations in today's schools. The acceptance and adoption of digital social networking tools by educators in these institutions tends to likewise follow the diffusion of innovations theory adoption curve. As an example, not too long ago, Internet sites such as YouTube were blocked by Internet filtering software at most schools across the country. When some schools began allowing access to this particular site, teachers who used this social content-creation platform were seen as technology adoption innovators. Today, schools that continue to block websites such as YouTube are seen as laggards—as is the teacher who refuses to use this digital innovation. This same pattern is evident with wikis and blogs. Today, it is not really innovative for schools and teachers to deploy a blog or host a wiki; it is simply a common, technological instructional tool. Most social media, however, is still on that cutting edge where schools tread cautiously and where educators venture cautiously.

Currently, there is a heated debate concerning whether teachers should be able to use social networking tools in their classrooms or even in the privacy of their own homes. Those who oppose the use of social networking sites by teachers usually focus their argument exclusively on the fact that schools cannot control the content of social networking sites and students may be exposed, intentionally or unintentionally, to images or content not appropriate to minor students. The Children's Internet Protection Act (CIPA), enacted in 2000, and the Family Educational Rights and Privacy Act of 1974 (FERPA) are often cited as a basis for this decision. CIPA, however, has recently been challenged by various groups, including the American Library Association (ALA) and the American Civil Liberties Union (ACLU), as impinging on the rights of adult users of the Internet. This argument is often quickly extended to the use of school computers after school hours. Making this case is understandable when coupled with the reality that the use of social networking tools often blurs the distinction between the private and the public as well as the educational and the social. The argument can be made that computers purchased and maintained with public funds should not be used for teachers' private online social interactions. School districts, however, are overstepping their bounds when restricting or denying teachers' use of social networking tools outside of school hours, without the use of school resources, and when the content is focused on their school. Across the country, however, many school officials are setting up zero tolerance policies that actively restrict the use of social networking websites by their teachers both inside and outside of the classroom.

NEGATIVE RESULTS OF IMPOSING RESTRICTIONS

School districts that restrict or deny teachers the right to post online content about their school on social networking sites, such as Facebook, on their own time and using their own resources are creating unconstructive and intrusive policies that violate the privacy rights of today's teachers. First, these policies deny teachers the right to create and participate in their own personal learning social network using technology. Second, these policies severely restrict opportunities for teachers to create positive relationships that may potentially foster higher personal and professional satisfaction with their school and students. Third, restricting the online content a teacher can post on social networking sites sends the wrong message that the school does not trust their teachers. Each of these three points is explored in more detail in this point essay.

The first negative result of school or district policies that restrict teachers from posting online content on social networking websites is based on restrictions to an individual teacher's lifelong learning pursuits. Personal learning networks, such as those found on today's social networking websites, are interactive groups of individuals whose goal is to foster discussion and understanding of issues in a robust, fluid manner that involves multiple levels of crowdsourcing as well as the rapid dissemination of information. Developing personal learning networks is based on the theory of connectivism. Connectivism posits that any individual is simply a single node in a weblike network where meaning is co-constructed and knowledge is cocreated. In today's digital society, a single person cannot keep up with the mass amounts and vast variety of information that is pertinent to their profession or personal life. Teachers can, however, quickly and easily connect with other educators by engaging in various online social networks. Discussing school issues on these social networking websites significantly expands opportunities for finding possible solutions to problems or additionally informing people's opinions of issues. For example, if an elementary teacher posts how his math class is having difficulty understanding mathematical ratios, sending a message via the social networking website Twitter asking for lesson plan ideas and resources might lead to replies that in turn may help the teacher create powerful learning experiences in the classroom. Additionally, if a principal is having difficulty gaining district support for a 1:1 school laptop initiative, she could join a particular professional network on a social networking website and engage in online conversations with other principals to discuss how other schools have navigated or are navigating this massive paradigm shift.

The professional development of teachers is often informal and self-guided. Informal learning is a space where authentic learning can germinate and manifest itself into action. Social networking sites offer one such space for personal learning networks to grow quickly and expand. By restricting what online content can be discussed in these informal learning spaces (i.e., outside school walls and away from school equipment), school officials are essentially placing limits on a teacher's access to lifelong learning opportunities. As a result, school officials are, in effect, blocking generative, real-time solution-generating processes.

Aside from placing restrictions on a teacher's personal professional development, today's school leaders inevitably will have to ask what skill sets and dispositions in a global and digital world they value in their teaching faculty. Does a school system want teachers who are behind in their use and adoption of modern digital technologies, such as the use of social networking websites? Or do today's school officials value and embrace teachers who are technological innovators, who use the most relevant modern technologies, and who can incorporate those digital resources across both their personal and professional lives? In the current era of perpetual budget cuts and limited funding, modern school districts need to ask if they want teachers who are self-directed, self-motivated, social learners, or if they want teachers who engage in only costly professional development offered or mandated by others. School districts must be more holistic and ask themselves, what are the specific organizational, communication, and learning potentials of these current technological tools, including social networking websites? Additionally, school districts must reflect on how well these tools can be used as a mechanism to move away from groupthink and toward the creation of a shared vision of change and collaborative problem solving in the educational process.

It is well known that approximately half of all new teachers quit within their first 5 years of teaching. Professional as well as personal satisfaction in the teaching field significantly impacts a teacher's choice of whether to abandon the teaching profession. Social networking websites provide new and struggling teachers with a productive venue to discuss, vent, brainstorm, and seek creative, appropriate solutions to their unique problems. Social networking websites also give more experienced teachers an opportunity to mentor new or struggling teachers through online-based communications. High stress levels early in an educator's teaching career are often centered on a combination of low pay, poor working conditions, inadequate coping skills, or simply lack of experience. By organizing the conversation to exclude potentially hot button topics, districts are potentially fueling dissatisfaction and angst. It is much more likely that by seeking support and solutions through the use of social networking sites about school issues, teachers can potentially find a solution; lower, or even alleviate, the high level of stress that comes from being a new teacher; and build and maintain supportive relationships.

The third negative outcome of policies that restrict teachers from posting online content on social networking websites is that it greatly minimizes trust between school leaders and teachers. Banning school-focused posts to social networking websites greatly impacts a teacher's trust of school administrators and sends a clear message of distrust in the teacher's ability to exercise proper discretion and responsibility when posting online content to social networking websites. This is not only ironic considering teachers are trusted with the most valuable of resources (i.e., children), it also sets into motion a destructive institutional cycle of mistrust and even fear.

It is true that instances of misuse of social networking websites by some teachers have occurred. Some recent examples of teacher misuse of social networking websites include the use of public blogs by educators who boast about taking days off and by teachers who lambast their administrators. There are also examples of teachers who misuse social networking websites that have negative impacts on students. For instance, teachers have engaged in personal, online conversations with students on social networking websites or have been found to be venting on social networking websites about a particular student's apathy or low motivation levels. These examples of teacher misuse of social networking websites make for strong rationalizations as to why some school districts create blanket zero tolerance policies that discipline teachers for using social networking websites. However, it is unfair to restrict all teachers from accessing social networking websites based on the poor judgment of relatively few teachers.

ADDITIONAL CONCERNS

Whether it is conducted face-to-face or online, communication is largely about reaching out to others for advice and assistance. It involves multiple layers of relational dynamics. Today's social networking websites are simply a modern means to communicate with a wider audience. School districts that put up a wall, proverbial or literal, between teachers and online professional communities are perpetuating negative relational dynamics. Organizational trust is fostered in knowing that one's voice is being heard. If a school district does not listen first and then respond, its representatives cannot expect to add value to the conversation and thus improve the organizational culture of the school. By not listening to the authentic voice of the teacher via social networking sites or whatever medium she chooses, school districts are simply drawing first, asking questions later. Thus, the online-based communication and learning power of social networks are essentially ignored.

Additionally, if teachers are not trusted to use these technological tools appropriately, who will guide students to be responsible "digital citizens"? Digital citizens are those individuals who have the proper knowledge, skills, and ethical dispositions to use today's digital technologies in a knowledgeable and responsible way. Who will teach students how to effectively communicate in a digital world? Who will guide students to make responsible choices with regard to creating and managing their digital footprint? Who will guide the students to create responsible, appropriate online content in a way that does not disenfranchise others or slander oneself? If school districts and individual schools do not allow teachers to model these positive and appropriate behaviors, then it is impossible to expect students to learn these critical skills of online etiquette themselves. Restricting social networking website use to only instructional purposes does not mirror the real, digitally engaged professional or social world. Schools often proselytize about the need to make education meaningful and create an education system that reflects the realities of the real, global workplace. Restricting what and where teachers direct their online posts, especially on their own time and using their own technological tools, sends a contradictory message to today's educators. That is, are schools saying they seek to prepare students for a world that values open, responsible communication and collaborative citizenship but in reality forces teachers to live in a closed, top-down, untrusting bubble that stymies and prosecutes certain forms of online-based communication?

How locality is defined has changed. Educators are no longer limited geographically to discussing school issues in local brick-and-mortar libraries, bookstores, music shops, or at the school's watercooler. Social networking websites allow today's teachers to find an online audience that they can communicate with for assistance in both their professional and personal lives. If school leaders effectively ban social networking websites in form or content, then they are sending the wrong message that they really do not care to meet the needs of today's teachers who work in a digital age. By banning open and honest communication through social networking sites, a probable scenario is that a teacher or group of teachers complains about working conditions on these social networking sites but does so anonymously. The complaint might be easy to address, but without communication, it soon snowballs into complete dissention. Does the anonymous complaint help the school, staff, or overall school culture? This is juxtaposed with school leaders that permit this type of online communication, where teachers take full responsibility for their actions. As a result, schools are able to track back the complaint and open the discussion to find an amenable and useful solution.

MOVING FORWARD

So how can educators, as a profession, move forward? Looking at the business industry may yield a useful model. In 2005, IBM crowdsourced guidelines from their employees who wanted to engage in social networking websites. Thus, the stakeholders were active participants in crafting their own acceptable use policy for social networking websites. Some essential elements of the IBM co-constructed acceptable use policy for the use of social networking websites included the following: trust employees to exercise personal responsibility, be transparent and honest with anonymity, content posted should be consistent with one's work since they are identified as being an IBM employee, own the online conversation by using the first person voice, use a disclaimer stating that online content represents the social network website user's opinions and not that of the institution, protect confidential information, respect copyright and fair use laws, do not comment or add to rumors, respect the online audience, add value to the conversation, own up to mistakes, and most important, ensure social networking website activities do not interfere with your regular job. Each of these points used by the IBM corporation in its acceptable use policies involving employee use of social networking websites is directly applicable to today's teachers who blog, host or contribute to wikis, create videos, or engage in social networking websites.

The act of restricting a particular teacher's voice concerning school-related online content on social networking websites without using district-owned technology goes much further than simply being a constitutional right of a teacher's freedom of speech or expression. This is a choice school officials make between restricting versus fostering human capital. Posting online content on the Internet is permanent. Once it is posted, the writer loses control of its location, its use, and its voice. Therefore, it is essential that schools proactively enact acceptable use policies that respect the teacher's voice. The policy and actions must place responsibility in the hands of the teacher by making them aware of the potential positive as well as negative impacts their online voices may have on the schools as well as on the students in their classrooms.

COUNTERPOINT: Bruce Umpstead
Michigan Department of Education

The recent impact of social networking websites has been international in scope. For example, much has been reported of the significance of social networking's role in the recent civil unrest in the Middle East, specifically Iran, Egypt, and Libya. So much so, the 2009 civil protest in Iran was called the "Twitter Revolution":

> There was one group in Egypt that was one of the key groups in getting people out on the street. . . . Last week in a matter of days they went from 20,000 fans to 80,000 fans. . . . We can see that these sites were used in order to get the word out about how to bypass checkpoints, how to get across bridges, how to get to places where people wanted to demonstrate. So it was a critical tool in getting people out into the streets. (Hudson, 2011)

However, the speed of communicating via social networking websites and the permanence of the content posted on such websites should concern today's school administrators. This counterpoint essay argues that teachers who use popular social networking websites, such as Facebook, to post online content involving school issues should be strongly dissuaded from doing so and even disciplined in many instances, even if the online messages were posted during the teacher's personal time and without the use of any school resources. The ethical and moral responsibilities of today's teachers require that some of their personal freedoms, including the ability to post online content about school-related matters on their own time and without the use of school resources on social networking websites, should be restricted.

SOCIAL NETWORKING WEBSITES: A CONCERN FOR TODAY'S TEACHERS

This counterpoint essay argues that, given their unique and important role as educators of legal minors, today's elementary, middle, and high school teachers should be restricted from and disciplined for posting online information involving school-related issues or concerns on social networking websites, even if this online information is posted on a teacher's own time and without the use of school resources. In 2005, when teacher Anna Land left her house for a bachelorette party held in conjunction with the annual Jobbie Nooner festival on Lake St. Clair in Michigan, she had no intention of establishing national notoriety, state case law, or local school district policy for teacher disciplinary action related to teacher use of social networking websites. According to the appellate case, Land was unaware that she was photographed drinking alcohol that was dispensed through an anatomically correct male mannequin. The young teacher was completely surprised and embarrassed to discover these pictures were posted on a social networking website when students began circulating the salacious photos two years after the party. The social networking site immediately took down the pictures at her request, but it was too late. To this day, a properly worded search on Google Images search engine retrieves the digital images that almost cost Land her teaching career.

After two years of unpaid administrative leave and immeasurable emotional strain, Land was reinstated to her middle school classroom after fighting through the Michigan Tenure Commission, district court, and court of appeals. The appeals court found she had violated no law and behaved within reasonable expectations given the adult event in which she participated. The decision appeared to turn on Land's lack of knowledge and approval of the posting of the pictures for public view. One has to wonder what the result would have been had Land posted the pictures to her personal Facebook social networking page or forwarded the pictures to friends using her mobile cell phone. Land was suspended without pay for two years for lewd behavior off school property. Fortunately for Land, the Michigan Court of Appeals found in her favor, determining that the behavior was legal and the personal information was posted without her consent or approval.

Land's case provides fair warning to educators everywhere of the need to act responsibly when creating and posting online personal information on the

Internet, especially on social networking websites, even when the content is created on their own time, without the use of school technology resources. The pervasive combination of social networking websites inside and outside of schools makes this an increasingly salient topic of professional practice. Issues of cyberbullying and sexting make the use of social networking websites a hot-button topic in education, especially when considering the important role provided teachers in our society. Respect and responsibility accompany the high moral standard assigned to those who educate our children. To reinforce the importance placed on the proper role-modeling by teachers, especially those teaching in elementary and secondary schools, many states have adopted ethics codes and many schools have enacted personnel policies that clarify and solidify lines of conduct for becoming today's educators. The best approach for educators to take would be to develop informed attitudes and practices regarding these guidelines and self-monitor and police the sharing of personal and professional information using social networking websites.

CYBERBULLYING AND SEXTING: THE DARK SIDE OF SOCIAL NETWORKING WEBSITES

Serious recent issues, such as cyberbullying and sexting, continue to plague the efforts of teachers eager to open up traditional classrooms and schools to social networking technologies. Perhaps the suicide of student Megan Meier of Dardenne Prairie, Missouri, is the starkest example of the dark side of social networking. News accounts reported that Megan committed suicide after an exchange of hostile online messages with a boy who had befriended her on Myspace, another social networking site. The boy's online persona, it turned out, was fake, a cybercharacter created by Megan's neighbors for the sole purpose of bullying her. Her tragic story served as a rallying cry for advocates calling for stronger online protections for today's students. The states of Arizona, Kansas, Massachusetts, Nevada, New Hampshire, and Oregon have currently passed anti-cyberbullying measures. Social networking websites, such as Myspace and Facebook, also tightened policies and strengthened cyberbullying protections.

Using social networking websites to bully someone online is a practice not reserved exclusively for adolescents. Unfortunately, the news is also full of accounts of poor adult online behavior on social networking websites, including by teachers. Online-based sexting is another hot-button topic related to social networking websites. A recent sexting case involving an eighth-grade student named Isaiah and two middle school classmates from Lacey, Washington, tells the story of the potential negative consequences of sexting.

As *The New York Times* reported, Isaiah and his friends were charged and arrested for disseminating child pornography, a Class C felony, for forwarding a naked photo of Margarite, Isaiah's 13-year-old former girlfriend. The text went viral, destroying Margarite's reputation and psyche in the process. Eventually, the charges were lowered to a gross misdemeanor of telephone harassment (i.e., bullying), and the sentence was reduced to community service, giving presentations to other students on the hazards of sexting.

The students and legal minors in the previous case were subject to prosecution, it turns out, not because they forwarded a naked picture, but because the person in the picture was a minor, under 18 years of age. Constitutionally, sexting is considered protected free speech if exchanged between two consenting adults, and it seems a widely accepted practice, even among people of retirement age.

SOCIAL NETWORKING AND TEACHER DISCIPLINARY ACTION

Because of the unique nature of their profession, today's teachers face higher expectations in their personal and professional life compared to most adults at-large in society today. Our society assumes high moral and ethical character demonstrated by the adults who educate our children. These expectations for proper teacher behavior are typically codified in state codes of ethics and teacher tenure laws that stipulate unbecoming conduct for which teachers can and should be disciplined. A recent incident in Paterson, New Jersey, involving a teacher's lapse in judgment when using social networking websites generated headline-grabbing attention.

The New York Times reported that a first-grade teacher was suspended with pay after posting to her Facebook page that "she felt like a warden overseeing future criminals" (Hu, 2011). The community was outraged at the lack of mutual respect shown by the teacher toward her students and their families. Her defamatory comments on a private personal website stirred significant parent acrimony and community outrage that led to disciplinary action. It appears the school district had sufficient grounds for disciplinary action based on this single online indiscretion when one considers how her conduct violated the New Jersey Professional Standards for Teachers and School Leaders (Librera, Eyck, Doolan, Brady, & Aviss-Spedding, 2004):

> *Standard 2: Human Growth and Development*
>   Teachers shall understand how children and adolescents develop and
>   learn in a variety of school, family and community contexts and provide

opportunities that support their intellectual, social, emotional and physical development.

Standard 3: Diverse Learners
Teachers shall understand the practice of culturally responsive teaching.

The teacher's story from Paterson, New Jersey, is placid in comparison to the bombastic circumstances surrounding teacher Natalie Munroe, who was suspended without pay from Central Bucks East High School in Bucks County, Pennsylvania, because of comments made on a personal weblog. *Time* magazine wrote of Munroe's situation:

> When high school English teacher Natalie Munroe had a bad day at school, she didn't just vent to her husband: she took it to her blog. Titled "Where are we going, and why are we in this handbasket?" and all but unknown to the world until earlier this month, Munroe's website served as a chronicle of her "utterly loathsome" students. In one post, she advises students to go get jobs with the trash company. In another, she calls them "rude, disengaged, lazy whiners." In yet another she doesn't mince words, proclaiming, "There's no other way to say this: I hate your kid." Now Munroe, who has been temporarily suspended from her position, finds herself in the middle of a swirling online debate—not over what she did, but over what she said about the sometimes harsh realities of the 21st century classroom. (Webley, 2011, ¶ 1)

While Munroe's attorney claimed First Amendment rights in the case, her online communications clearly violated Pennsylvania's Code of Professional Practice and Conduct for Educators, which calls for professional educators to abide by the following expectations:

- Consistent and equitable treatment of students, fellow educators, and parents
- Respect for the civil rights of all and not discriminate on the basis of race, national or ethnic origin, culture, religion, sex or sexual orientation, marital status, age, political beliefs, socioeconomic status, disabling condition, or vocational interest
- Value of diversity in educational practice
- Impartation of principles of good citizenship and societal responsibility
- Exhibition of acceptable and professional language and communication skills in oral and written communications with parents, students, and

staff that reflects sensitivity to the fundamental human rights of dignity, privacy, and respect

- Appropriate judgment and communication when responding to issues within the educational environment

The cases of the Paterson, New Jersey, first-grade teacher and Natalie Munroe have not been litigated at this writing; however, these educators may face what I believe will be tenure commissions and courts less favorable than those in Michigan because they willfully posted incendiary content online for public consumption.

SCHOOLS STRENGTHENING PERSONNEL REGULATIONS

Currently, public school districts are wasting no time reacting to this litigation by strengthening personnel regulations and acceptable computer use policies that govern educator and student use of social media. Reese-Puffer Schools, a small school district in west Michigan, provides a recent example. The school district made local news by drafting a social media networking conduct policy. Steve Edwards, district superintendent, was generous enough to share a draft of the policy and explained that the district was attempting to eliminate the posting of questionable activities and commentary by teachers when using social media and prohibit fraternization between teachers and students through social technology and mobile technologies that could lead to illegal misconduct.

CONCLUSION

Many schools continue to ban the use of social networking sites by teachers and students on school property, even as more and more schools adopt educational technology that incorporates social networking technologies. This counterpoint essay has highlighted several instances that provide fair warning to educators of the need to act responsibly when using social networking websites, regardless of whether teachers are creating and posting personal information for student consumption or creating content for purely private use on their own time and without the use of school resources. It is even fair to say that teachers must even more vigorously regulate their use of social networking websites based on being in the education profession. The posting of online information becomes a permanent record. The lasting legacy of this online information poses unique and serious challenges to today's educators. In many cases, teachers are seen as role models in the community. Similar to police officers who are always identified in that role whether or not they are officially on duty, many teachers are always identified in their role as educator, whether or not they are in the classroom. This special role of educators justifies the fact that school administrators should be able to discipline teachers for online content about the school even if these online postings were done on a teacher's own time and without the use of any school resources.

Ultimately, it makes sense that educators would adopt safe social networking website practices. These practices include removing students from personal social networks, refraining from posting defamatory comments about students, administrators, and the community, and avoiding the sharing of information and photos that are morally questionable or sexually suggestive. While these safeguards represent heightened restrictions of personal expression for today's teachers, they provide means of satisfying the high ethical and moral requirements placed on teachers by society as educators of our children. These heightened ethical and moral requirements placed on today's teachers properly justify the increased restrictions placed on teacher's online content involving school matters on social networking websites.

FURTHER READINGS AND RESOURCES

Brady, K. P. (2008). The promises and pitfalls of social networking websites. *School Business Affairs, 74*(9), 24–28.

Edwards, S. (2011, March). Social media networking conduct. *Reese-Puffer School's Employee Manual*, Section 5201 (draft).

Hu, W. (2011, April 2). Paterson teacher suspended over a post on Facebook. *The New York Times*, p. A17. Retrieved from http://www.nytimes.com/2011/04/02/nyregion/02facebook.html

Hudson, J. (2011, January 31). The "Twitter Revolution" debate: The Egyptian test case. *The Atlantic Wire*. Retrieved from http://www.theatlanticwire.com/global/2011/01/the-twitterrevolution-debate-the-egyptian-test-case/21296

Librera, W. L., Eyck, R. T., Doolan, J., Brady, J., & Aviss-Spedding, E. (2004). *New Jersey professional standards for teachers and school leaders*. Retrieved from http://www.nj.gov/education/profdev/profstand/standards.pdf

Moore, L. (2011, March 12). Teachers' Facebook pages face scrutiny in Reeths-Puffer. *The Muskegon Chronicle*. Retrieved from http://www.mlive.com/news/muskegon/index.ssf/2011/03/teachers_facebook_pages_face_s.html

National School Boards Association. (2007). *Creating and connecting: Research and guidelines on online social and educational networking*. Retrieved from http://www.nsba.org/site/docs/41400/41340.pdf

Pennsylvania Code of Professional Practice and Conduct for Educators: http://www.pacode.com/secure/data/022/chapter235/chap235toc.html

Webley, K. (2011, February 18). How one teacher's angry blog sparked a viral classroom debate. *Time*. Retrieved from http://www.time.com/time/nation/article/0,8599, 2052123,00.html#ixzz1L3nObEQo

Court Cases and Statutes

Children's Internet Protection Act, P.L. 106–554, 114 Stat. 2763 *et seq.* (2000).
Family Educational Rights and Privacy Act, 20 U.S.C. § 1232g (2006).

Should school administrators have greater authority to discipline students for acts of cyberbullying and cyberharassment?

POINT: Philip T. K. Daniel, *Ohio State University*

COUNTERPOINT: Patrick D. Pauken, *Bowling Green State University*

OVERVIEW

According to the most current research available at the Cyberbullying Research Center, estimates of the number of youth who suffer from cyberbullying abuse and harassment vary widely, ranging from a low of 10% to more than 40%, depending on the age of the student and how cyberbullying abuse and harassment are formally defined. According to Sameer Hinduja and Justin W. Patchin, cyberbullying research experts and codirectors of the Cyberbullying Research Center, cyberbullying is defined as when someone "repeatedly makes fun of another person online or repeatedly picks on another person through email or text message or when someone post something online about another person they don't like." More generally, cyberbullying has been defined as the use of communication-based technologies—including e-mail, cell phones, text messages, instant messaging, and most recently social networking sites—to facilitate deliberate, repeated, and hostile behavior by an individual or a group toward another. Nonetheless, it is clear that the negative outcomes associated with the cyberbullying of other students are a growing problem in today's schools. Additionally, the exact role of school administrators when it comes to disciplining students for acts of cyberbullying is under debate.

This chapter examines the debate regarding what authority today's school administrators have in terms of disciplining students for acts of cyberbullying. As communication via the Internet and other electronic media has become habit for so many students, the act of bullying has likewise evolved to now occupy the virtual as well as the physical environment. This new form of bullying, where students can harass or intimidate their fellow students through electronic means, has been termed *cyberbullying*. Cyberbullying, which is sometimes referred to as online social cruelty or electronic bullying, may involve sending mean, vulgar, or threatening messages or images; posting sensitive, private information, and/or lies about another person; pretending to be someone else to make that person look bad; or intentionally excluding someone from an online group. Some scholars believe that cyberbullying is now the modern form of bullying. Based on the rising incidences of abuse and suicide, some physicians and medical organizations have described cyberbullying as an emerging public health problem. Nonetheless, many educators are currently unsure and/or unaware of whether and when they have legal authority to regulate student expression and behavior in the form of cyberbullying.

While school officials appear to have their hands tied by prevailing American jurisprudence, elected officials have been somewhat more responsive. Quite a number (45 of 50) of states have enacted antibullying educational legislation. Of those, 31 states have antibullying laws that include electronic harassment, and 6 states have antibullying laws that specifically mention cyberbullying. Although this legislation is a step in the right direction, problems do exist. Most important, such legislation lacks consistent language among states that would uniformly recognize the authority of educators to regulate student conduct that takes the form of cyberbullying. In addition, there is little uniformity of language in general and a great disparity of what behavior is actionable or protected.

In his point essay, author Phillip T. K. Daniel (Ohio State University) argues that today's school administrators must be equipped with the legal authority to discipline students who cyberbully other students when this online abuse and harassment has a negative impact on the school environment. According to Daniel, three primary legal developments—the "substantial disruption" test of a leading landmark student free speech case decided by the U.S. Supreme Court, the use of zero tolerance discipline policies, and the expansion of state-level, anti-cyberbullying legislation—have provided school administrators increased authority to discipline students for acts of cyberbullying.

First, Daniel argues that school administrators must properly determine whether the cyberbullying activities "materially and substantially interfere with the requirements of appropriate discipline in the operation of the school or the rights of others." In other words, Daniel argues that in the landmark student free speech case, *Tinker v. Des Moines Independent Community School District* (1969), the U.S. Supreme Court gave school officials legal guidance in determining a "material and substantial disruption test" indicating that school officials may discipline student speech, even off-campus speech, such as online speech, if that speech materially and substantially disrupts classwork or the overall educational community.

In addition to the legal justification afforded today's school administrators to discipline cyberbullying acts if those acts materially or substantially interfere with the safe and efficient operation of the educational environment, Daniel argues that zero tolerance discipline policies are other means by which school officials can increase their authority to discipline students for cyberbullying acts. According to Daniel, the primary goals of zero tolerance disciplinary policies are to protect the overall health, safety, and welfare of students and school personnel. While zero tolerance policies were originally intended to minimize incidents of school violence, these policies have evolved over time to include nonviolent student offenses, including cyberbullying. Daniel maintains that today's school administrators may justify the use of zero tolerance policies in disciplining students for acts of cyberbullying if a sufficient nexus can be established between the student's cyberbullying behavior and the school context.

Daniel indicates that the third legal justification for the increased authority of school administrators to discipline students for acts of cyberbullying is related to the fact that a number of states have recently passed anti-cyberbullying statutes to protect students. Daniel highlights Massachusetts's antibullying legislation as illustrative of one that not only increases the authority of school administrators to discipline students for cyberbullying but also assists greatly in the identification, documentation, and reporting of cyberbullying incidents in Massachusetts elementary through high schools. Daniel encourages other states to adopt antibullying legislation that includes cyberbullying along with regulating incidents of traditional bullying and harassment.

In his counterpoint essay, Patrick D. Pauken (Bowling Green State University) agrees that cyberbullying is an issue for today's school administrators but indicates that equipping administrators with increased legal authority only addresses part of the problem linked with incidents of the cyberbullying of other students. Instead, Pauken argues that much of the cyberbullying problem lies in a lack of morality or providing enough opportunities for today's students to engage in civil, ethical behavior. More specifically, Pauken maintains that today's school leaders must encourage more moral leadership and civility as alternatives to increased disciplinary measures as a means to control the cyberbullying problem in today's schools.

According to Pauken, the existing research indicates that it is fairly common practice for school administrators to attempt to regulate student conduct of the use of various technologies through law and policies, including acceptable use policies and antibullying codes. However, Pauken questions the effectiveness of antibullying laws and policies as a means to significantly change student behavior. Instead, Pauken argues, what is really needed is creation and maintenance of student learning environments that encourage model agency among school administrators, teachers, staff, and students. In other words, school administrators need to play a vital role in the cultivation of a moral agency that provides ample opportunities for students as well as staff to engage in ethical behavior with one another. Instead of more restrictive laws that provide school administrators with greater authority to discipline students for acts of cyberbullying, a commitment by school administrators to build an ethical school culture by rewarding ethical behavior is a much more effective method of addressing the negative behaviors of students who engage in the cyberbullying of other students. Clearly, the debate of whether today's school administrators should have greater authority to discipline students for acts of cyberbullying will continue as incidents of cyberbullying continue to escalate in schools across the nation.

Kevin P. Brady
North Carolina State University

POINT: Philip T. K. Daniel
Ohio State University

A ll educators should be concerned with the harm that emanates from online-based harassment, such as cyberbullying. Today's school administrators must have the legal authority to discipline students when this activity negatively impacts the school environment. Research demonstrates, for example, that there are direct connections between cyberbullying and suicidal thoughts among children who are the targets of this activity. Students tend to feel victimized and vulnerable, and they in turn become isolated from peers and family, leading to social problems and other difficulties. An important outcome of cyberbullying victimization is the development of psychopathological behavior in the victim; thus the expression and behavior in turn may transform the victim into a future victimizer.

Although the term is often associated with students in school, particularly among adolescents and even preteens, cyberbullying encompasses any activity where a person or people use technology to intimidate, send hurtful messages, or otherwise engage in hostile behavior that has the intent or effect of being harmful. Since the bullying and harassment takes place in cyberspace, cyberbullying requires the use of electronic communication devices, such as computers, mobile phones, or other Internet-access-granting devices.

DIFFERENCES BETWEEN BULLYING AND CYBERBULLYING

Five important differences exist between traditional student bullying and cyberbullying that are worth noting. They include the following:

1. *The victims of cyberbullying, including students and school staff, have profound difficulty escaping the torment.* Cyberbullies are able to send messages much more quickly and to much wider audiences. Whereas traditional methods of schoolhouse bullies confined the victimization to mostly face-to-face interactions, the Internet now allows cyberbullies to reach their intended targets all day, every day. A recent article published in the *Journal of Adolescent Health* reported a staggering 50% increase in online harassment of youth from 2000 to 2005.

2. *Another difference concerns the power of anonymity.* In practice, cyberbullies are capable of hiding their identities, or having their identities protected by

Internet service providers. This veil of secrecy allows cyberbullies to communicate aggressive and hurtful comments that they might not otherwise communicate in person.

3. *The distance between a cyberbully and his or her victim also plays a role in both incentivizing the bully and desensitizing bystanders.* Since cyberbullies operate from behind their electronic devices, they rarely witness the effect of their actions on their victims, enabling them to pitch derogatory and hurtful language at their victims while disregarding the consequences of such behavior.

4. *Cyberbullying also differs from traditional bullying with regard to the role that bystanders play.* While traditional bullying involves a number of bystanders serving different functions, a cyberbully has more power to limit who the bystanders are and what roles they assume.

5. *The consequences of cyberbullying can often be far more permanent than those associated with traditional bullying tactics.* Research shows that cyberbullying causes psychosomatic problems in its victims, and that victims may in turn strike out at unsuspecting others or even hurt themselves.

STUDENT FREEDOM OF SPEECH AND EXPRESSION IN TODAY'S SCHOOLS: A LEGAL OVERVIEW

Over time, legal decisions from United States courts have constructed jurisprudence for student free speech rights in the schoolhouse context that can be described as complex, somewhat dissociative, and in certain instances contradictory. Today's traditional legal framework for student free speech and expression leaves cyberbullying's student victims in a legal gray area, where school administrators and relevant criminal codes are essentially unable to offer them any protection from their online peer tormentors.

The First Amendment to the U.S. Constitution provides students who are disciplined by public school officials for their speech a means to reverse or stop such disciplinary punishments. In the landmark student free speech case, *Tinker v. Des Moines Independent Community School District* (1969), the U.S. Supreme Court announced that school officials may not prohibit symbolic speech, political speech, speech that protests the government, or even the silent speech of students, unless the expression would "materially and substantially interfere with the requirements of appropriate discipline in the operation of the school or the rights of others."

In the *Tinker* case, the Court gave general guidance as to what would not qualify as a material and substantial disruption, but it did not specify what *would* be sufficiently disruptive to warrant censorship. Additionally, the *Tinker*

Court tangentially informed educators that the ruling may also affect off-campus activities that are capable of causing school disruption, stating "conduct . . . *in class or out of it,* which for any reason—whether it stems from time, place, or type of behavior—[that] materially disrupts classwork or involves substantial disorder or invasion of the rights of others is, of course, not immunized by the constitutional guarantee of freedom of speech."

THE "SUBSTANTIAL DISRUPTION" TEST AND STUDENT CYBERBULLYING CASES

Not surprisingly, lower courts have also differed in their most basic interpretations of *Tinker's* controlling language, which has resulted in contradictory holdings. In *Layshock v. Hermitage School District* (2010), for example, the Federal Court of Appeals for the Third Circuit recognized that a student had violated the school's code of conduct regarding unauthorized use of the school's website. It ruled, however, that entering the school district's website to retrieve the principal's photograph and use it without authorization (as opposed to, by comparison, breaking into an office) did not supply enough of a nexus to support a finding of a substantial school disruption. On the other hand, in *J.S. v. Blue Mountain School District* (2010), the same court found that a profile of a school principal that had been created on Myspace was said to be unprotected speech because the student's off-campus cyber-composition did cause substantial school disruption. The court found that because the student had lied about creating the site, along with the fact that there had been a reported downturn in the behavior of the student body because of the profile, such circumstances did cause a substantial disruption of the school. The court also found that the website could cause foreseeable additional disruption, because the profile made allegations of sexual misconduct that bore on the principal's professional reputation.

The Third Circuit agreed to rehear both the *Layshock* and *J.S.* cases *en banc,* meaning that the original decisions issued by three-judge panels would be reviewed by the full 14-member court. Following the review, in a unanimous decision, the court once again affirmed the lower court's decision in the *Layshock* case for essentially the same reasons. In the *J.S.* case, however, by an 8 to 6 majority, the court reversed the lower court's ruling. Here a sharply divided full court disagreed with the panel's conclusion that the false profile would cause substantial disruption to or material interference with the educational process. Since the Third Circuit's decision is binding only in Delaware, New Jersey, Pennsylvania, and the Virgin Islands, litigation will likely continue in other jurisdictions until a definitive decision is handed down by the U.S. Supreme Court.

It should be noted that other courts that have interpreted *Tinker*'s "substantial disruption" standard in the cyberbullying context have devised a variety of factors to help guide them in their decision making. Both the Central District of California and the Eastern District of Missouri have stated that if school administrators or teachers were pulled away from their normal duties to deal with and mitigate the effects of a student's speech, this circumstance weighs in favor of a finding of a substantial disruption. Similarly, the Pennsylvania Supreme Court found a substantial disruption based on evidence that the emotional harm to and subsequent absences of a targeted teacher undoubtedly caused substantial disruption in her classroom and, accordingly, across the school. If the off-campus online speech contains anything considered threatening or violent, according to both the Supreme Court of Pennsylvania and the Western District Court of Pennsylvania, it is more likely that a substantial disruption will be found.

More recently, in *Doninger v. Niehoff* (2011), the Federal Court of Appeals for the Second Circuit found substantial disruption when members of the student council accessed the e-mail account of a parent and sent a mass e-mail to staff and students in the school and to parents protesting the location of a student function. In addition, numerous letters were sent and phone calls were made to school personnel by other students. Moreover, the plaintiff in the decision wrote an entry in her public blog referring to school officials as "douchbags" [sic]. Her expressive behavior resulted in being prevented from running as senior class secretary. Reacting to a First Amendment violation claim, the Second Circuit granted qualified immunity to administrators ruling that these extracurricular service rights were "not clearly established" at the time of the disruption and that the student had no First Amendment right "to engage in such behavior while serving as a class representative."

Altogether, the novelty of cyberbullying in schools, combined with the miniscule amount of case law available that directly addresses cyberbullying issues, has left the schools with a unique and difficult challenge as they attempt to create policies to protect students from the consequences of cyberbullying that are also capable of withstanding judicial scrutiny. When faced with cases involving cyberbullying victims that are either teachers or school administrators, lower courts have generally adopted the substantial disruption framework. Although the right of students to attend school free from psychological harm has rarely been discussed in the courts, most likely due to the fact that cyberbullying case law is dominated by situations involving adult victims, it presents a promising analytical framework for school personnel to wield against cyberbullies' potential First Amendment claims.

ZERO TOLERANCE STUDENT DISCIPLINE POLICIES AND CYBERBULLYING

Zero tolerance legislation is a means by which the federal government, along with a number of states, seeks to protect the health and welfare of students and school personnel. While zero tolerance themed legislation appeared prior to 1999, there is no doubt that the massacre at Columbine High School in April 1999 spurred a national conversation that yielded zero tolerance laws all across the United States. The term *zero tolerance* has come to reference school- or district-wide policies that mandate predetermined, typically harsh consequences or punishments for a wide degree of rule violations.

Even though zero tolerance policies were initially intended to send a "tough on violence" message to students and parents, their scope has been expanded piece by piece. Over time, these policies have come to regulate nonviolent offenses, including bullying and cyberbullying. For cyberbullying, this expansive application now means that school personnel have the authority to discipline students whenever a sufficient nexus can be found between the student's virtual behavior and the school context.

For example, the State of California promotes one of the most comprehensive state policies. For example, under the aegis of the state's zero tolerance law, school officials have the power to suspend or expel students for any of the following activities: extortion; theft; damage to property; threatening or intimidating another student, including by electronic means; the use of obscenity, profanity, or vulgarity; or the defying of school staff. All of these terms may be amply defined. For example, California's code not only punishes the possession of "any controlled substance" but also the possession of any device for preparing, testing, or measuring controlled substances. The term *sexual harassment* is very broadly defined, as it includes unwelcome sexual advances, requests for sexual favors, and any verbal or visual conduct of a sexual nature in an education setting.

These regulations cover all activities that take place to and from school or any school activity, and discretion is left to school officials to determine what constitutes "school grounds" or a "school activity." California public school personnel have interpreted state codes expansively. In one recent California case, a student was recommended for suspension and then ultimately expulsion by an assistant principal for fighting under the school district's zero tolerance code (*T.H. v. San Diego Unified School District*, 2004). A hearing panel found that the student engaged in willful force attempting to cause bodily injury. The student claimed that the state zero tolerance policy violated the

United States Constitution in that it did not permit the assistant principal to recommend a lesser punishment and that, under other legal circumstances, the administrator could have done so. The California Court of Appeals for the Fourth Appellate District disagreed, finding that although the zero tolerance procedures adopted by the school district used language that was different from the language of California's state zero tolerance code, this did not result in a justiciable inconsistency. The court ruled that deference must be given to school districts to carry out the will of the law whenever the health, safety, and welfare of students are at stake.

The California Court of Appeals for the Second District has also endorsed granting school districts flexibility as they seek to achieve particular objectives. In a case involving a dispute over the authority to award points for citizenship and whether a superintendent usurped his powers, the court found that any administrative decision involving a program or school activity that was not in conflict with, inconsistent with, or preempted by law was consistent with proper discretion under California law (*Las Virgenes Educators Association v. Las Virgenes Unified School District*, 2001). That is to say that so long as there are no state regulations or laws to the contrary, a state public school has the authority to issue *any* disciplinary action within the bounds of its student code of conduct in punishing severe bullying or cyberbullying.

Though zero tolerance policies are increasingly controversial, dangerous activity in the school context requires strong and effective action on the part of school personnel, and zero tolerance policies are a reflection of this great need. Protecting the safety of students requires that school administrators be flexible in their responses to harmful behavior. California's code and subsequent judicial decisions should be viewed as model responses to the cyberbullying epidemic.

THE IMPACT OF STATE ANTIBULLYING LEGISLATION ON CYBERBULLYING

A number of states have passed antibullying and even anti-cyberbullying statutes to protect students. The legislative language for some of these states is somewhat vague. One state, however, provides an excellent model that denotes some explanation and, perhaps, a blueprint for emulation.

Antibullying legislation in Massachusetts defines bullying as "written, verbal or electronic expression or a physical act or gesture or any combination thereof, directed at a [school] victim . . ." (An Act Relative to Bullying in Schools, 2010). The Massachusetts statute is alone among the states in containing explicit anti-cyberbullying provisions built into the antibullying provisions, with off-campus applicability. The broad coverage effectively addresses the criticism that state legislation has been largely ineffective in reducing incidents of bullying or cyberbullying because it focuses on specific incidents instead of forcing schools to implement a whole-school approach to bullying. Massachusetts also has one of very few state statutes that require identifying, documenting, and reporting incidents of cyberbullying—not merely disciplining the students involved. These provisions take aim at the tragic fact that most cyberbullying in schools goes unreported. This broad discretion gives schools the power to both punish those responsible and to address the underlying systemic causes of cyberbullying at the same time.

Regardless, cyberbullies will continue to push the envelope and challenge the authority of school administrators to punish speech that has heretofore been made almost sacrosanct by lower court interpretations of the *Tinker* case. In the absence of a U.S. Supreme Court decision, states may consider following the example that Massachusetts has set in "wide-netting" control of cyberbullying by declaring that school districts, through codes of conduct and acceptable use policies that are protected by comprehensive state statutes, may counteract expressive behavior that infringes on the rights of cyberbullied victims or that substantially disrupts the education process.

Following the lead of states such as California and Massachusetts, legislatures should enact anti-cyberbullying statutes within or alongside their own antibullying statutes. A mere difference in geographic origin should not overshadow the fact that both on-campus and off-campus can cause the same level of disruption in school. States that continue to tailor their laws to the current legal standards propagated by *Tinker* enthusiasts may be jeopardizing the welfare of their students.

CONCLUSION

Cyberbullying in today's schools is quickly becoming a worldwide epidemic, and the United States may be at the epicenter of its disastrous consequences. The First Amendment's protections, originally invoked by students wishing to express their political views in the *Tinker* case, have unfortunately been overemphasized by federal district courts, whose opinions have in turn taught school personnel to be wary of disciplining cyberbullies. More troubling, the jurisprudence that these lower courts has developed now insulates cyberbullying conduct that nonetheless potentially threatens the lives of student victims.

This point essay has three recommendations for assisting today's school administrators in addressing the cyberbullying problem in today's schools. First, legislators, school officials, and judges must be aware of the effects of cyberbullying to create much-needed policies that will protect students and discipline cyberbullies. Second, more attention must be paid to the importance of zero tolerance legislation, and the benefits that stem from empowering school administrators with the force of the law. Model legislation and judicial decision making can be found in California, where local officials are granted sufficient latitude in dealing with bullying. Third, states should adopt new anti-bullying legislation or modify their existing legislation to include cyberbullying alongside traditional bullying. The Massachusetts legislature has produced model antibullying legislation that seeks to prevent harmful speech in the school context regardless of its geographic origin. Although cyberbullying may be a recent phenomenon, judges, legislators, and school administrators can curb its destructive influence by proactively pursuing these recommendations.

COUNTERPOINT: Patrick D. Pauken
Bowling Green State University

In his 1998 book *Civility,* Stephen Carter made the following statement: "In contemporary America, we tend to rush toward legislation and regulation— in short, toward coercive means of correction—whenever we spot a problem and believe we have found the solution" (p. 284). In an era plagued by pervasive, dangerous, and often tragic bullying and cyberbullying among young people, there is no question that teachers, school administrators, and other education leaders must play roles in the discipline and education of bullies, in protection and care for victims, and in the creation and maintenance of environments conducive to safety, learning, and positive growth. In furtherance of these roles played, Carter, in his previous statement, makes a necessary point. The responses we offer cyberbullying must be swift, and they must send a message of deterrence, but they also must be long-lasting and send a message of hope for the future.

For at least two reasons, increased legislation and regulation is flawed and incomplete. First, with the present guidance from legislatures and courts, school administrators have sufficient legal authority to discipline students for cyberbullying. Much of this counterpoint essay will address the legal authority school leaders already have in this regard. Second, increased legal authority to discipline students addresses only part of the student cyberbullying problem. Bullying is not solely the result of a lack of rules. It is also the result of a lack of morality and a lack of positive, forward-moving opportunities for children to engage in civil, ethical behavior. The final part of this counterpoint essay will encourage moral leadership, moral education, and civility as alternatives (or at least supplements) to student discipline.

EXISTING STATUTORY AND JUDICIAL AUTHORITY TO DISCIPLINE STUDENTS FOR CYBERBULLYING

For years now, school leaders have attempted to regulate the conduct of students and their use of technology, typically through acceptable use policies and expanded discipline, antiharassment, and antibullying codes (Daniel & Pauken, 1998; Daniel & Pauken, 2002). These leaders are often guided by state and federal statutes and related case law.

State Statutes

Nearly all states and the District of Columbia have enacted laws specifically dealing with bullying and harassment in schools. These laws define applicable terms and require schools to adopt and enforce antibullying policies. According to Ohio Revised Code Annotated section 3313.666(A) (2011): "harassment, intimidation, or bullying" means

> any intentional written, verbal, or physical act that a student has exhibited toward another particular student more than once and the behavior both: (a) causes mental or physical harm to the other student; and (b) is sufficiently severe, persistent, or pervasive that it creates an intimidating, threatening, or abusive educational environment for the other student.

The required policy must include, at a minimum, procedures for reporting, documenting, and investigating the alleged incidents; procedures for notifying the parents or guardians of students involved; strategies for protecting alleged victims; and disciplinary procedures for students guilty of harassment, intimidation, or bullying.

Ohio's antibullying law is similar in many respects to the laws of several other states. But two aspects of the law are worthy of additional comment. First, many states' antibullying provisions make particular reference to technology and cyberspace. Ohio's statute does not include such a reference. The provision's language, however, is easily read to include cyberbullying. There is no explicit restriction in the statute to student conduct that occurs on the physical premises of a school or during school activities. The statute, instead, appears to target the effects of harassment, intimidation, and bullying, regardless of when and where it originates. Therefore, applications of harassment, intimidation, and bullying via electronic media appear viable under Ohio's law. The same can be said for many other states' statutes.

Second, the necessary provisions for student due process include an explicit mention that due process and discipline "which shall not infringe on any student's rights under the first amendment to the Constitution of the United States," according to Ohio Revised Code Annotated section 3313.666(B). As free speech claims are fairly common among students who are disciplined under these state laws, the reference to the First Amendment in Ohio's antibullying law gives leaders further guidance in the enactment and implementation of antibullying policy. As the next section explains, student expression in school settings has been guided very readily by four landmark Supreme Court decisions, and several recent lower court decisions involving students and cyberspace.

Guidance From the U.S. Supreme Court

In *Tinker v. Des Moines Independent Community School District* (1969), the Supreme Court struck down a school district's ban on black armbands worn by students who wished to protest the Vietnam War. The Supreme Court held that public school administrators may not restrict the silent, passive, political speech of students unless that speech substantially disrupts the operation of the school, materially interferes with school discipline, or infringes on the rights of others. In its discussion, the Court stated, "it can hardly be argued that either students or teachers shed their constitutional rights to freedom of speech or expression at the schoolhouse gate" (*Tinker*, 1969, p. 506). The Court held that undifferentiated fear of disturbance is not enough to overcome individual rights to freedom of expression. In other words, administrative action in light of such student expression must be caused by more than the mere desire to avoid the unpleasantness that accompanies an unpopular viewpoint. As loudly as the *Tinker* case rings for students and free speech, the decision also speaks loudly for authority to maintain discipline. With this ruling, and as seen in several recent cases involving student conduct online, school administrators still retain wide discretion to determine whether there is sufficient evidence of material or substantial disruption or whether such disruption can be reasonably forecast under the circumstances.

In 1986, the Court spoke again in *Bethel School District No. 403 v. Fraser*. In the *Bethel* case, a high school junior delivered a speech at a school-sponsored assembly nominating a fellow student for elective office. During the speech, the student referred to his candidate in terms of a graphic, explicit sexual metaphor. Many of the 600 students in attendance laughed; many hooted and hollered; several made physical gestures relating to the words; and others sat there, stunned and bewildered. The student was suspended for three days and was removed from consideration as a graduation speaker. He brought suit. The Supreme Court ultimately held for the school: "It was perfectly appropriate for the school to disassociate itself to make the point to the pupils that vulgar speech and lewd conduct is wholly inconsistent with the 'fundamental values' of public school education" (*Bethel,* 1986, pp. 685–686).

The *Bethel* Court noted that the rights of students in schools are not coextensive with the rights of adults in other settings. As such, the determination of what student speech is appropriate or inappropriate, when spoken in a classroom or in a school assembly, properly rests with the school board. According to the Court, the objective of public education is "the inculcation of fundamental values necessary to the maintenance of a democratic political system" (p. 681). Among these values are civility in public discourse and respect for the rights of others.

Two years later, in *Hazelwood School District v. Kuhlmeier* (1988), the Court gave schools the authority to exercise editorial control over student speech in school-sponsored activities, so long as the restrictions are related to legitimate pedagogical concerns. In the *Hazelwood* case, three high school students filed suit against their public school district and principal after the principal cut two pages of the school-sponsored newspaper to avoid the publication of two articles the principal felt were objectionable, invasive, and inappropriate. The Supreme Court held for the school, stating that "[e]ducators do not offend the First Amendment by exercising editorial control over the style and content of student speech in school-sponsored expressive activities so long as their actions are reasonably related to legitimate pedagogical concerns" (*Hazelwood,* 1988, p. 273).

Admittedly, the *Hazelwood* case is less applicable to cases of cyberbullying, as the bully's conduct is rarely, if ever, a part of school-sponsored activities. But schools must be watchful, so as not to give the impression that they tolerate such conduct. School administrators may exercise greater control over school speech that members of the public might perceive to bear the imprimatur of the school.

Finally, in June 2007, in *Morse v. Frederick,* the U.S. Supreme Court held that a school principal did not violate the First Amendment free speech rights of a student when she suspended the student for unfurling a 14-foot homemade banner with the phrase "BONG HiTS 4 JESUS" across the street from his high school during a school-sanctioned activity. The student argued that the speech was student-generated, nondisruptive, and displayed off school premises. The principal (Morse) and the school argued that the speech violated school policy that prohibited students from displaying messages promoting the use of illegal substances. Morse claimed the sign was inconsistent with the educational mission of the school, and argued that failure to act as she did would give the impression that the school condoned such speech. Frederick, the student, claimed that his speech was designed to be meaningless and funny. He was simply hoping to get on television. Acknowledging these noticeable differences in the interpretation of the banner, the Supreme Court adopted Morse's reading: "we hold that schools may take steps to safeguard those entrusted to their care from speech that can reasonably be regarded as encouraging illegal drug use" (*Morse v. Frederick,* 2007, p. 2622). The majority in the *Morse* case gave educators credit for taking on their necessary roles and gave them the leeway to act reasonably in the face of conduct such as Frederick's.

Application to Student Cyberbullying

For years, when presented with questions of Internet, cyberspace, and other electronic conduct of students, school leaders had to look to old law for help. *Morse v. Frederick* is the first student free speech case decided by the Supreme Court in the cyberspace era. On its own, *Morse*'s decidedly narrow opinion (addressing, it seems, only speech relating to the advocacy or glorification of illegal drug use) offers a little help. Along with the *Tinker, Bethel,* and *Hazelwood* cases, more help is offered. Add state statutes and school policies on bullying and cyberbullying, and much more guidance is offered. In fact, with these laws, school administrators are fully equipped with the authority necessary to discipline students for acts of cyberbullying.

The number of reported lower court cases involving incidents of cyberbullying and other online conduct of students is relatively low at this point; but the decisions are instructive, striking a good balance between individual rights and institutional authority. A central question in most of these cases is whether the school has the authority to discipline at all, given the fact that, in so many cases, the conduct occurs away from school premises and/or after school hours. In situations involving such incidents, the argument that the school lacks authority to discipline generally fares well. For example, in *Killion v. Franklin Regional School District* (2001), a student e-mailed a "top ten list" of disparaging remarks about his school's athletic director to several classmates. The student author was suspended for 10 days after a hard copy of the list was found at school. It was undisputed that a classmate was the one who brought the hard copy to school. The student and his family filed suit alleging both due process and free speech violations. The court found in favor of the student, in part, due to the fact that the student's conduct occurred off premises and that the speech was not disruptive.

Cases similar to *Killion* followed, involving derogatory, controversial, and/or lewd and vulgar comments directed at school employees or classmates, but now made and posted on personal websites (*Beussink v. Woodland R-IV School District,* 1998; *Coy v. Board of Education of North Canton City Schools,* 2002; *J.S. v. Bethlehem Area School District,* 2002; *Mahaffey v. Aldrich,* 2002), blogs (*Doninger v. Niehoff,* 2011), cell phone texts (*Wisniewski v. Board of Education of Weedsport Central School District,* 2007), message boards (*Flaherty v. Keystone Oaks School District,* 2003), web-based social networks (e.g., Myspace or Facebook) (*Evans v. Bayer,* 2010; *J.S. v. Blue Mountain School District,* 2010; *Layshock v. Hermitage School District,* 2010), or YouTube videos (*J.C. ex rel. R. C. v. Beverly Hills Unified School District,* 2010; *Requa v. Kent School District No. 415,* 2007).

Without substantial disruption to school or to the rights of others, or reasonable likelihood of it, courts hold that a school has no authority to punish. In *Mahaffey v. Aldrich* (2002) and *Beussink v. Woodland R-IV School District* (1998), for example, students created webpages on home computers and, while the content on the sites contained language and images of vulgarity and violence (including language critical of the school), there was no evidence of substantial disruption. The student who posted her displeasure over school decisions to a publicly accessible blog was not as fortunate (*Doninger v. Niehoff,* 2011). The student who posted a YouTube video of his teacher was similarly unlucky, with the court upholding his suspension as well (*Requa v. Kent School District No. 415,* 2007), while the students who posted a video that contained disparaging remarks about a classmate won their case, with the court finding no disruption (*J.C. v. Beverly Hills,* 2010).

Finally, two divergent cases involving fake Myspace pages created by students about their schools' administrators also illustrate the importance of location and effect of student online speech. In *Layshock v. Hermitage School District* (2010), the court found that because the fake profile, which contained references to sex, drugs, and alcohol, was created off premises and caused no substantial disruption at school, the school had no authority to discipline. The court in *J.S. v. Blue Mountain School District* (2010) came to the opposite result, finding that the fake profile, which contained similarly harsh content, had caused some disturbance at school. The court in *J.S.* held that potential impact of the content was enough to satisfy the *Tinker* disruption test. *Layshock* and *J.S.* have since been reheard by the full Third Circuit Court of Appeals. After the rehearing, the court stuck with its original decision in *Layshock* but came to a different conclusion in *J.S.* On rehearing, the court held that school officials had failed to show that there was a potential for substantial disruption.

Many of these results may indicate that schools need additional legal authority to discipline cyberbullying. I disagree. Almost certainly, under the current state of the law, both statutory and judicial, schools will be able to connect student cyberbullying to the school and make a successful argument that bullying activity is disruptive, at the very least, to the victim(s) and perhaps to the school as a whole. When the school leaders can show actual or potential substantial disruption at school, regardless of where the conduct originated, the school will have the authority to punish. In addition to the location and effect of student conduct (applying *Tinker*), schools can also point to the content (applying *Bethel* and *Morse*). The *Bethel* Court held that it was appropriate for school leaders to determine that lewd and vulgar speech was contrary to the educational mission of the school. And in *Morse*, the Court gave great credence and leeway to the school leader's "reasonable interpretation" of the meaning of the student's controversial speech. In the world of cyberbullying, the tendency of school leaders to err on the side of the bullying victim(s) and argue that the perpetrator's message has an actual or reasonably likely disruptive effect is very real. And courts may follow suit, disagreeing with the student perpetrator who argues that the message was meant to be harmless commentary. Content-based arguments target harmful conduct closer to its core. There is little question that the "fundamental mission" language from *Bethel* is a powerful tool for school leaders when combating the creativity of inappropriate student speech.

MORAL EDUCATION AND MORAL AGENCY

The current balance in the courts on cases involving student speech in cyberspace is an appropriate one, leaving school administrators necessary authority over cyberbullying and protecting the constitutional rights of students. Student speech that is published off campus; does not cause any disruption to the work of the school or to the rights of others; is not lewd, vulgar, threatening, or advocating illegal or dangerous behavior is generally protected under the First Amendment. But as stated at the outset, regulation of student behavior in reactive, punitive form does not address all of what bullying projects. According to Raymond Fisman (2006), "Changing the law is helpful, but not by itself sufficient to induce change in a corrupt world" (p. 40). What is truly needed to address cyberbullying cannot be legislated from afar with levels of authority higher than those that currently exist. Instead, what is needed is the creation and maintenance of learning environments that encourage and model moral agency among administrators, teachers, staff, and students. Current codes and court decisions may decrease the number of infractions. But the actor's personal code of ethics plays a role as well. So what we need is not additional regulation; we need moral education that includes opportunities for young people to engage in ethical behavior (Cheung & Lee, 2010; Ellwood & Davies, 2010; Steutel, 1997). Or, as the Supreme Court in *Bethel* asserted, the inculcation of values (e.g., civility and respect) is truly the work of the schools.

Aristotle says that living a moral life is a matter of doing well (*eudaimonia*, or happiness), and doing well is a matter of applying appropriate guidelines, or moral virtues, to instances that require them. For Aristotle, moral virtue is acquired by repetition of virtuous acts:

> [W]e acquire the virtues by first practicing them. . . . [W]e become just by performing just acts, temperate by performing temperate acts, brave by performing brave acts. . . . If this were not so, there would have been no need for a teacher; all would have been *born* good or bad at their respective skills. . . . Thus, in short, dispositions arise from like activities. (1963, pp. 28–29)

Aristotle's *Ethics* should not be read to indicate that virtue is attained by mere habit. Virtuous people not only act the right way, but they do so "for the right reasons and with the proper accompanying emotions" (Milliken, 2006, pp. 320–321). This is where "moral education" plays a significant role. How we are taught makes a difference. According to Aristotle, we can't do "good" acts unless we do them (1) with knowledge that they are good, (2) with the choice of the good acts because they are good (for their own sakes), and (3) as a person of "good character" would do them (Aristotle, 1963, p. 32; see also Milliken, 2006, pp. 321–322). Educators must focus their energy not on punishment, but on teaching and modeling ethical behavior. Do we become ethical by doing ethical things, or merely by refraining from doing unethical things? At the risk of making it sound easier than it is, it is my argument that we become ethical by doing ethical things, and that ethical people do not engage in bullying behaviors. Moral agency entails a responsibility to act ethically—to do ethical things. The call to educators, therefore, is not to encourage more restrictive law, but instead to build an ethics culture in their schools by teaching and modeling the practice of ethics and by providing opportunities and inspiration for others to do the same. Become ethical by doing ethical things, and the students, teachers, staff, parents, and community members will follow. Inevitably they will model.

FURTHER READINGS AND RESOURCES

Aristotle. (1963). *Ethics* (J. Warrington, Trans.). New York: J. M. Dent & Sons. (Original work written 350 BCE)

Carter, S. L. (1998). *Civility: Manners, morals, and the etiquette of democracy.* New York: Basic Books.

Cheung, C., & Lee, T. (2010). Improving social competence through character education. *Evaluation and Program Planning, 33,* 255–263.

Cyberbullying Research Center: http://www.cyberbullying.us

Daniel, P. T. K. (1998). Violence and the public schools: Student rights have been weighed in the balance and found wanting. *Journal of Law and Education, 27,* 573–614.

Daniel, P. T. K., & McCormick, S. (2009). Technological advances, school expression, and the authority of school officials. *Education Law Reporter, 248,* 553–578.

Daniel, P. T. K., & Pauken, P. D. (1998). Authority, rights, and issues on the way to using the information highway: Cyberspace and schools. *Journal of Urban & Contemporary Law, 54,* 109–155.

Daniel, P. T. K., & Pauken, P. D. (2002). The electronic media and school violence: Lessons learned and issues presented. *West's Education Law Reporter, 164,* 1–43.

David-Ferdon, C., Feldman Hertz, M., & Electronic Media. (2007). Violence and adolescents: An emerging public health problem. *Journal of Adolescent Health, 41,* A1–A4.

Ellwood, C., & Davies, B. (2010). Violence and the moral order in contemporary schooling: A discursive analysis. *Qualitative Research in Psychology, 7,* 85–98.

Fisman, R. (2006, May 22). Reforming Tony Soprano's morals: Carrots and sticks alter corrupt behavior less than you might think. *Forbes, 177*(11), 40.

Kim, Y. S., & Leventhal, B. (2008). Bullying and suicide: A review. *International Journal of Adolescent Medicine and Health, 115*(2), 357–363.

King, A. (2010). Constitutionality of cyberbullying laws: Keeping the online playground safe for both teens and free speech. *Vanderbilt Law Review, 63,* 845–884.

Milliken, J. (2006). Aristotle's aesthetic ethics. *The Southern Journal of Philosophy, 44*(2), 319–339.

Sourander, A., Klomek, A. B., Ikonen, M., Lindroos, J., Luntamo, T., Koskelainen, M., et al. (2010). Psychosocial risk factors associated with cyberbullying among adolescents. *Archive of General Psychiatry, 67*(7), 720–728.

Steutel, J. W. (1997). The virtue approach to moral education: Some conceptual clarifications. *Journal of Philosophy of Education, 31*(3), 395–407.

Willard, N. (2007). The authority and responsibility of school officials in responding to cyberbullying. *Journal of Adolescent Health, 41,* S64–S65.

Court Cases and Statutes

An Act Relative to Bullying in Schools, Chapter 92 of the Acts of 2010, codified at 71 M.G.L.A. § 370. Retrieved from http://www.malegislature.gov/Laws/SessionLaws/Acts/2010/Chapter92

Bethel School District No. 403 v. Fraser, 478 U.S. 675 (1986).

Beussink v. Woodland R-IV School District, 30 F. Supp.2d 1175 (E.D. Mo. 1998).

Coy v. Board of Education of North Canton City Schools, 205 F. Supp.2d 791 (N.D. Ohio 2002).

Doninger v. Niehoff, No. 09-1452-cv, 09-1601-cv, 09-2261-cv, 2011 U.S. App. LEXIS 8441 (2d Cir. Apr. 25, 2011).

Evans v. Bayer, 684 F.Supp.2d 1365 (S.D. Fla. 2010).

Flaherty v. Keystone Oaks School District, 247 F. Supp.2d 698 (W.D. Pa. 2003).

Hazelwood School District v. Kuhlmeier, 484 U.S. 260 (1988).

J.C. ex rel. R. C. v. Beverly Hills Unified School District, 711 F. Supp. 2d 1094 (C.D. Cal. 2010).

J.S. ex rel. H. S. v. Bethlehem Area School District, 807 A.2d 847 (Pa. 2002).

J.S. v. Bethlehem Area School District, 569 Pa. 638, 807 A.2d 847 (Pa. 2002).

J.S. v. Blue Mountain School District, 593 F.3d 286 (3d Cir. 2010), *vacated, reh'g en banc granted,* 2010 U.S. App. LEXIS 7342 (3d Cir, Apr. 9, 2010), 2011 WL 2305973 (3d Cir. 2011).

Killion v. Franklin Regional School District, 136 F. Supp. 2d 446, 455 (W.D. Pa. 2001).

Las Virgenes Educators Association v. Las Virgenes Unified School District, 102 Cal. Rptr. 2d 901 (Cal. App. 2001).

Layshock v. Hermitage School District, 496 F. Supp. 2d 587 (W.D. Pa. 2007), *affirmed* 593 F.3d 249 (3d Cir. 2010)*, rehearing en banc granted, opinion vacated* (3d Cir. April 9, 2010), *affirmed* 2011 WL 2305970 (3d Cir.).

Mahaffey v. Aldrich, 236 F. Supp.2d 779 (E.D. Mich. 2002).

Morse v. Frederick, 127 S. Ct. 2618 (2007).

Ohio Rev. Code Ann. §3313.666 (2011).

Requa v. Kent School District No. 415, 492 F. Supp.2d 1272 (W.D. Wash. 2007).

San Rafael Elementary School District v. State Board of Education, 87 Cal. Rptr. 2d 67 (Cal. App. 1999).

T.H. v. San Diego Unified School District, 19 Cal. Rptr. 3d 532 (Cal. App. 2004).

Tinker v. Des Moines Independent Community School District, 393 U.S. 503 (1969).

Wisniewski v. Board of Education of Weedsport Central School District, 494 F.3d 34 (2d Cir. 2007).

11

Should administrators have greater authority to discipline students for false posts about school personnel on social networking websites?

POINT: Curtis R. Nash, *University of Dayton*

COUNTERPOINT: Korrin M. Ziswiler, *University of Dayton*

OVERVIEW

For the overwhelming majority of today's middle and high school students, online communication is a significant method of their daily communication with peers as well as the outside world. The fairly recent and growing popularity of online social networking websites, such as Facebook and Myspace, have only reinforced the fact that many students are comfortable communicating with each another within an online environment. As direct evidence of social networking website's popularity, especially among middle and high school students in the United States, a 2007 study by the National School Boards Association (NSBA) revealed that a staggering 96% of surveyed students with online access reported accessing and using a social networking website. However, scores of school administrators across the country have not welcomed the use of social networking websites, mainly due to the potential student safety and privacy concerns associated with student use of social networking websites and the potential negative impact on the school. For example, recent statistics indicate that approximately half of U.S. public schools have taken some formal disciplinary actions as a method to prevent students from accessing these social networking websites on school premises.

By definition, social networking websites are websites where individuals can post online profiles, such as messages, photographs, or videos, and, when invited to do so, view the online profiles of others who are members of a particular social networking website, such as Facebook or Myspace. Once a person has created an online profile on a social networking website, he or she can become part of larger online social networks by linking their personal online profile with others who have similar interests, such as schools attended or favorite professional sport teams.

In this chapter, authors Curtis R. Nash (University of Dayton) and Korrin M. Ziswiler (University of Dayton) debate the contentious, and legally undecided, issue of whether school administrators should have greater authority to discipline students for false online posts about school personnel on a social networking website. In essence, the issue involves striking the proper balance between students' free speech rights and school administrators' duty and responsibility to maintain order and discipline in their schools.

In his point essay, Nash maintains that today's school administrators should be given increased authority to discipline students who post false information about school personnel on social networking websites, whether the student's online statements were written on school grounds or off-school grounds. According to Nash, the key legal determinant is not whether the student's online speech takes place on or off school grounds. Instead, school administrators need to appropriately determine whether the student's false online statements involving school personnel caused a "material and substantial disruption" in the operation of the school.

As evidence, Nash cites two recent Third Circuit decisions from Pennsylvania, *Layshock v. Hermitage School District* and *J.S. v. Blue Mountain School District*. Both cases involved students who posted false online information about school personnel on a popular social networking website. While the initial legal decisions in the two cases differed, the judges in both cases reasoned that in order for school administrators to properly discipline students for posting false online content about school personnel on social networking websites, the students' online speech must have a potential for "foreseeable substantial disruption of the school." Nash argues that, in many instances, student false online postings about school personnel on social networking websites can be determined to be disruptive within a school environment. When this becomes the case, Nash argues, school administrators have the proper legal authority to discipline students for this behavior regardless of whether the student created the online posting at the school or in the privacy of his or her own home.

In addition to being potentially disruptive to the school environment, Nash makes the argument that student online postings on social networking websites not only disseminate quickly to large groups of online followers, but online speech remains permanently in the public domain of the Internet. While social networking sites are becoming a popular way for today's students to vent their frustrations, many students are unaware of the lasting legacy of their online speech and expression. The permanent nature of online speech, Nash argues, also should give today's school administrators greater authority to discipline students for their false online postings about school personnel on social networking websites.

In her counterpoint response, Ziswiler argues that today's school administrators should have considerably less authority to discipline students for false online posts about school personnel on social networking websites. Ziswiler's primary argument is that disciplining students for their online speech and expression on social networking websites fails to address the main cause of the problem. According to Ziswiler, it is much more important that today's school administrators provide teachable moments and play a significant role in educating students in the responsible and ethical use of the Internet. Ziswiler argues that the fear of increasing school administrator authority to discipline students for false online statements about school personnel on social networking sites is that school leaders will overstep their bounds. More specifically, Ziswiler maintains, increased disciplinary authority will allow school administrators to interpret merely offensive student speech, which is currently protected, and incorrectly label it as slanderous or defamatory student speech, which is not protected. Additionally, Ziswiler argues that increasing school administrators' authority to discipline students for online speech on social networking websites limits the rights of parents to discipline their own children for this type of behavior.

Both authors agree that disciplinary actions imposed by school administrators for students posting false online comments about school personnel on social networking websites is a reactive approach to dealing with a specific type of student behavior. In his point essay, Nash maintains that this type of reactive behavior is usually positive. Moreover, providing today's school administrators with greater authority to discipline students for the posting of false information on social networking websites does not restrict school leaders from creating and cultivating programs that address the need to educate students about the responsible and ethical use of the Internet, specifically social networking websites. Even with all the education in the world, Nash argues, administrators must have in place both the proper disciplinary tools and authority because not all students will become good "digital citizens." Since school administrators need to protect the entire school from even the potential of disruption, they must be given the proper legal authority to discipline students for their online behaviors.

Overall, this chapter centers on how school administrators cultivate good digital citizenship among students. Would increased disciplinary measures in the form of student suspensions and expulsions act as a proper deterrent to bad student online behaviors? Can school officials teach responsible and ethical Internet behavior? Both authors agree on the end goal: students who behave responsibly and ethically when using today's social networking websites. The disagreement arises regarding how we successfully get to that point.

This issue remains contentious and is worth watching since it is likely to reach the U.S. Supreme Court in the not-too-distant future. The Third Circuit recently revisited the question and issued new decisions in both the *Layshock* and *J.S.* cases. In each case, the court overturned disciplinary action taken by school authorities against students who had created false profiles of their principals that were unflattering and even lewd. Since the profiles were created on home computers, the court ruled that school officials were limited in their abilities to discipline the students, even though the profiles were posted on social networking sites that could be accessed at school and specifically targeted school personnel.

Kevin P. Brady
North Carolina State University

POINT: Curtis R. Nash
University of Dayton

Student speech and expression cases involving today's social networking websites fall under what is commonly known as the *Tinker* standard (*Tinker v. Des Moines Independent Community School District,* 1969) in which a "material and substantial disruption" in a school must be proven in order for school administrators to discipline certain student speech or expression (Paulson, Policinski, Haynes, Hudson, & Villager, 2011). Such a disruption in a school environment is inherent in today's social networking websites because of social networks' innate ability to rapidly disseminate messages to a wide online audience. Also, such a disruption exists with today's social networking websites because they are in the public domain and a permanent electronic record of every online conversation is saved and archived. Thus, since false statements communicated on social networking websites remain permanent, and since those messages can be communicated quickly and widely, such a "material and substantial disruption" exists. This point essay takes the position that school administrators should be given greater authority to discipline students who post false online information about school personnel on social networking sites.

According to Nancy Willard (2011), the current director of the Center for Safe and Responsible Internet Use, there are a growing number of students using today's social networking websites, including Facebook, Myspace, Twitter, LiveJournal, and many others over the past few years. Willard describes the process and function of social networking websites, in which students register and establish online profiles that list an individual's personal information and photos on these social networking websites. Additionally, students make online connections or links with other members who share interests or connections. Finally, Willard suggests that students who use these social networking websites engage in many forms of communication, as well as information sharing, including viewing one another's personal web pages, blogs, and discussion groups.

Willard further states that the harmful or illegal behavior of today's users is often associated with these social networking websites, but the social networking website technologies themselves are generally not the problem. That is, social networking websites do not actively promote or condone negative behavior, such as posting false information about school employees. As such, with millions of active members on social networking websites, the owners of these websites cannot be expected to effectively regulate the online behaviors of all their members. Given that so many students actively use social networking websites, instances of harmful, negative, and illegal behavior on the part of students through social networking websites has pervaded schools, which has manifested in both disciplinary issues between students and school authorities as well as increased the possibility of litigation over these issues.

STUDENT FREE SPEECH AND EXPRESSION

Prior to the Internet, there had been a wide array of disciplinary cases brought before the courts involving student speech and expression in schools. The heart of these court proceedings centers on a student's First Amendment right to free speech and expression. A student's right to free speech has been curbed in some areas, including their speech and expression in school-sponsored publications; instances of vulgar, lewd, obscene, and otherwise offensive speech; or when a material and substantial disruption in the school takes place.

To date, three separate categories of student free speech and expression have been developed by the U.S. Supreme Court. As stated previously, cases involving student speech fall into one of three categories of legal standards established by the court (Paulson, Policinski, Haynes, Hudson, & Villager, 2011). Each one deals with particular aspects of student speech and is applied to cases accordingly. The first category is called the *Fraser* standard and is often used in student free speech cases involving vulgarity, lewdness, obscenity, or other offensive speech. The second category refers to the *Hazelwood* standard and applies to school-sponsored publications, and the third category of student speech falls under the *Tinker* standard.

The Fraser standard refers to the Supreme Court's decision in *Bethel School District v. Fraser* (1986) where a high school senior gave a speech filled with sexual innuendoes in front of the student body. The school found that the student had violated school policy and, thus, suspended him. The American Civil Liberties Union (ACLU) sued the school district on behalf of Fraser and the case eventually made its way up to the Supreme Court. The Court ruled in favor of the school district, noting that the school's policy on disruptive behavior did not violate Fraser's First Amendment rights. Commonly, the Fraser standard is used in cases involving vulgarity, lewdness, obscenity, and other offensive speech (First Amendment Center, 2011).

The second category of school speech, outlined by the First Amendment Center (2011), the Hazelwood Standard on school-sponsored speech, came from *Hazelwood School District v. Kuhlmeier* (1988), where the Supreme Court ruled that public school administrators can limit what appears in school-sponsored student publications, such as a school-sponsored student newspaper. The *Hazelwood* case centered on content printed in a high school newspaper that was published as part of a journalism class. The principal at the school was given an advance copy of the paper that included articles about teenage pregnancy and divorce. The principal, concerned about the anonymity of those interviewed for the stories and that the content may be too mature for the student audience, decided to delete those articles from the school paper.

Finally, the remainder of student free speech falls under the earlier *Tinker* standard (First Amendment Center, 2011). The *Tinker* standard was enunciated by the Court in *Tinker v. Des Moines Independent Community School District* (1969). The dispute developed when Tinker, Tinker's sister, and a friend, wore black armbands to their school to protest the Vietnam War. The school principal adopted a formal policy banning armbands in school. The students were suspended but were allowed to return after agreeing to comply with the school policy. Tinker, his sister, and friend all violated the policy on return from suspension, and, thus, were suspended again. The parents sued the school district. The case made its way to the Supreme Court, and in a 7 to 2 decision, the Court ruled in favor of Tinker. Furthermore, the Court found that the First Amendment applied to schools and that school administrators would have to prove that a material and substantial disruption in the school would take place in order for the speech of students to be disciplined.

COURT RULINGS REGARDING STUDENT SPEECH ON SOCIAL NETWORKING WEBSITES

Courts have ruled that most cases involving student speech on social networking websites fall under the third category, as made evident by recent court decisions, *Layshock v. Hermitage School District* (2007) and *J.S. v. Blue Mountain School District* (2010). In both of these cases, the lower courts found that in order for school administrators to be able to properly discipline students for their speech on social networking websites, a material and substantial disruption of school must be apparent.

John Cannan (2010) details these two similar and complex court cases that originated in Pennsylvania. Cannan notes that on the same day, two separate panels of the U.S. Court of Appeals for the Third Circuit issued two rulings that reached very different conclusions on whether it is legally permissible for a student to be disciplined by school administrators for statements posted on the social networking website, Myspace.

Cannan notes that in both cases students made parody profiles of their high school principals on Myspace outside of school. In both cases, the students responsible for creating the faux profiles were discovered and subsequently disciplined by school administrators. The parents of the respective students believed that their child's First Amendment right of free speech was violated, and, thus, sued the respective school districts. When discussing the first ruling in *Layshock,* Cannan states that the lower court ruled in favor of the student, finding that his First Amendment rights had been violated; whereas, in *J.S.* the lower court ruled in favor of the school district. Both rulings were appealed to the Third Circuit.

The Third Circuit upheld the lower court's ruling in *Layshock,* contending that school administrators can only discipline students when there is a foreseeable and substantial disruption of school. A different panel also upheld the lower court's ruling in *J.S.,* finding that the explicit content on the Myspace page coupled with the capability to spread the content to a large audience both in and out of school could lead to a substantial disruption of school. To settle the apparent disparity between the two rulings, the Third Circuit agreed to review the earlier versions *en banc,* meaning that the cases were reviewed by the full court rather than a three-judge panel.

Following the rehearing, the court issued decisions in favor of the students in both cases. In a unanimous opinion, the appeals court once again upheld the trial court's decision in the *Layshock* case, rejecting the school district's argument that there was a sufficient nexus between the parody and school to warrant its disciplinary action. A divided court (8 to 6) in the *J.S.* case affirmed part of the lower court's original decision but reversed other aspects. In essence, on review, the full court was not convinced that school officials could discipline the student for creating a lewd parody of her principal off campus. In each of these cases, the court was unwilling to extend school officials' authority to discipline students for actions that took place off campus, even though those actions targeted school personnel.

The issue is far from settled, as an appeal to the U.S. Supreme Court is likely. Even so, it remains that for school administrators to discipline student speech because of content posted on social networking websites, a foreseeable and substantial disruption of the school must be proven. In order for a substantial disruption to be determined, the court must assess whether or not the speech of the student materially and substantially interfered with appropriate discipline in the school setting (*Tinker v. Des Moines Independent Community School District,* 1969). In other words, only speech that does not disrupt the classroom environment or invade the rights of others is protected. Since false postings about school personnel on social networking websites can be deemed disruptive, it seems reasonable that school administrators should have carte blanche authority (complete discretion or authority) to discipline such behavior.

RAPID DISSEMINATION AND PERMANENT
LEGACY OF ONLINE COMMUNICATION

Not all social networking sites are alike. Twitter, for example, enables quick dissemination of information that reads like headlines to those who follow a particular account. Facebook, on the other hand, allows users to create personal profiles and to connect with "friends." Another example, YouTube, is a forum in which individuals can upload videos of nearly any nature for viewing by the public. The list of social networking websites could go on, but the point is that even though these websites are not alike in form, they function similarly. That is, social networking websites create a forum in which messages can be rapidly disseminated to a widespread audience.

For example, in the *Layshock* case, the statement of the facts indicated that the student's false profile of the school principal spread quickly and reached, most (if not all) of the school. The parody profile was able to reach such a vast audience because of the inherent function of all social networking websites. That is, a message created by a website member can be seen by the "friends" or contacts that individual has on a particular site. However, the message does not end there. The message can be forwarded on to second-, third-, or even fourth-hand parties. The chain is seemingly endless, and the message can be sent faster than a blink of an eye. Additionally, the forwarding of these messages is not necessarily intentional. For example, a message can be passed on to a second-hand party through Facebook if a first-hand party simply adds a comment under the original post. Furthermore, many of these social networking websites are linked. For example, an individual can link his or her Twitter account to Facebook so that information can be shared with users of both websites.

Not only can false information be quickly passed on through social networking websites to a vast audience, these sites are public domain and a permanent record of material posted is maintained. For example, the terms of service for Facebook imply that the site can keep and use copies of user content even if the user deleted the information or closed his or her account (Sarno, 2009). In other words, a false statement about school personnel posted on a social networking website is recorded indefinitely, and, thus, it has the potential to be disseminated to the population and to create a disruption.

Traditionally, students would pass on messages through word-of-mouth, note passing, flyers, and so on. These traditional channels of communication did not produce a permanent record that could be passed on or used at any moment or brought up at some time in the distant future. In other words, false messages created and transmitted through traditional channels of communication have a short shelf life, whereas false messages created and disseminated on social networking websites remain there indefinitely and, thus, can lead to a disruption any time after their creation.

Consider the cases of *Layshock* and *J.S.* In both cases, a parody profile was created of school personnel, albeit off campus. A record of this false information remains in the database of Myspace and on the hard drives of anyone who saved the information before it was taken down from the website. That is, there is potential for this information to reemerge and create a disruption in the school. However, if these students spread the false statements through conversation in the lunch room or through a note circulated during homeroom, such endless potential for disruption would not exist because traditional channels of communication do not create a permanent record.

As one can see, when a student makes false comments about school personnel on social networking websites, the comments can potentially be seen by a seemingly limitless population in a short amount of time. Moreover, these comments are never fully destroyed, and remain in the public sphere indefinitely. Therefore, school administrators have greater authority to discipline students for false posts about school personnel on social networking websites. Further, many of the false profiles have the potential to damage the victim's reputation and professional standing. Since they can never be fully removed, the damage can never be undone. In addition, the false postings can cause lasting emotional harm to the victim.

CONCLUSION

It can be argued that social networking websites have become the new note passing in school. That is, instead of circulating rumors by traditional channels, such as word-of-mouth or note passing, the channel of social networking websites is the new commonplace way for students to spread gossip. It can also be argued that, much like note passing, posting rumors and gossip (false information) on social networking websites is a way in which students vent their frustration with school personnel.

While spreading gossip might be a form of blowing off steam, when done through social networking websites, a serious problem arises. As argued in this point essay, these websites provide a forum in which information is spread rapidly and to a wide audience. In addition, information posted on these websites can never fully be deleted, and thus a foreseeable disruption to the school exists, unlike false information spread through traditional channels of communication.

Another argument against granting greater authority to school administrators to discipline students for posting false information about school personnel on social networking websites is that it is reactionary and that it does not proactively work to educate students about the dangers and pitfalls of these sites. It is true that granting administrators greater authority to discipline students for such violations is reactionary; however, giving administrators authority to discipline students does not take away their ability to create programs that would educate students about these sites and the potential harm they can cause themselves and others. Additionally, even if they create proactive measures, administrators must have the tools to discipline because not all students will learn from the proactive measures, and the potential disruption that could occur to the school because of such false information posted on these websites is so vast.

A final argument used against giving greater authority to school administrators to discipline students for their false posts about school personnel on social networking websites is that such discipline is purely punitive and not educational. However, such greater authority to discipline students does not necessarily equate to punitive measures only, such as probation, suspension, or expulsion, in which the student may be more than happy to miss school days. Administrators can use these instances as teachable moments in which a suspension is coupled with a computer ethics class, research project, or mediation with the individual that the student harmed so the student can see how his or her false posts actually affected the school personnel.

In all, regardless if this new technology is students' channel of choice to vent their frustration with school personnel versus traditional channels of communication, the point still remains that false information posted on social networking websites presents a disruption to the overall school environment. Also, granting administrators more authority to discipline students who post false online content to social networking sites does not take away their ability to proactively engage students so that these disruptive situations do not occur in the first place. Finally, giving this increased disciplinary authority does not inhibit administrators from employing educational discipline instead of using purely punitive means.

COUNTERPOINT: Korrin M. Ziswiler
University of Dayton

This counterpoint essay argues that today's school administrators should have considerably less authority to discipline students for false posts regarding school personnel on social networking websites. Not only is increasing the authority for schools to discipline students for posting false online statements overstepping the legal bounds of parental rights to deal with such situations, but it has also been decided by the Supreme Court to be unconstitutional due to the infringement of students' First Amendment free speech and expression rights. More important, school administrators should not be allowed to increase their authority to discipline in these instances, particularly because their methods of punishment neither address the root cause of the problem nor create teachable moments that could positively impact the student body as a whole. However, it is critical in this technological and digital age for schools to begin taking a role in educating students concerning the social responsibility of being respectful and ethical digital citizens as the use of social networking sites continues to grow.

LEGAL RULINGS REGARDING STUDENT ONLINE POSTINGS

The seminal legal decision supporting student free speech in schools is *Tinker v. Des Moines Independent Community School District* (1969) in which the U.S. Supreme Court first established students' free speech rights within a school setting. In the *Tinker* case, three students decided to partake in a program that local antiwar supporters had initiated by wearing black armbands in silent protest of the Vietnam War. The local school board discovered the students' intentions and convened to develop a policy that stated that any student caught wearing a black armband would be requested to remove it or face suspension. On arrival at school, John Tinker, a 15-year-old student, was suspended after refusing to take off the black armband. The Tinker family filed a legal suit against the school claiming that the enforced suspension was a violation of First Amendment rights. Although lower courts supported the school's decision; in the *Tinker* case, the Supreme Court ruled that students do not "shed their constitutional rights to freedom of speech or expression at the schoolhouse gate" (p. 506). Additionally, the *Tinker* ruling set the legal precedent on a school's right to implement punishment on students if substantial disruption of classroom activities occurs due to the student's free speech actions. A clear definition of substantial disruption is needed while we are on this topic. Substantial disruption is not the presumption that disruption may occur. There actually has to be some proven disruption or *substantiated* forecast that it will occur in order for this reasoning to warrant a school assigned punishment.

Though the *Tinker* case is often used as a framework to support a student's free speech rights in a school setting, the complexities of student free speech and expression issues are amplified in situations where students can access the

Internet to post online comments off campus or not on school premises. In these situations, a different legal precedent is generally used, *Bethel School District No. 403 v. Fraser* (1986). The original *Fraser* court case involved an appeal over school punishment of a student for making a lewd speech that was laced with sexual innuendos at a mandatory school event. Matthew Fraser was suspended, and his parents sued the school. The Court in this case ruled in favor of the school and disagreed that Fraser's First Amendment rights had been violated. This was the first case to support school regulation of free speech when substantial disruption was absent. The Supreme Court asserted that despite the fact that no substantial disruption was created, the student's lewd speech had a captive audience of students while, at the same time, the school was attempting to instill morality and appropriate behavior in its students.

Although the rulings have been split in the many cases filed on the basis of *Fraser,* the case is often used by school districts when attempting to extend the scope of their authority to regulate student free speech. Three factors must be present to apply *Fraser* to student free speech. First, there must be a captive audience. Second, the speech must contain lewd or sexual content. And finally, the school must need to distance itself from the student's speech (Tomain, 2010). In other words, the school has a good reason to not want to be associated with the content of the speech.

According to an analysis of legal precedents in the area of online student free speech by Joseph A. Tomain in a 2010 law review article titled "Cyberspace Is Outside the Schoolhouse Gate: Offensive, Online Student Speech Receives First Amendment Protection," published in the *Drake Law Review,* the online environment cannot be governed by schools under this legal precedent for two reasons. First, because there is an absence of a captive audience or a need for a school to reasonably dissociate itself from online content, the *Fraser* ruling cannot be applied. Second, online postings are not geographically bound. Therefore, the analysis in the *Drake Law Review* contends, it does not matter where a student posts or accesses this online material; its boundaries are not geographical but are between an online and real world. The analysis further contends that students' free speech rights should not only be protected to promote the development of their individuality but, further, false speech, including content that schools deem contentious or rude, is also protected by the First Amendment.

Other legal cases have also addressed the concept of geographical boundaries for posting and accessing online material by students. In the case *Coy v. Board of Education of Canton City Schools* (2002), the court ruled that school administrators could not punish a student for creating and publishing a webpage from the student's home with lewd content in it, even if the student accessed this particular website from school. The webpage did not have a captive audience, and, although the content related to school, it was not disseminated at a school-sponsored event. Finally, in *Emmett v. Kent School District* (2000), the court ruled that the suspension of a student for putting a parody obituary of other students online was not appropriate under the *Fraser* ruling, even though the site had connections to students of the school and was a product of a school-related assignment. Taken together, these cases demonstrate that the courts have deemed punishment of student free speech that occurs off campus beyond the scope of school involvement and not punishable, even if it has connections to the school environment.

In a recent legal proceeding decided in February 2011, a federal magistrate, Barry Garber, denied a Florida principal's request to dismiss a lawsuit brought forth by a student who was suspended for creating a Facebook page that criticized her high school teacher. Garber supported his ruling with legal precedent established in *Layshock v. Hermitage School District* (2010) that determined that a school could not punish a high school student for creating a fictitious profile of a school principal from a computer after hours at his grandmother's house. Though this profile was accessed by other students, it was never accessed on campus. The Third Circuit stated in its ruling that, "It would be an unseemly and dangerous precedent to allow the state in the guise of school authorities to reach into a child's home and control his/her actions there to the same extent that they can control that child when he/she participates in school sponsored activities" (2010, p. 260).

A full 14-judge panel of the Third Circuit recently reviewed its previous decision in *Layshock* along with a seemingly contrary decision in *J.S. v. Blue Mountain School District* (2010). In each of these decisions, the appeals court essentially reaffirmed its earlier ruling in *Layshock* that school administrators do not have the authority to discipline students for off-campus behavior, even when that behavior can reach into the school itself. In the two cases before it, the court was not convinced that the students' behavior, creating unflattering and false parodies of their school principals at home, had the potential to create a substantial disruption in school sufficient to warrant discipline.

The cases and examples previously cited clearly show that even children have First Amendment rights protected under the U.S. Constitution. Furthermore, although schools state that they assert punishment under *en loco parentis* (meaning that they are acting as a parent when parents are not present) and to maintain order in the school environment, the courts have shown that this does not hold true when a student is off campus and there is no disruption in the school environment. Finally, the rulings in the aforementioned cases demonstrate schools cannot punish student free speech on the basis of disagreeing with or not liking what the student has to say, especially if substantial disruption is not clearly proven. The First Amendment of the Constitution protects offensive speech that has little or no usefulness to society just as much as it protects outrageous political rhetoric or societal critique.

THE SLIPPERY SLOPE OF STUDENT ONLINE SPEECH

The fear that arises with school involvement in restricting false or slanderous statements online (also referred to as cyberbullying) is that there is a distinct possibility that schools will overstep their bounds and encroach on areas of student free speech. The danger lies in schools attempting to interpret the difference between what is merely offensive speech (nonthreatening in nature), and slanderous or defamatory speech. First Amendment rights protect offensive speech, while threatening or slanderous speech is not protected. Additionally, when schools insert themselves into the contentious position of deciding which student postings are "false" and which are student opinion or venting of frustration, student free speech is inevitably jeopardized. Moreover, when schools possess the increased authority to discipline student online behaviors, an *obligation* to police this online realm arises; a task that is daunting in nature and scope. Former staff attorney with the National School Boards Association, Thomas Hutton, put it best when he stated, "Once you've asserted your authority to do something, there's an argument that you've asserted the responsibility to do something" (Taylor, 2007, p. 36). Schools neither have the resources nor need the additional responsibility that this increased authority creates.

The extension of schools' authority also robs parents of their right to discipline their children as they see fit. In essence, schools would be encroaching on parental rights to discipline children, a major infringement of parental control over their children. *In loco parentis* gives the school the duty of acting as a parent when the student is in their charge, not when the student is at home or under the supervision of their parents. This is not to say that parents are devoid of responsibility in supervising their children on the Internet. Parents need to become more involved in monitoring their children's online lives to protect them from harm from others or from their own immature behaviors.

To examine the root cause of the increasing phenomenon of posting false or derogatory online statements, it is necessary to consider what a typical teenager is managing on a daily basis. A number of factors could negatively affect how they think, feel, and express themselves. Hormones are raging out of control, and students are searching for their own identity and voice and are constantly attempting to assert some sort of control over their lives. Teenagers are facing peer pressure, family issues, and increasingly complex social situations in their real lives and in virtual ones on social networking websites. They are at risk for cyberbullying from peers, which often is unnoticed by authority figures around them and has resulted in student suicides, depression, and emotional damage. Many times, these posts are a cry for help, for attention, or for clarity at a time when the world does not makes sense. Is it a wonder that kids today attempt to push back in an antiauthority way against those that they feel have abandoned or misunderstood them?

If censorship is allowed to occur on social networking websites, one of few outlets where students are able to freely express themselves (good, bad, or indifferent), there is a strong possibility that increased and exceedingly violent acts will result. The angst that accompanies the teenage years is nothing new, but the ways in which students discharge these feelings have taken increasingly violent turns in recent times. School shootings have become alarming recurrences in society and illustrate how far students will go when they are ignored or stifled. Schools and parents often ignore or repress students' attempts to assert their voice, online or in the real world, to maintain authority, or because they do not have the time, patience, or knowledge to deal with these behaviors. Today, social networks and online forums allow students a place to express how they are feeling—their anger, frustration, confusion, and happiness—in an indirect way.

CONCLUSION

According to Shaheen Shariff (2008), author of *Cyber-Bullying: Issues and Solutions for the School, the Classroom and the Home,* the punishment imposed by school administrators for students posting false or offensive online comments is a reactive approach to dealing with this behavior that focuses more on the school system maintaining a positive image than effectively dealing with the problem of making false statements about other people. Most often, punishment for this type of student behavior takes the form of suspension from school for extended lengths of time. Not only do some students view this as a positive reinforcement, suspension does nothing to address the root cause of this misguided act or curb student behavior if schools and parents do not take advantage of the teachable moment that this behavior presents.

Shariff goes on to say that school administrators are notably more focused on the lack of control they have over technology, their inability to effectively regulate this forum, and the potentially negative ramifications to their public image for not enacting swift and harsh punishment of these behaviors than they are on addressing what is actually going on in a student's life that caused this conduct to occur. In addition, as school administrators attempt to increase their abilities to govern student activity in cyberspace, it can create oppressive and intolerant school environments where students are unable to vent their feelings of frustration. Instead of taking a punitive approach, schools should use these instances to educate the whole student body about the effects of irresponsible online posts, how they affect others, and the serious ramifications that can ensue from these seemingly innocuous acts.

Stakes continue to rise in the efforts to punish false online posts made by students about teachers and schools. In some cases, teachers will even go as far as filing personal lawsuits against students for posting false or defamatory statements about them online. In such situations, it is important to keep one thing in perspective: The students in question here are mentally, emotionally, and legally children. Is it really the belief that dragging teenagers through a legal process is the most effective way to deal with or punish this situation? These types of proceedings could haunt students for the rest of their lives, to punish them for a decision that in many cases they were not mentally or emotionally mature enough to control. In any situation, dragging a minor through judicial proceedings is a drastic measure to only be broached in the direst circumstances. Since teenagers are not developed enough to comprehend the long-term ramifications of their impulsive actions, it would seem this course of action punishes students for lack of adult attention, supervision, and intervention that is necessary during these confusing and vulnerable times in their lives.

School administrators have to comprehend that today's generation views their online persona as an extension of themselves, with endless possibilities for creative and expressive outlets. This online presence for students is now an extension of their identity; a way for them to express feelings and sentiments that they may not be confident enough to share in the physical world. With this amazing outlet comes an immense amount of power, which most adolescents are not capable of policing on their own. Schools and parents need to share in the accountability of providing perspective, education, and guidance concerning appropriate behavior in cyberspace.

It should be the duty of schools, teachers, and parents to educate students concerning the proper and responsible use of today's social networking websites and the Internet in a conscionable way. Online programs and curriculum are currently available to assist teachers in educating students on how to be moral and considerate citizens in the modern technological society. By instructing students how to behave in this boundless digital environment, schools not only proactively fight online bullying of all sorts, but they provide students with a framework of how to operate in this realm as its presence increases in society.

FURTHER READINGS AND RESOURCES

Cannan, J. (2010, March 30). *United States: Federal appeals court panels address whether students' punishment for Myspace pages violates First Amendment free speech protections.* Retrieved from News and Events website: http://www.loc.gov/lawweb/servlet/lloc_news?disp3_l205401888_text

First Amendment Center. (2011). *Bethel School Dist. No. 403 v. Fraser, 478 U.S. 675 (1986).* Retrieved from http://www.firstamendmentschools.org/freedoms/case.aspx?id=35

Paulson, K., Policinski, G., Haynes, C. C., Hudson, D. L., & Villager, T. (2011, April 20). *How do school officials and the courts apply free-speech court standards?* Retrieved from the First Amendment Center website: http://www.firstamendmentschools.org/freedoms/faq.aspx?id=12992

Sarno, D. (2009, February 16). Facebook founder Mark Zuckerberg responds to privacy concerns. *Los Angeles Times.* Retrieved from http://latimesblogs.latimes.com/technology/2009/02/facebook-founde.html

Shariff, S. (2008). *Cyber-bullying: Issues and solutions for the school, the classroom and the home.* New York: Routledge.

Taylor, J. (2007, Spring). Legislation targets "cyber bullies." *Student Press Law Center, 28*(2), 36. Retrieved from http://www.splc.org/news/report_detail.asp?id=1329&edition=42

Tomain, J. A. (2010). Cyberspace is outside the schoolhouse gate: Offensive, online student speech receives first amendment protection. *Drake Law Review, 59*(1), 97–180.

Willard, N. (2011, Fall). *Schools and online social networking.* Retrieved from http://www.nea.org/tools/9279.htm

COURT CASES AND STATUTES

Bethel School District No. 403 v. Fraser, 478 U.S. 675 (1986).

Coy v. Board of Education of North Canton City Schools, 205 F. Supp.2d 791 (N.D. Ohio 2002).

Emmett v. Kent School District, 92 F. Supp. 2d 1088 (W.D. Wash. 2000).

Hazelwood School District v. Kuhlmeier, 484 U.S. 260 (1988).

J.S. v. Blue Mountain School District, 593 F.3d 286 (3d Cir. 2010), *vacated, reh'g en banc granted,* 2010 U.S. App. LEXIS 7342 (3d Cir, Apr. 9, 2010), 2011 WL 2305973 (3d Cir. 2011).

Layshock v. Hermitage School District, 496 F. Supp. 2d 587 (W.D. Pa. 2007), *affirmed* 593 F.3d 249 (3d Cir. 2010), *rehearing en banc granted, opinion vacated* (3d Cir. April 9, 2010), *affirmed* 2011 WL 2305970 (3d Cir.).

Tinker v. Des Moines Independent Community School District, 393 U.S. 503 (1969).

Should public schools promote themselves on social networking sites, such as Facebook and Twitter?

POINT: Steven M. Baule, *North Boone Public School District, Poplar Grove, Illinois*

COUNTERPOINT: Robert Stewart Mayers and Geraldine R. Johnson, *Southeastern Oklahoma State University*

OVERVIEW

The use of popular commercial social networking sites, including Facebook, Myspace, and Twitter, is continually growing at a phenomenal rate, especially among the nation's middle and high school students. For example, a recent survey from the Pew Research Center's Internet and American Life Project revealed that approximately 73% of online teens are using social networking sites as a primary method of their online communications (Hampton, Goulet, & Rainie, 2011). Today's social networking sites are defined as web-based technology tools that allow users to develop a public online persona, or profile. This online profile allows users to electronically communicate with other users of a particular social networking site with whom they share a connection, such as a certain professional sports team or music group, and view as well as comment on their list of communications with other members of the group. The terms *social network sites* and *social networking websites* are often used interchangeably.

Social networking sites have dramatically altered the way people communicate on the Internet. In addition to individuals, an increasing number of private and public companies and organizations have used social networking sites as a modern means of advertisement. Despite the popularity of today's social networking sites, however, recent media coverage has drawn attention to some real concerns associated with the use of social networking sites by legal minors, namely students, due to privacy and safety issues. Based largely on privacy and safety concerns involving students, some members of the educational community have been reluctant to allow both teachers and students access to these technologies in schools. In fact, many school districts across the country have actively developed policies banning the use of social networking sites in school facilities.

In this chapter, the point and counterpoint authors debate the contentious issue of whether public schools should promote themselves on today's social networking sites, such as Facebook and Twitter. In his point essay, Steven M. Baule, a superintendent at the North Boone Public School District in Poplar Grove, Illinois, argues that school officials need to take full advantage of today's social networking sites because they are a relatively inexpensive and efficient way for educators to positively promote schools to the community. Baule argues that the way schools traditionally communicated with parents and the larger community was costly and usually involved mass mailings. Today, school officials could simply put an online post of an important school-related event on a popular social networking site, such as Facebook or Twitter, and electronically link the news of the school-related event to the school's existing website. According to Baule, the advanced technologies of social networking sites naturally facilitate quicker and more effective communication with a larger audience of educational stakeholders compared to the traditional methods of using mass mailings or print newspapers.

While Baule maintains that the advantages of using social networking sites as a means to positively promote today's schools far outweigh any potential disadvantages, he mentions two possible considerations that school officials must consider. First, school officials must be aware of families with students in the school that do not have Internet access at their home. Families that do not have Internet access must receive hard copies of all school-related news and activity announcements so they are not left out. Second, school officials must receive proper professional development to effectively and safely use social networking sites for the purpose of positively promoting the school. According to Baule, it is not only beneficial for school officials within a particular school to receive professional development in the use of social networking sites but that professional development and collaboration within a larger, online social network is even more effective.

In their counterpoint essay, coauthors from Southeastern Oklahoma State University, Robert Steward Mayers and Geraldine R. Johnson argue that today's popular social networking sites pose significant risks and drawbacks for school officials. In their counterpoint essay, the authors highlight three primary shortcomings of today's social networking sites that make them unsuitable for school environments: a lack of Americans with Disabilities Act (ADA, 1990) compliance, the potential to be used for inappropriate online relationships, and the current lack of clear legal guidance from the courts relating to the use of social networking sites.

Counterpoint essay coauthors Mayers and Johnson's first exception to the use of social networking sites by school officials to promote schools argues that these online sites are not in compliance with the ADA. As a result, they argue that people with disabilities, such as blindness and spinal cord injuries, are unable to access the information on social networking sites. While the authors agree that school districts have the ability to develop websites that are ADA complaint, the majority of today's popular social networking sites are not ADA compliant. Second, Mayers and Johnson argue that there have been a growing number of recent cases involving inappropriate online relationships between teachers and students on popular social networking sites. Third, Mayers and Johnson maintain that the current legal status regarding the use of social networking sites in school environments is unclear. The authors argue that in this current economic downturn, school officials who choose to use social networking sites run the risk of giving the district unwanted litigation-related costs.

In this chapter, both the point and counterpoint essay authors ask a similar question: Do the advantages of using social networking sites as means to promote today's public schools outweigh the disadvantages of using such sites? Clearly, the point and counterpoint authors arrive at different conclusions. However, one point is agreed on in this debate. Today's popular social networking sites have revolutionized the way people communicate in online environments, and the users of these sites are increasingly young students in today's classrooms.

Kevin P. Brady
North Carolina State University

POINT: Steven M. Baule
*North Boone Public School District,
Poplar Grove, Illinois*

Social networking sites are changing the way people communicate in online environments. Currently, more than 400 million people worldwide use Facebook, which is the most popular social networking website. More than 26 million people have accounts with the social networking website Twitter. Seven million people are using StumbleUpon, a more recent social networking site that calls itself a "social discovery network." Clearly, the number of people using social networking sites is growing significantly, and current usage indictors reveal that the use of social networking sites is not a passing technology fad. The interactive social networking sites that comprise what many people call web 2.0 are growing exponentially. For example, in a recent National School Boards Association (NSBA) survey, more than half of the students using social networking sites said that they use these sites as a means to help complete and improve their school work (National School Boards Association, 2007).

In this point essay addressing whether public schools should promote themselves on social networking sites, I argue that schools should take full advantage of social networking sites as a constructive means to improve both communication and professional development among educators. Historically, accurate communication has been a time-intensive as well as expensive task for schools. However, the use of social networking sites is a relatively inexpensive and efficient way for today's schools to effectively communicate with parents as well as the larger community. Traditionally, school districts have overwhelmingly relied on mass mailings as a means to provide important news or information to the parents of students attending schools in the district. This traditional print media form of communication generally requires schools to pay for a direct mailing to parents. Second, schools often send out press releases or work with the local media to communicate with the public.

COMMUNICATION

Postal mailings are generally expensive ventures when school officials consider the collective costs associated with the use of staff time, material-related costs, and postage. Today's school officials should consider the alternative of posting a brief summary of an important school-related event or issue on a social networking site, such as Twitter or one of the other popular social networking sites, that would electronically link a particular notification to a letter or news release on the school's website. If today's school officials can embrace the use of social networking sites and actively encourage parents and other important educational stakeholders to sign up for online notifications through e-mail, schools will be increasingly more effective and timely in communicating with their multiple constituencies.

Today's existing print media outlets are changing dramatically in the face of online social networking technologies. A current example is the changing nature of the print newspaper. Recently, traditional print newspaper readership is down significantly according to several sources. Historically, local newspapers are where most of the school news had previously been covered. As readership declines for traditional print media, it makes effective communication even more difficult for schools who are still using this medium as their primary media outlet.

Media currency is another hurdle for traditional print media. Many local papers devote significant attention to school news. Often, however, the lead time to get news into print in weekly or biweekly papers makes them significantly less effective for important, time-sensitive news. Mailings are the other traditional communications tool that schools have used to inform the public about school-related news and events. Mailings to all postal patrons are generally expensive for even the smallest school districts, and often such mailings are recycled before they are opened. With the current economic downturn, large mailings of school newsletters to all stakeholders are often being eliminated because of current budgetary constraints.

This perfect storm of the decrease in traditional print newspaper readership coupled with the cost of mass mailings of school newsletters makes it particularly difficult for schools to communicate effectively using traditional print media. However, there is a relatively simple solution for today's schools to dramatically and effectively improve communication with the greater community: the use of social networking sites. Schools can inexpensively reach large audiences of stakeholders as well as the wider community when they use social networking sites effectively.

Social networking sites allow for communicating with three primary stakeholder groups for schools: parents, alumni, and the at-large community. Historically, parents are the easiest group to communicate with because of the direct connection parents have with the school through their children. Sending materials home with students generally works through the elementary years. However, once students enter middle and high school, parents cannot always rely on students to carry information home in a timely manner. Social networking sites are an easy way to communicate with parents and remind them of upcoming events on a daily basis. Posting the school's daily announcements to a social networking site, such as Facebook, can help parents work as partners to ensure that students are prepared for upcoming school events, such as picture day, final exams, or a guest speaker.

Social networking sites are an excellent way to keep parents in the loop on what is happening in the school without any additional cost and nearly no additional effort on the part of school staff. Social networking sites are inexpensive ways to send reminders about where to look for school closing information, parent-teacher conferences, and a host of other events. Social networking sites can further help parents and schools work more effectively together. Online posting to social networking sites can also assist in making sure that noncustodial parents receive the same information that custodial parents receive without additional cost to the school district.

Similarly, social networking can be set up directly for students. For instance, many high school students and middle school students have pocket-sized, Internet-capable devices. A school district can allow students to sign up for digital copies of daily announcements or even the lunch menu as a text message. Teachers can send online text messages of reminders for homework and other long-term project due dates or give final review reminders about quizzes or exams.

Alumni, however, are one of the most difficult groups for many schools to communicate with, as well as gather information on. Social networking sites are almost tailor-made to assist schools with keeping in contact with alumni. For example, setting up a basic profile on the social networking site Facebook can encourage former graduates to connect with their school by selecting a "Like" option on the school's page. Once this online connection has been established, it is possible to communicate with alumni and solicit information, including survey information. Reunion information can easily be distributed, and alumni are an excellent potential source of fund-raising for many schools. The online networking aspects of most social networking sites can help schools track down more elusive alumni who have moved away from the area. Overall, social networking sites are an excellent vehicle for connecting schools and their former students.

Social networking sites are also a good way to communicate with the wider community beyond simply parents. Blogs, tweets, and Facebook updates are all useful ways to keep the wider community up-to-date as to what is going on in the school. The traditional quarterly or semiannual school district newsletter is quickly becoming extremely expensive. Postage alone is an expensive proposition for many of today's financially strapped schools.

Connecting with other community groups, parent and booster organizations, and other local governments can help to create a positive, supportive culture for the school online as well as in the schools and at school events. Announcing fund-raising events, student performances, and athletic contests via social media can assist in raising attendance, increasing funds generated via donations and gate receipts, as well as enhancing the standing of the activities in question. Well established, credible social media sources that have been providing information about a school can be invaluable when a crisis arises or when it's time to pass a referendum. Elections and other high-profile events, such as the hiring of a superintendent or the closing of a school, often bring out a number of bloggers or others who take to the Internet to deliver their messages. If the school already has a strong social media communications structure in place, it is much easier for the school to provide accurate information and combat disinformation and rumors that often arise in such situations.

The obvious downside to such Internet-based electronic communication is that some families simply don't have access to those resources. In the registration process, schools need to allow families the ability to indicate that they don't have access to the Internet and would prefer hard copies of announcements and other key communications from the district. This type of safety net will ensure that those without access to the Internet are not left out.

A key concept in effectively using social media is to ensure that the district's subscriptions are managed by the end users. The school needs to use systems where the parent or community member submits their e-mail address and subscribes.

PROFESSIONAL DEVELOPMENT

Professional development is another way for schools to effectively use social media. The concept of the professional learning community that has been promoted as an important stimulus for improving instruction within schools can be expanded in a geometric way by the use of professional learning networks based on social media. If it is a good thing for teachers within a building or department to take time to share and collaborate to improve instruction, it stands to reason that the same type of professional collaboration and sharing within a wider online social network could become even more powerful.

One of the keys to using online social networking sites for professional development is finding the right tools for the task at hand. Although Facebook has its uses as a general communication medium for schools, other social networking sites, such as Edmodo, Ning, and Wikispaces, provide much more appropriate online environments for professional development targeted for those in the education profession. For example, Yahoo Groups hosts more than 500 groups specifically focused on some aspect of teacher professional development. The social networking site Yahoo Groups allow members to share e-mail, post files, and conduct surveys on a specific topic of mutual interest.

Within a school district, setting up a wiki or a Google Docs site can facilitate the sharing of lesson plans, assessment instruments, and presentations between teachers of a similar grade level or subject area. Teachers can share and compare documents and lessons as well as look for ways to cooperatively improve instruction across all classrooms of a given grade level.

At professional conferences, for example, more teachers are using the social networking site Twitter as well as other popular social networking sites to share information about sessions and speakers in real time. This allows teachers in other sessions or even at school to ask questions, share, and virtually participate in ways that were not possible only a few years ago. Presenters can use the same technologies to get immediate feedback from participants and extend their reach to those who were not able to get to a particular session.

The social networking site Twitter allows users to virtually see who other online Twitter users are following. Often the online connections made to other users via these relationships allow users to further develop a professional network and find access to new resources. Many professional organizations, such as the Illinois Association of School Administrators (IASA), have a professional development director who is constantly tweeting new programs and services of which he has become aware. Following some Twitter accounts is like reading a "best of" digest of current professional publications.

StumbleUpon is another social networking site that has a great deal of potential for today's educators. It is essentially an online search engine that allows a user to enter a topic and get results (websites) that have been recommended by other users on a particular topic. It also allows a user to follow other online users. For instance, a lead teacher or department chair could use the social networking site StumbleUpon to mark a number of professional blogs or webpages that he or she wished the department could read prior to a committee or department meeting.

Skype is a type of social networking site that can be used to bring experts into in-services or faculty meetings for little or no cost as compared to having to deal with hotel costs, airline schedules, or even traditional phone calls. In some cases, Skype can be used to follow up with those same experts in real time. Schools that use webinars as a way to reduce travel-related costs or extend the shrinking professional development dollar are in fact embracing social networking technologies. When a teacher or administrator can participate in a two-hour webinar and then be in the school building for the rest of the day instead of being away from the school where they cannot work directly with students, the use of social networking sites makes complete sense.

All of these professional development options allow for school administrators and teachers to make new contacts and expand their support network of educators. As teaching is a profession where much professional time is spent only with students and without colleagues or mentors, it makes good sense for a school to embrace social networking technologies as a way of fostering professional development and innovation within the classroom. For instance, school administrators can use social networking technology tools, such as SurveyMonkey or Zoomerang, to receive detailed feedback on in-service presentations. Administrators, teacher committees, or even school board members can gather input from staff, parents, and students about proposed changes to policies or programs using these same tools. The ability of these online social networking tools to gather and disaggregate data is quite impressive. Human resources staff can use social networking sites to promote a particular school's job openings to reduce advertising costs associated with the use of traditional print media. Additionally, reviewing the social networking pages of prospective hires is not a bad idea either.

CONCLUSION

In all, social networking sites and tools provide schools with exceptional opportunities to increase communication with all the major educational stakeholder groups, from students to alumni and from parents to local business owners. The real possibilities of online social networking sites to support school- or district-wide staff development initiatives and to support the individual professional growth of all staff are nearly limitless. The educational and cost-saving benefits of today's social networking sites are significant for schools and should not be ignored.

COUNTERPOINT: Robert Stewart Mayers and Geraldine R. Johnson
Southeastern Oklahoma State University

S ocial networking sites, such as Facebook and Twitter, are the online media of choice for communication for millions of people. But are these social networking sites the best choice for today's public schools to use to positively promote themselves as well as stay in touch with others? This counterpoint essay argues that social networking sites are not effective technologies for schools to use as beneficial means of promoting themselves. As with any modern technology, there may be ways to constructively use social networking sites to promote a public school. However, there are also considerable risks and drawbacks to using social networking sites. These risks and drawbacks are reasons why so many schools block access from their computer networks to social networking sites. Examples of major reasons for public schools not to use social networking sites include the lack of Americans with Disabilities Act of 1990 (ADA) compliance of these networking sites and the inherent dangers of social networking to stakeholders, particularly the potential for inappropriate use by school officials and students. Moreover, the current lack of clear guidance from the courts concerning legal issues that may arise from the use of social networking is yet another reason why schools should not use social networking sites.

LACK OF AMERICANS WITH DISABILITIES ACT COMPLIANCE

School districts across the nation expend considerable effort to ensure complete access to all school district facilities and resources as required by the ADA. Although the ADA was passed in 1990, the courts are now being asked to apply the ADA to 21st-century technologies. According to Dan Goldstein, legal counsel for the National Federation of the Blind, not even one-half of the Internet is currently ADA compliant. People who suffer from disabilities such as blindness, cerebral palsy, and spinal cord injuries are unable to access much of the information on the Internet.

Much of the difficulty in gaining ADA compliance on the Internet stems from the language of Article III of the ADA, which requires compliance for any entity that is an "actual, physical" place. Whether or not cyberspace qualifies for ADA protection under that definition is a matter of disagreement among the federal courts. In 1994, the First Circuit Court of Appeals held in *Carparts Distribution Center, Inc. v. Automotive Wholesaler's Association* (1994) that if a person who purchases health insurance in a brick-and-mortar building is covered under ADA, then a person purchasing the same insurance via the telephone or by mail should be afforded the same protection despite not having entered an "actual, physical" place to make the purchase. In the 2006 court case, *National Federation of the Blind v. Target*, this conclusion was extended to include online websites that conduct business through the Internet. In contrast, the federal trial court for the southern district of Florida ruled in *Access Now, Inc. v. Southwest Airlines* (2002) that Title III of ADA did not apply to websites. On appeal, the Eleventh Circuit dismissed the case against Southwest Airlines based on legal defects in the appeal. A school district has the ability to build websites that are ADA compliant. Since most social networking websites are not ADA compliant, it does not make sense for schools to unnecessarily wade into this potential legal quagmire.

POTENTIAL FOR INAPPROPRIATE ONLINE RELATIONSHIPS

In mid-2011, there were approximately 750 million active Facebook users, and half of them log in to Facebook at least once each day. With 500 million active users in early 2010, the number of active Facebook users has increased by 50% in approximately 18 months (Facebook, n.d.). Furthermore, 48% of 18- to 34-year-olds check Facebook when they wake up (Digitalbuzz Blog, 2011). At the same time, inappropriate relationships between teachers and students are beginning to take place in school systems across the nation.

For example, recent cases involving the inappropriate online relationships between teachers and students have taken place in at least 40 states across the country. Currently, the majority of the 50 states have legal statutes that criminalize online teacher relationships with students. Such charges can potentially include sexual assault or sexual abuse. Such inappropriate relationships often begin online. In a 2004 study that was prepared for the U.S. Congress titled "Educator Sexual Misconduct: A Synthesis of Existing Literature," author Charol Shakeshaft estimates that approximately 5 million students in the United States have been sexually assaulted by an educator. The explosion of social networking site use combined with the staggering number of reported inappropriate student–teacher relationships has caused many school district officials to strongly consider and even adopt social networking site use policies for both school staff and students.

In 2009, a new law in Louisiana went into effect requiring every school district in the state to develop policies "to regulate electronic communications between school employees and students" (Louisiana Revised Statutes, 2009). The law requires that employees who communicate electronically with students be required to use school-provided devices that must be tracked by the school district. The Louisiana law also provided that any electronic communication with students using technology-enabled devices that do not belong to the school must be reported. Violation of the policy could lead to employee termination.

In 2010, the teachers union in Manatee County, Florida, filed suit challenging the constitutionality of the district's newly proposed policy regulating teacher speech on social networking sites, such as Facebook and Twitter. Specifically, the free speech and expression policy prohibits teachers from posting online any negative comments or unfavorable photos about the district, its employees, or students on teachers' social networking user sites. The policy was proposed in response to a situation where two Manatee County teachers were disciplined for inappropriate use of the Internet in communicating with students.

Inappropriate online communications between teachers and students, such as those in Manatee County, Florida, seem to justify the need for formal policies restricting the use of social networking sites. Recently, Dailyrecord.com reported that a veteran teacher in New Jersey had criminal charges brought against him because of sexually explicit online conversations he had with middle school students on Facebook. In another case in Brownsville, Pennsylvania, a high school Spanish teacher was suspended for 30 days for posting online pictures of a male stripper at a bachelorette party she hosted for a colleague.

However, not all inappropriate relationships are of a sexual nature. Cyberbullying, or online-based bullying and harassment, has become all too common in today's public schools. According to the Cyberbullying Research Center, nearly 20% of all middle school students in the United States report they have been cyberbullied at least once. In New York, a sixth-grade teacher is facing termination after an inappropriate online post about her students. The day after one of her students drowned at a beach, the teacher wrote, "After today, I'm thinking the beach is a good trip for my class" and "I hate their guts." A high school English teacher in the Central Bucks School District in Pennsylvania was suspended for using a social networking site to describe her students as "frightfully dim," "lazy," "sneaky," and "rude." The teacher also said one female student seemed "smarter than she actually is."

As technology continues to evolve, the number of individuals who are susceptible to cyberbullying also continues to increase at an alarming rate. The task of monitoring online communications on today's social networking sites is daunting for school officials. It does not seem wise for public schools to create even more opportunity for online-based misconduct by attempting to promote themselves using a popular social networking site, such as Facebook or Twitter. In this current economic downturn, most of the country's public school financial resources are increasingly scarce and must be used wisely.

Another strong argument against the use of social networking sites as a source of online advertisement by public schools are the potential financial and human costs of having to navigate the legal issues that can arise related to the online environment. These legal costs can financially impact districts as well as take away needed resources in the classroom.

LEGAL ISSUES

Financial resources for today's public schools are scarce. Using social networking sites require schools to potentially become involved in legal issues that have yet to be clearly defined by U.S. courts. Unfortunately, the possibility of significant human and capital resources being tied up in litigation is all too real. Unlike traditional websites that can only be edited by those authorized to do so, social networking websites are designed to actively allow the public to participate. This brings into question what types of speech and expression students, teachers, administrators and patrons are allowed to engage in within an online environment. To date, the U.S. courts have delivered mixed messages in this area of the law that have left school districts little in the way of guidance as it relates to regulating social networking sites for use by school officials and students.

Two recent court cases in Pennsylvania help illustrate issues surrounding online student speech and expression in social networking sites. In *Layshock v. Hermitage School District* (2010) and *J.S. v. Blue Mountain School District* (2010), trial courts were asked to determine whether or not school officials could sanction students for using pictures of their principals taken from their respective school websites to build fake Myspace pages that contained potentially damaging yet false information about the principals. In the *Layshock* case, the trial court decided the officials of Hermitage School could not sanction Layshock for the false Myspace page since it merely was "parody." The court in the *J.S.* case, however, took a different view when it decided that J.S. could be sanctioned for her speech, reasoning that J.S.'s speech was so vulgar it offended community values. Furthermore, the court reasoned that due to the potential harm to her principal's professional reputation, J.S.'s speech could not be afforded First Amendment protection. To reconcile these two seemingly conflicting legal opinions, both cases have been reviewed by the full Third Circuit Court of Appeals. The court essentially upheld the *Layshock* decision but reversed portions of the decision in *J.S.*, holding that school authorities could not discipline the student for her actions. The history of these cases shows how the law is not clearly settled in this area.

In 2009, two high school sophomore girls who posted racy photographs of themselves on the popular social networking site Myspace were suspended from extracurricular activities at their school for the entire 2009 to 2010 school year. The students sought to pursue legal remedy as a class action suit. A trial court representing the Fort Wayne Division of the Northern District of Indiana ruled the complainants lacked the "numerosity" and adequate class representation necessary to support certification as a class. The court went further by stating that certifying a class for this type of complaint was legally untenable because the fact-specific nature of each claim would require each case to be decided on its own merits.

In Florida, a student, Katherine Evans, started a Myspace group titled "Ms. Sarah Philips is the worst teacher I've ever met" and was disciplined by her principal for cyberbullying. The judge in the case ruled that Evans's speech was protected because it did not cause any on-campus disruption and was not lewd or threatening and did not advocate illegal or dangerous behavior. However, the judge did admit that it was not clear what legal precedent should control in this case. Evans received $1 in nominal damages, $15,000 in attorney fees, and an order of the court requiring the school to expunge all references to the Myspace page and the resulting suspension from her record. So, where is that magic line that separates protected from nonprotected online student speech? If federal judges cannot agree, how useful are their legal opinions in making social networking sites a safe vehicle for school officials, including both teachers and administrators, to use in communicating with their students?

Teacher speech is no more clearly defined than student speech when using social networking sites. In 2007, the Ohio Education Association (OEA), a subsidiary of the National Education Association, issued a memo warning teachers about the use of Myspace online profiles and actively discouraged teachers from using them. The OEA's memo warned that online content from a teacher's Myspace profile could be used as evidence in adverse employment proceedings.

Approximately 1 year later, in *Spanierman v. Hughes*, the Federal District Court in Connecticut upheld the termination of a nontenured teacher for posting a Myspace page in which the teacher posted online pictures of nude men and held personal, online conversations with students. Although the teacher argued disparate treatment because other teachers who maintained Myspace pages were not similarly disciplined, the court disagreed. The judge in the case held that the content of the teacher's personal social networking site was not analogous to the online content of other teachers' pages and thus no disparate treatment had occurred. The court also rejected the teacher's free speech claim since his conduct was likely to be disruptive to the school.

Exactly how far a school district can go in regulating the online speech of students or teachers is currently not clear. The courts have used both the *Tinker* "substantial and material disruption" standard as well as the *Bethel v. Fraser* "lewd and vulgar" standard. Yet no definitive legal standard for online student or teacher speech has emerged. Attempts to adjudicate teacher online speech issues have largely been based on statutory state ethics codes in states where they exist or potential criminal statutes.

In considering the use of social networking sites as a means to promote themselves, a school district should ask the question, "What can be accomplished with social networking sites that cannot be accomplished using a traditional online website?" Additionally, does the potential of using social networking sites outweigh the financial costs in terms of litigation and the tension among school administration, teachers, students, and parents? As a viable alternative, traditional websites can provide students and parents with homework assignments, lesson plans, field trip information, and, through the use of a secure, password-protected system, access to a student's grades. Simultaneously, a traditional website with password-protection carefully regulates the online communication among a school's users.

CONCLUSION

This counterpoint essay argued that today's social networking sites are not effective means for schools to promote themselves. Social networking sites, by their very nature, are interactive. Even in school-administered social networking site accounts, the potential for inappropriate online relationships between teachers and students and, by extension, the legal issues and nightmares that accompany those situations, are very real issues and concerns for school officials. Due to the ability of social networking site users to "friend" one another, the chain reaction among individual user accounts, including from school-owned and operated to one or more private accounts, can occur easily. The transition in cyberspace from a school-owned social networking account to a personal, or individual, social networking user account all too often is mirrored by a transition from an appropriate and legal relationship to an inappropriate one. Even with the flurry of effort currently underway in many states and school districts to craft protective and effective policies for the use of social networking sites, their use by schools for public relations is an online minefield no school needs to navigate.

FURTHER READINGS AND RESOURCES

Brady, K. P. (2010). Lifting the limits on social networking sites. *The School Administrator,* 67(2), 8.

Digitalbuzz Blog. (2011). *Facebook statistics, stats and facts for 2011.* Retrieved from http://www.digitalbuzzblog.com/facebook-statistics-stats-facts-2011

Facebook. (n.d.). *Statistics.* Retrieved from http://www.facebook.com/press/info .php?statistics

Ferrera, G. R., Reder, M. E. K., Bird, R. C., Darrow, J. J., Aresty, J. M., Klosek, J., et al. (2011). *Cyberlaw: Text and cases* (3rd ed.). Mason, OH: South-Western College.

Hampton, K. N., Goulet, L., & Rainie, L. (2011). *Social networking sites and our lives.* Washington, DC: Pew Research Center's Internet & American Life Project.

Hinduja, S., & Patchin, J. W. (2009). *Bullying beyond the schoolyard: Preventing and responding to cyberbullying.* Thousand Oaks, CA: Corwin.

Jacobs, T. A. (2010). *Teen cyberbullying investigated: Where do your rights end and consequences begin?* Minneapolis, MN: Free Spirit Publishing.

Kessler, S. (2010). *The case for social media in schools.* Retrieved April 18, 2011, from http://mashable.com/2010/09/29/social-media-in-school

National School Boards Association (NSBA). (2007). *Creating and connecting: Research and guidelines on online social—and educational—networking.* Retrieved June 29, 2011, from http://www.nsba.org/Services/TLN/BenefitsofMembership/Publications/ Creating-and-Connecting.pdf

Shakeshaft, C. (2004). *Educator sexual misconduct: A synthesis of existing literature.* Washington, DC: U.S. Department of Education.

Social Media Schools. (2008). *Should your school be using social media?* Retrieved June 29, 2011, from http://socialmediaschools.com/should-your-school-be-using-social-media/2008/11

Court Cases and Statutes

Access Now, Inc. v. Southwest Airlines, Co. 227 F. Supp.2d 1312, 1322 (S.D. Fla. 2002).

Americans with Disabilities Act of 1990, 42 U.S.C. §§ 12101-12213 (2006) as amended by ADA Amendments Act of 2008, PL 110-325, 122 Stat. 3553 (2008).

Carparts Distribution Center, Inc. v. Automotive Wholesaler's Association, 37 F.3d 12 (1st Cir. 1994).

J.S. v. Blue Mountain School District, 593 F.3d 286 (3d Cir. 2010), *vacated, reh'g en banc granted,* 2010 U.S. App. LEXIS 7342 (3d Cir, Apr. 9, 2010), 2011 WL 2305973 (3d Cir. 2011).

Layshock v. Hermitage School District, 496 F. Supp. 2d 587 (W.D. Pa. 2007), *affirmed* 593 F.3d 249 (3d Cir. 2010), *rehearing en banc granted, opinion vacated* (3d Cir. April 9, 2010), *affirmed* 2011 WL 2305970 (3d Cir.).

Louisiana Revised Statutes, Title 17, § 81(Q) (2009).

National Federation of the Blind v. Target. 452 F. Supp. 2d 946 (N.D. Cal. 2006).

Spanierman v. Hughes 576 F. Supp 2d 292 (D. Conn. 2008).

13

Do new technologies have the potential to transform education by replacing current teaching methods?

POINT: Jill Castek, *University of California, Berkeley*

COUNTERPOINT: Margaret Hagood, *College of Charleston*

OVERVIEW

As this chapter shows, thoughts about use of new technologies present some of the most varied and divided questions in education research and classroom practice. On a far side of that divide are idealists who believe that new technologies can radically transform public education, as they have other areas, such as biotechnology. To the idealists, digital tools provide means for viewing various media, collaborative network learning, and so forth. To others, new technologies are a great equalizer; nearly anyone can construct a level of product that a few years ago was only within the capacity of a few people with specialized training.

From a more moderate perspective are optimists who place hope on the promises of new technologies, particularly those of the Internet and its accompanying virtual learning environments and resources, novel means of assisting students who struggle with academics, and ways to connect with others in their immediate as well as wider surroundings. In her counterpoint essay, Margaret Hagood (College of Charleston) takes such a position in showing many of the benefits that can be found in the uses of new technologies, but cautions that new technologies are not the key to successful instruction.

Taking the middle ground are pragmatists who draw from the technologies of the moment as simply tools to address an immediate need or problem, such as employing an education software program that adds or delivers content outside the ability or resources of a school, such as a language program to assist a student who speaks a different language than those in the classroom. In her point essay, Jill Castek (University of California, Berkeley), as does Hagood in her counterpoint essay, highlights possible education benefits of new technologies, but points to the many unrealized potentials of those tools when actual classroom pedagogies are examined.

Moving further along the scale of perspectives, there are skeptics who often reject new trends and favor older technologies and methods that have stood the test of time or are a product of their direct experience. For example, a skeptic might argue that the pen, writing tablet, blackboard, and book—once extraordinary technologies—are more than sufficient tools in the hands of an expert teacher to effectively teach curriculum content to students. To them, reaching beyond these basic materials and methods is a nebulous area that is simply not necessary for them to explore.

Finally, there are the dissidents who, for various reasons, flatly reject the hopes and promises of the idealists and optimists. For instance, new forms of communication distance people from others as well as from nature. From these four camps of opinion, new technologies have potential, for better or worse. Yet, to actualize the potential of novel ideas, tools, and materials for enhancement in education is often a difficult task.

The enhancement to curriculum and instruction that new technologies afford—the notion that guides the present chapter—is sometimes a matter of degree. In various respects, the matter of degree is tied to overall issues in education. For example, as shown throughout the present book series, the belief that public education in the United States is in need of radical reform has been a key issue over recent years. This conviction is fueled by reported national student achievement scores that are flat at best, and dismal at worst. New technologies skeptics point out that computers and similar tools have been a part of many of the nation's classrooms for some time but have had little overall effect on teaching and learning. In response, optimists counter that although sophisticated digital tools are available in classrooms, they have been grossly underutilized by teachers who lack the proper skills to use new technologies effectively. Further, students in some schools may have little time to devote to learning and using new technologies since their school time is taken by other, more conventional practices ranging from worksheets and tests to hands-on experiential learning.

Even so, reform is about change, often radical change. In the ilk of such change is the work of Bill Gates, founder, former CEO, and code writer of Microsoft, who, in partnership with IBM, revolutionized computing practices and placed the PC into the laps of millions of users. Gates has left his posts at Microsoft, and he is now an education reform advocate. In a February 2011 *Washington Post* opinion piece, he wrote about how to "flip the curve" in public education by increasing class sizes and reducing spending costs. Although not expressed by Gates, placing his business and new technologies background alongside schooling practices suggests another possible dimension of radical reform that could appeal to avid digital enthusiasts: the human teacher, at least in part, could be replaced by computerized learning platforms, artificial intelligence, and innovative software.

An illustrative case of teacher replacement appeared in a July 2010 *New York Times* article, which shows how science fiction can become science fact (Carey & Markoff, 2010). In experimental classrooms in the United States, sophisticated teaching robots with artificial intelligence, abilities to track human movement and expression, and speech recognition abilities, have recently been "hired," as the reporters described it, to instruct children. Similarly, students can now take three-dimensional tours through online museums and examine archaeological sites, representations of government buildings such as the White House, and so forth. Also using a computer, children can ponder and rotate digital objects and interact with multiple spaces and virtual teachers, among other things. Additionally, they can play and learn processes through what James Gee (2008) described as "serious games" that are related to "serious learning."

A skeptic might argue that these experiences cannot replicate important human qualities, such as subtle gestures, expressions, and feelings. However, the lines between the virtual and real world increasingly blur. To the pragmatist, these devices can possibly be effective for instructing children in some of the most basic school skills, such as beginning word and number identification, which could free teachers' time to address more sophisticated and thought-provoking curriculum material. In the end, these virtual environments, artificial intelligence, and robotics might be appealing to policymakers because of state budget deficits that affect public education funding.

The answer to whether new technologies enhance classroom instruction might also be a matter of place and pace. On one basic scale, having seemingly endless resources in a computer file versus storing and retrieving resources from conventional file cabinets could make instructional planning and delivery easier. Conversely, sifting through a plethora of teaching materials can be daunting. On a broader scale, affluent communities may be more likely to have access to the newest technologies, and savvy users of them, than other places. In the United States, there have been efforts to close the "digital divide" by providing computers, Internet access, software, and so on to schools (Negroponte, 2005). Still, divisions based on local economies continue, as have lingering questions about the utility and impact computers and new technologies have had, and will have, on overall teaching practices and student learning.

A. Jonathan Eakle
The Johns Hopkins University

POINT: Jill Castek
University of California, Berkeley

Internet-connected computers and portable digital devices have the potential to become the defining technologies for literacy and learning in the 21st century. However, for teachers in today's classrooms, this potential has not been fully realized. As such, this point essay explores the potential technology holds for transforming classroom instruction and reasons why this promise remains untapped in K–12 education. This point essay concludes with a discussion of the changes that need to take place for the promise of new technologies to be more fully realized.

EXPLORING THE POTENTIAL OF NEW TECHNOLOGIES TO TRANSFORM TEACHING AND LEARNING

New technologies offer educators opportunities to transform teaching and learning. However, the value of any new technology depends on how purposefully it is used (Bauer & Kenton, 2005). When put to best use, computers can support inquiry learning, provide access to a wealth of information, offer creative ways to share content and ideas online, and extend learning experiences to prepare students for their futures. Each of these potentials, and the ways classrooms fail to take advantage of them, are explored in the following sections.

Computers Support Inquiry Learning

Despite the advent of new technologies that have given rise to new pedagogies, most of our classrooms remain traditional as teachers introduce ideas that students are expected to later produce on assignments, tests, and projects. In contrast, teaching with the Internet and infusing the use of new technologies through the curriculum creates an environment where inquiry learning can be more fully embraced. With the strategic use of computers, students can learn to locate their own resources, access content in flexible ways, and engage with a wide variety of information presented in multiple formats. Inviting students to explore the full range of information available to them online assists them in accessing knowledge; however, the scope of what new technologies makes possible extends far further. Students can readily contribute to the resources available online and are able to distribute their new knowledge widely through online networks.

Inquiry learning encourages students to use their creativity and exercise choice. Online resources promote connections to the real world and provide instant access to simulations, animations, and visual enhancements. These resources can also connect students to experts through video conferencing platforms, networking websites, and webinars. Instead of being asked to produce one right answer, online inquiries lead to multiple solutions that, when shared, benefit the whole group of learners. Yet, school-based curricula are not often organized in ways that make inquiry learning possible. Many curricular programs tend to employ highly structured approaches to whole-group teaching that is geared toward mastery of a set number of skills that are introduced, reinforced, and assessed in a given sequence.

Computers Provide Access to a Wealth of Information

The Internet provides instant access to vast amounts of information. This appears to motivate students to explore a wide range of resources, making it possible to deeply investigate the topics that are the most interesting to them. Even so, in light of the seemingly infinite amount and range of information that each student can access, navigating resources on the Internet requires students to be skilled in making informed choices about what they explore. Thus, the Internet is both a much richer context for content learning and also a much more complicated one. To take advantage of the resources the Internet makes available to students, they must learn to skillfully select, evaluate, manage, and organize information efficiently. Assisting students in acquiring these skills is a significant and important way that teachers can be helpful. They can guide students as they work to gather, organize, and analyze information. In addition, these resources can help students learn to communicate strategically, work successfully in collaborative teams, and learn effectively from online resources. On the other hand, new technologies enable students to work with greater autonomy, collaborate with peers, and gain access to information related to their own interests. Exploring ideas in this way has the potential to increase students' investment in their own learning processes.

At the same time, school-based curricula are not often organized to provide access to the abundance of information that can be found online. Instead, teachers frequently provide specific texts for students to read rather than allowing them to locate several resources and then choose which ones to skim and which ones to read in depth. In fact, the primary way teachers convey concepts is by providing material found in textbooks and similarly traditional curricular resources. Such so-called offline materials are often outdated and explore only a single perspective, which limits opportunities for students to learn to recognize quality resources and sort them out from those that are less valuable. In addition, these offline materials provide few authentic opportunities to engage in the critical evaluation of ideas while exploring ways in which authors shape ideas and persuade readers to accept their way of thinking. Exposure to a wide range of online resources and the ability to make choices gives rise to the sort of critical thinking that educators value the most.

Computers Facilitate Ways to Share Content and Ideas Online

With the wide variety of networked applications that permeate the Internet today, learners can explore, create, and share ideas in dynamic ways (Leu, O'Byrne, Zawilinski, McVerry, & Everett-Cocapardo, 2009). Video creation and editing software, for example, allows students to create and share multimodal presentations that illuminate concepts or tell stories in unique and compelling ways. Digital cameras allow students to capture images and embed them into classroom websites, blogs, Glogs, or other networked spaces. Online collaboration environments such as Edmodo and presentation tools such as VoiceThread make it possible for groups of students to collaborate on projects simultaneously, even when they do not share the same physical learning space. Through these digital platforms, students have more opportunity to use their creativity to explore ideas and share what they know; and teachers have greater flexibility to monitor and support student learning.

More often than not, schools remain composed of traditional classroom arrangements where the teacher is the sole voice of authority, lectures at the front of the class, and addresses the class in a homogenized manner. Instruction is targeted for the students who are in the middle range of abilities and less attention is given to inattentive or more advanced students who might already have learned the material. The teacher might ask a few students to come to the front of the room to solve a problem, while the rest are encouraged to watch. While no teacher strives to teach in this way, the reality of these tendencies in U.S. classrooms remains intact. New technologies might have the potential to transform education, but that promise is far from being realized because teaching methods have not changed in response to the dynamic learning environments new technologies have made possible.

Computers Extend Learning Experiences That Prepare Students for Their Futures

Computers hold considerable potential to supplement the textbooks, trade books, and student-created resources traditionally found in classrooms for problem solving, inquiry, project-based learning, and collaborative work. This goal often leads to students' searching for information on the Web, sharing ideas digitally, and preparing reports and presentations using word processors, computer graphic tools, and multimedia presentation software.

However, school-based curricula are not often organized to prepare students for their futures. Many school curricula do not take advantage of different representations of knowledge, including those found in graphics, digital models, simulations, or interactives. Although these resources are freely available to educators and students on the World Wide Web, educators lack a centralized digital portal where such enhancements are stored and made widely available. In fact, high-speed Internet access in many schools is limited, at best. In other schools, it is controlled and even censored. These types of resources enhance students' understanding of content; yet the widespread use of such resources remains largely untapped.

WHY IS THE POTENTIAL OF NEW TECHNOLOGIES UNTAPPED IN K–12 EDUCATION?

Some U.S. schools are ill equipped in terms of providing students access to computers, new technologies, and other digital devices. In school districts that serve poor economic communities, there may not be a single computer in a classroom, let alone high-speed Internet connections, cutting-edge software, and access to a knowledgeable teacher who can guide students in using technology to maximize learning. Although the reasons for these inequities lie outside the scope of this point essay, it is important to recognize that the gap in economic resources between communities has had a notable effect on the general failure of schools to realize the potential of new technologies for teaching and learning. Further, despite the potential for enhancing instruction, when adequate computers are found in schools, even up-to-date multimedia computers with high-speed Internet access are often not used in ways that significantly enhance teaching and learning. For example, students are often provided computer time for rote drill-and-practice exercises, to complete online quizzes associated with popular computer programs, such as Accelerate Reader or Read 180, or simply as an unguided, free-choice reward activity when their assigned academic work is completed. Additional examples include the use of computers as terminals for word processing practice or as a means of accessing games or other extension activities on CD or DVD. Despite sustained research and development demonstrating the positive benefit of using new technologies throughout schooling, a significant disconnect remains between the potential of computers in education and the ways that they are currently being used or not being used.

WHAT WOULD IT TAKE FOR EDUCATORS TO MORE FULLY REALIZE THE PROMISE OF COMPUTERS AND NEW TECHNOLOGIES?

Increased Opportunities for Professional Development

Teachers play a critical role in school reform efforts. Yet there is much to be learned about how to support teachers in successfully integrating technology into teaching, learning, and assessment. To date, teachers have not received adequate training and support for integrating technology into day-to-day classroom instruction (International Reading Association, 2009). Training in the benefits and uses of new technologies must begin in pre-service teacher education programs and occur continuously as an important component of professional development in K–12 schools.

Insofar as the new technologies that surround us continually evolve, training itself will not fully ensure that all teachers will develop a firm grasp on the pedagogy needed to design and conduct meaningful learning opportunities that use new technologies. Thus, *sustained* professional development efforts are needed. For example, nurturing professional learning communities made up of those who are technology savvy as well as those who are novices may provide critical peer assistance. By affording time to explore new ways of using technologies, to reflect on their teaching practice, and to share ideas about new technology program implementation, teachers will be much more likely to use technology in ways that enhance student learning.

Shared Goals

When it comes to articulating the educational purposes computers serve in classrooms, many different views within a school district, and beyond, may abound. However, when educators embrace a common vision and a shared set of goals, they take a first step in what is vitally important to the success of any educational initiative. The educational community at large needs to view technology as a means of meeting established goals, not as a new or separate set of goals. Working toward well=thought-out and publicly embraced objectives will head off challenges such as conflicting expectations, educational approaches, and criteria for evaluating impact.

Transformation of Traditional Teaching Practices

To embrace the full range of possibilities for learning that new technologies make possible, traditional teaching practices need to be transformed. A gap is widening between the way youth engage with digital media and the way technology is used to address curriculum standards. To help close this gap, greater emphasis needs to be put into creating learning environments that take advantage of networked, multimodal, and social tools and techniques that engage learners in supporting each other's construction of knowledge within and beyond school. Hagood's counterpoint essay draws attention to the fact that traditional teaching practices fail to explicitly address the "cultural competencies necessary to engage in participatory communities." Hagood goes on to assert that "various technologies require different rules of engagement, which often are not intuitive and therefore must be taught." For these reasons, targeted teaching practices that move beyond traditional instructional methods must become a regular part of classroom learning so that students can skillfully acquire these essential skills.

Transformation of the School Culture

The culture surrounding computer use at a school plays a significant role in the acceptance or rejection of technology among teachers (Hew & Brush, 2007). Developing a learning culture that promotes the use of new technologies and the adoption of new teaching practices involving those technologies are important factors in successful efforts. This requires teachers to think flexibly about organizing daily activities that involve computers, which can be a challenge in some schools where human and material resources are limited.

Cross-Curricular Connections

Framing the Internet as a literacy issue will speed Internet integration into the classroom and help avoid resistance, which is common in schools, and lead to full-scale new technology integration. Adopting a specific focus on technology-rich instruction across content areas will encourage the use of new technologies as an integrated set of skills and strategies that enhance student learning (Gray, Thomas, & Lewis, 2010). These skills are a vital part of learning in the 21st century and require full integration spanning from preschool to grades K–12 and beyond.

Fully Addressing the Common Core State Standards

The Common Core State Standards provide an overview of capacities expected of 21st-century individuals. These new standards assert that students should be able to use technology and digital media strategically and capably and employ technology thoughtfully to enhance their reading, writing, speaking, listening, and language use. For example, students are expected to conduct online searches to acquire useful information efficiently; draw information from multiple print or digital sources to locate an answer to a question quickly or solve a problem efficiently; gather relevant information from multiple print and digital sources and assess the credibility and accuracy of each source; and use technology to produce, publish, and interact with others while also recognizing the strengths and limitations of various technological tools. These standards suggest that strategic knowledge about how and when to use various technologies to communicate ideas is an essential component of reading and writing in today's networked world.

While many schools are not yet positioned to fully address these goals, it seems evident that reform efforts will soon be under way to meet the charge these standards set forth. Implementation will require the development of a new generation of educational leaders who are able to support their students in learning as well as support their colleagues in teaching strategically with technology.

NEXT STEPS

While new technologies hold tremendous potential to enhance teaching and learning, turning that potential into reality is a complex and multifaceted task. It requires the development of new teaching practices as well as the adoption of new mindsets. Despite the fact that computers and digital devices are ubiquitous and widely used, the integration of new technologies in school classrooms has not become a natural outgrowth of the use of technology in our daily lives. Few teachers are knowledgeable about how to guide their students in developing online reading, writing, and collaboration skills in today's networked world. If we are to realize the potential of new technologies in education, it is imperative that we support teachers' understanding of the profound changes taking place in literacy and its ripple effect on educational settings.

Success in meeting this goal will be defined by a unified and clear educational vision. Carefully planned long-term commitments are required. The U.S. Department of Education has released a new National Educational Technology Plan that guides the use of information and communication technologies in transforming education (National Education Technology Panel, 2010). It calls for a revolutionary transformation rather than evolutionary tinkering of the educational system and encourages educational communities to use new technologies in school in ways that reflect how they are used in nearly every aspect of modern life. The plan provides a set of concrete goals that can inform state and local educational initiatives. If these initiatives are realized, we can look forward to substantial reforms that will aid educators in using technology strategically to enhance student learning.

COUNTERPOINT: Margaret Hagood
College of Charleston

Technologies in educational contexts have historically served the purposes of improving communication, productivity, and efficiency of learning. Among these technologies are the printing press, the telephone, and the television. All of these technologies have changed the way that information was produced for, distributed to, and consumed by audiences.

New technologies, including computers, the Internet, cell phones, e-book readers, hand-held devices, and gaming consoles and accessories, have opened wide access to information and various forms of learning. These new technologies are characterized by customization, interaction, and user control. Thus, new technologies have not only advanced the access to information for users, whereby improving communication capabilities, but these have also allowed users to develop their own queries and to pursue their own interests and goals, affecting the efficiency of learning and transforming classroom instructional practices. These tools are powerful enough to have changed the ways that people communicate, think, produce, and consume information, and they have propelled the knowledge revolution to a level where information and access can be ever-present to many people. However, new technologies are not the magic bullet of improved classroom instruction. They do not, and should not, replace foundational learning and teaching methods, but must be used in conjunction with foundational learning tools.

NEW TECHNOLOGIES AND CLASSROOM INSTRUCTION

New technologies of the early 21st century have moved away from distributive models of knowledge used in 19th- and 20th-century classroom instruction. To be sure, the concepts of knowledge and learning have changed because of new technologies. Rather than learning in a didactic and teacher-controlled environment—where the transfer of knowledge is from teacher to student, which was characteristic of the Industrial Revolution and its production line economy—new technologies allow teachers to focus content instruction on the inquiry of students' ideas and on teacher and student knowledge creation. New technologies also allow users to access information and content and to communicate with others instantly and in practically any imaginable setting. Further, new technologies are integrally tied to forms of social interaction, whereby users create their own content, share it with others, and use content to engage others' attention, conversation, and friendship in both face-to-face (f2f) and online contexts. And, perhaps most important to the educational setting, uses of new technologies are not age specific. Very young children to adults use new technologies as part of their day-to-day lives.

New technologies are significant for classroom instruction for two reasons. First, these technologies have changed the ways in which we think. Access to information abounds on the Internet, as well as in other mass media, and people must have the skills and strategies necessary not only to locate the information but also to evaluate its usefulness, to judge its merit and credibility, and to synthesize it so that it can be meaningfully utilized. Users must be able to act quickly and efficiently in implementing these skills and strategies because the various new technologies not only provide users with heaps of information, but they also compete with one another for users' attention. Second, access to information has also changed how people learn. No longer do students have to wait to learn information presented by teachers following a specific curriculum and its scope and sequence. Instead, users with access to new technologies proactively search for information on a just-in-time basis, obtaining information as and when it is needed. As such, users of new technologies expect to have information, some of which has been created very recently and other material that has been present for centuries, at their disposal and to be able to sift ably through it for what is of interest to them at that particular moment.

LITERACY AND COMMUNICATION

New technologies have also changed views of literacy and have affected how we communicate with one another. Literacy has historically been defined as the ability to read and write and that was assumed to include only printed language texts. However, the advent of new technologies that include printed texts, graphics, visual data displays, photographs, embedded videos, audio tracks, and animations/simulations, to name only a few, have helped expand the definition of literacy to include the ability to read, write, and communicate with a variety of print as well as nonprint materials, such as pictures. Indeed, users of technologies must be able to read and to write with printed words alongside images, sound, and other media. They must also learn how to maintain their focus on the material and tasks at hand, avoiding texts and content unrelated to their set goals for reading and/or writing.

In this way, new technologies have touched the forms and functions of literacy within the content we learn and how we learn it. Users now must be able to navigate through and with new technologies, decoding and encoding a variety of multimodal texts individually and in formal and informal community groups. The multimodal access to information and content has also changed the ways that we communicate with one another. Communication now is varied via e-mail, text, phone, video conferencing, vlogging/blogging; and it is also in many cases instantaneous. These new technologies have broken down boundaries that have tied people to a specific location and have given people freedoms to forge global connections that take place in real time.

As such, it is of great importance to consider the ethical responsibilities teachers and learners have when working with new technologies. Users must consider not only the technological tool to communicate and the genre for the literacy to be used, but they must also form understandings of the social skills and cultural competencies necessary to engage in participatory communities that are afforded by access to the technological tool at hand. Communication using these various technologies requires different rules of engagement, which often are not intuitive and therefore must be taught. It is crucial, then, that classroom instruction includes engagement in reflective activities where participants must consider the rules of the community and the protocol for membership within the community, whether it is a face-to-face interaction or a more distanced one, such as through a blog. Sometimes that instruction and learning is done among teachers and pupils in formal education settings, but often these processes take place less formally, outside of traditional education settings, such as among young people communicating protocol through instant messaging.

Indeed, changes in communication, teaching, learning, literacy, and community access reflect our changing world. In part because of these changes, new technologies have shifted education and instruction out of the confines of a school and classroom and into the world, providing opportunities for users to develop skills to function in societies and to work differently than they would if restricted to merely classrooms. No longer are users only consumers of technologies. Instead, today users are also designers and producers of content. As designers, consumers, and producers, users actively engage in their own learning and the sharing of the content they produce with others. In such cases, users develop their own teacher–student or mentor–mentee relationships with others through their engagement with new technologies.

Uses of new technologies are also part of socially situated practices supported by skills, strategies, and stances that enable the representation and understanding of ideas using a range of modalities that are embedded within new technological tools. Competent users of new technologies understand how to select appropriate tools to meet their learning needs, and they also plan how to use a variety of new technologies to represent various ideas. For education to be relevant to students and teachers, classroom instruction and learning expectations must adapt and change for both teachers and students so as to keep pace with the workings of new technologies in out-of-school spaces. The benefits of instructional practices from using new technologies abound for both teachers and students.

BENEFITS OF NEW TECHNOLOGIES IN THE CLASSROOM

Access to and uses of new technologies in classroom instruction yield more well-rounded and expanded roles for teachers and students. Because content is ubiquitous online and there are many ways to access the same information, such as through online streaming video, pictorial depiction, and reading of scanned primary documents, teachers no longer must act as the sole owners of content and the transmitters of knowledge. Instead, teachers become facilitators of student learning or coaches (of sorts), instructing and mentoring students on how to learn rather than imparting the knowledge they deem important.

In a similar and reciprocal way, new technologies can diminish passive learning. Rather, students are active participants and contributors to propel their knowledge and understanding of content. This redeveloped and recalibrated relationship between teacher and students results in shared responsibility for teaching and learning and in the creation of new meaning. In a redefined teacher-student relationship, content learning can be catered to students' interests and needs. Students can help shape the curriculum and their own learning based on personal learning goals that connect to and extend beyond relevant content area curriculum standards.

New technologies also exponentially improve access to resources, which can be infused into classroom instruction. With Internet connections and computers, wireless multimedia tablets, or smart phones, mobile access to information for teachers and students gives anytime, anywhere, anyhow learning capability. For teachers, this means a connection to a network of other professionals with whom to communicate and collaborate through online interaction between individuals and within online learning communities. Online resources also give teachers access to a seemingly endless array of content that can be used to enliven a course of study or to expand a textbook description or to give alternative perspectives not represented in a classroom or through a single source, which more often than not is a textbook or similarly static instructional resource with comparatively dated information to what is available through the Internet. For students, access to information changes how and when they learn. With access to new Internet technologies, schooling as a process of learning is no longer confined to a building and a classroom. Instead, online access allows for flexibility across time and space so that learning can become more flexible and content can be perused and developed in greater depth.

New technologies in the classroom provide opportunities for varied learning opportunities as well. Students' needs may be met through flexible grouping options that are supported by new technologies. For example, students can work on self-paced tasks using technologies that assist with foundational literacies. Drill and practice games and digital simulations can help students develop content and process knowledge and can provide them with immediate feedback, which is often motivating and can lead to students' improved academic performance. Using computer technologies in this way frees up a teacher's time to work with other students in individualized or small, cooperative groups on tasks that require uses of new technologies that engage the learner in higher-level analysis and synthesis. For example, groups can create a digital story that summarizes the findings of global warming using online and print-based references. In this instance, students could also integrate content from their local environments, such as how global warming might be affecting natural resources in their communities, by collecting digital photographs, and so forth. Thus, new technologies provide a smorgasbord of learning opportunities for the development of important skills through drill and practice, synthesis, analysis, and evaluation. In short, new technologies in classroom instruction bring the wider world into a walled space, providing a boost for teachers to engage students through innovative and relevant technological tools, which makes learning more interactive and provides enhanced potential for improved retention of content and processes that are relevant to students' lives.

Online access also takes the walled space of the classroom out into the world, giving students a larger audience with whom to collaborate and to share. On the Internet, students can match up with others working on drill and practice exercises, thus moving an individual activity into a group space. Likewise, social networking websites on the Internet provide the space for group work to be shared with audiences much larger than the classroom or school community.

THE REAL KEY TO SUCCESSFUL CLASSROOM INSTRUCTION

Research has shown that new technologies can, indeed, help improve teaching and learning when used wisely. However, classroom instruction is only as good as the instructors who teach in those rooms, regardless of whether those rooms are real brick-and-mortar or virtual ones, such as those of online learning communities. Hence, teacher–student relationships are the key to successful classroom instruction using new, as well as older, technologies. It is crucial to understand that simply having access to the tools of new technologies and an adequate supportive infrastructure are not enough.

For classroom instruction to be successful with new technologies, teachers must have training on the tools and proper ongoing support. Training for successful implementation includes time for teachers to learn about the technologies, including the related theories and research related to the technologies. It also includes a period of time for teachers to use the technologies in their own lives, without having to immediately apply them to classroom instruction. And only when teachers have developed facility with the technology and been given time to think through appropriate classroom uses for enhancing instruction, learning, and teacher–student relationships should they then include it in classrooms, relating the technology to content area standards. Further, once technologies are implemented in classrooms, teachers need outlets for continued professional development and support. These outlets might be formal, such as in professional development course offerings, or informal, as in the joining of an online community of teacher users of content to share ideas and to garner support.

Classroom instruction using new technologies must also connect foundational literacy practices, such as the ability to decode words for reading and writing print, to comprehend authorial intent, to summarize, and to write a cohesive paragraph with new literacies practices, such as the ability to download music, to splice video, to analyze a visual image, and to compose a shorthand text message. Teachers and students must share the responsibility to instruct each other on the nuances of the literacy practices so that foundational and new literacy practices can work in unison via new technologies. They need to be able to use technologies in ways to build relationships with students where both teachers and students engage collaboratively in teaching and learning how to use tools.

New technologies are not a fad or an educational quick fix. They are here to stay, but they should not replace traditional instructional methods. The question with regard to new technologies, therefore, is how and to what extent these technologies should be used in schools to ensure that current instruction is meaningful and relevant to students' lives.

FURTHER READINGS AND RESOURCES

Bauer, J., & Kenton, J. (2005). Toward technology integration in the schools: Why it isn't happening. *Journal of Technology and Teacher Education, 13*(4), 519–546.

Carey, B., & Markoff, J. (2010, July 10). Students, meet your new teacher, Mr. Robot. *The New York Times.* Retrieved from http://www.nytimes.com/2010/07/11/science/11robots.html

Gee, J. P. (2008). "Learning and games." The ecology of games: Connecting youth, games, and learning. In K. Salen (Ed.), *The John D. and Catherine T. MacArthur Foundation series on digital media and learning* (pp. 21–40). Cambridge: MIT Press.

Gray, L., Thomas, N., & Lewis, L. (2010). *Teachers' use of educational technology in U.S. public schools: 2009.* Retrieved from National Center for Educational Statistics website: http://nces.ed.gov/pubs2010/2010040.pdf

Hew, K. F., & Brush, T. (2007). Integrating technology into K-12 teaching and learning: Current knowledge gaps and recommendations for future research. *Educational Technology Research and Development, 55*(3), 223–252.

International Reading Association. (2009). *New literacies and 21st century technologies: A position statement.* Newark, DE: Author. Retrieved from http://www.reading.org/General/AboutIRA/PositionStatements/21stCenturyLiteracies.aspx

Ito, M., Horst, H., Bittanti, M., Boyd, D., Herr-Stephenson, B., Lange, P. G., et al. (2008). *Living and learning with new media: Summary of findings from the Digital Youth Project.* Chicago: MacArthur Foundation Digital Media and Learning Project.

Jenkins, H. (2006). *Confronting the challenges of participatory culture: Media education for the 21st century.* Chicago: MacArthur Foundation.

Lenhart, A., Arafeh, S., Smith, A., & Rankin Macgill, A. (2008). *Writing, technology and teens.* Washington, DC: Pew Internet & American Life Project.

Leu, D. J., O'Byrne, W. I., Zawilinski, L., McVerry, J. G., & Everett-Cocapardo, H. (2009). Expanding the new literacies conversation. *Educational Researcher, 38,* 264–269.

National Education Technology Panel. (2010). *Transforming American education: Learning powered by technology.* Washington, DC: U.S. Department of Education. Retrieved from http://www.ed.gov/technology/netp-2010

Negroponte, N. (2005, November 18). One laptop per child. *The Economist.* Retrieved February 6, 2011, from http://www.economist.com/node/5134619

Rushkoff, D. (2010). *Program or be programmed: Ten commands for a digital age.* New York: OR Books.

Salomon, G., & Schrum, L. (2007). *Web 2.0: New tools, new schools.* New York: International Society for Technology in Education.

INDEX

Note: Bolded numbers refer to volume numbers in the Debating Issues in American Education series.

Espelage, Dorothy L., **5:**69
E-SPLOST. *See* Education special purpose
local option sales taxes
Establishment Clause
accommodationist approach, **4:**123,
4:124, **4:**131, **4:**132
ethnocentric charter schools and, **1:**21,
1:29–31
extension to states, **4:**xvii, **4:**44–45, **4:**71,
4:98
government aid to religious schools and,
4:4, **6:**255
interpretations, **4:**21–22, **4:**98–99,
4:159–160
moments of silence as violations, **4:**67
motives, **4:**44, **4:**82, **4:**97
prayer in schools as violation of,
4:35–36, **4:**45–47, **4:**48, **4:**49,
4:61–62
released time programs and, **4:**xxiv
religious holidays and, **4:**204–207,
4:210–212
religious materials distribution in public
schools, **4:**251, **4:**257
See also Church-state separation;
Coercion test; Endorsement test;
First Amendment; *Lemon*
(tripartite) test
Ethics
academic integrity, **5:**127, **5:**132,
5:135–138
of administrators, **7:**99–100
of counselors, **3:**23
digital citizenship, **10:**34, **10:**38,
10:143–144, **10:**176–177, **10:**190,
10:221
diversity and, **7:**99–100
expectations of teachers, **10:**147,
10:148–151
moral education and, **10:**170–171
new models, **2:**208–209
in school cultures, **10:**156, **10:**171
See also Academic dishonesty; Moral
values
Ethnic identities, **1:**28, **1:**32, **3:**24–25
See also Cultural differences; Minority
students
Ethnic minorities. *See* Achievement gaps;
Diversity; Minority students
Ethnocentric charter schools, **1:**19–33
advantages, **1:**20–21, **1:**28, **1:**32
Afrocentric, **1:**25

constitutionality, **1:**xxiii, **1:**20, **1:**21,
1:25–26, **1:**29–32
criticism of, **1:**21, **1:**49, **1:**50
curricula, **1:**6–7
reasons for choosing, **1:**20–21
religious groups and, **1:**25–26,
1:29–30, **1:**50, **1:**133–134
segregated, **1:**31–32
Ethnocentric schools, **1:**21, **1:**25–26
See also Native American schools
ETS. *See* Educational Testing Service
Eugenics movement, **2:**65
Eurocentrism, **2:**134–137
Europe
immigrants in, **2:**131–132
public and private school comparisons,
1:154, **1:**158–159
school governance in, **7:**259
school year lengths, **1:**248
European Union, Year of Creativity and
Innovation, **2:**155
Evans, Katherine, **10:**205
*Everson v. Board of Education of Ewing
Township*
child benefit test, **4:**xix, **4:**6, **4:**11, **4:**18
dissent, **4:**10
Establishment Clause extension to
states, **4:**xvii, **4:**98
legacy, **1:**31, **4:**27–28, **6:**272
majority opinion, **4:**xviii, **4:**1–2, **4:**5–6,
4:9–10, **4:**21
wall metaphor, **4:**1–2, **4:**27, **4:**45
Evertson, Carolyn M., **5:**150
Every Child Matters (ECM; U.K.), **7:**53
Evidence-based model (EBM) of school
funding, **6:**206–207, **6:**208,
9:207–208
Evidence-based practices (EBP), **5:**243,
5:244, **8:**117, **8:**118
Evolution
Darwinian theory, **4:**187–188, **4:**190,
4:191, **4:**195–196
instruction in, **4:**187
public views of, **4:**197–198
Scopes Monkey Trial, **4:**xxv, **4:**185, **4:**196
state laws on teaching, **4:**185, **4:**196–197
weaknesses of theory, **4:**187–191
*A.A. ex rel. Betenbaugh v. Needville
Independent School District*, **4:**268,
4:274
Excessive entanglement. *See Lemon*
(tripartite) test

identification of students, **2:**163–166,
2:168–169, **6:**105–106
individualized, **2:**159, **2:**163–164, **2:**166,
2:167
legal requirements, **6:**xxiv–xxv
mandates, **6:**110, **6:**113, **6:**115–116,
6:117, **6:**119
need for, **2:**163, **2:**165
response to intervention model,
2:163–164
school sizes and, **6:**116–117
societal benefits, **6:**237–238
teachers, **2:**159, **6:**122–123
See also Advanced Placement courses;
International Baccalaureate
courses; Magnet schools
Gifted students
ability grouping, **3:**150, **3:**163, **3:**164
in arts, **2:**160, **2:**163
career choices, **2:**159–160, **2:**165
creativity, **2:**165, **2:**166–167,
2:168–169, **2:**171–172
definition, **2:**162–163
differences among, **2:**164–165
in general education, **2:**163
identification of, **2:**163–166,
2:168–169, **6:**105–106
mentoring of, **2:**159, **2:**174
number of, **6:**113–114
overexcitabilities, **2:**171
private services, **6:**114
in Science, Technology, Engineering,
and Mathematics, **2:**159–160,
2:164–166, **2:**167
talent development, **2:**158–159,
2:164–165
Gilbert, David, **1:**59
Gillespie, Lauren Nicole, **3:**179
Gilligan, Carol, **2:**196
Gillis, Lisa, **10:**87
Gimbert, Belinda, **10:**124
Gintis, Herbert, **3:**70
Gitomer, Drew H., **2:**99
*Givhan v. Western Line Consolidated School
District,* **8:**199
Glennan, Thomas, **7:**170
Global competition
in education, **9:**57–58, **9:**218,
9:226–227, **9:**236–239
impact on education, **7:**213,
7:215–216, **7:**247
impact on school funding, **7:**209

increase in, **7:**213
in science, technology, engineering, and
mathematics, **2:**90–106
standards and, **9:**20–35
vocational education and, **1:**217
See also International comparisons;
Market competition
Globalization, definition, **2:**131
Goe, Laura, **9:**142
Goetz v. Ansell, **4:**147
Gogol Bordello, **2:**211–213
Goldman, Daniel, **2:**245
Goldman Sachs, **9:**111, **9:**234
Goldman v. Weinberger, **4:**275
Goldstein, Dan, **10:**201
Goldstein, Thalia, **2:**150
Golly, Annemieke, **5:**237
Good News Club, **4:**53–54
*Good News Club v. Milford Central School
District,* **2:**202, **4:**xxvi–xxvii, **4:**49,
4:81, **4:**234, **4:**236–237, **4:**245, **4:**246,
4:253, **4:**261
Goodman, Ken, **2:**73
Goodman, Yetta, **2:**73
Google, **10:**16
Gordon, June, **3:**262, **3:**263
Gordon, Rebecca, **5:**41
Goss v. Lopez, **5:**xviii–xix, **5:**49, **5:**195,
5:200, **5:**204, **5:**206
Governance
administration and, **7:**xxiii
centralized, **2:**19, **2:**24, **7:**178, **7:**246,
7:255–260, **7:**261–262
choice programs and, **1:**105–106
decentralized, **6:**76–77, **7:**246,
7:255–256, **9:**124–125
definition, **7:**249
democratic, **2:**18, **2:**24–25, **7:**178,
7:257–258, **9:**17
effects of business interests,
7:165–184
effects of charter schools, **7:**xxvi–xxvii,
7:130–146
federal role, **7:**xix–xx, **7:**xxi, **7:**40–56,
7:112, **7:**248–250
history, **7:**xvii–xxiii, **7:**1–3, **7:**6–7,
7:12–13, **7:**255–256
issues, **7:**xxiii–xxviii
managerial, **7:**180–182
parental involvement, **9:**267, **9:**270,
9:271–274
politicization, **7:**xxiii